"An exploration of life at the edge.... Bardach's meditations on slavery tap into the wall of pain and insight that feeds songs of freedom everywhere."

—Paul Goldberg, *New York Times Book Review*

"This is an extraordinary book even in an age such as ours in which published revelations about the totalitarian regimes of Hitlerian Germany and Stalinist Russia are themselves not unusual.... Written in gripping and utterly engaging prose ... [it] should be read by anyone seeking to understand this very violent century."

—*History Book Club*

"Riveting ... it is often hard to remember that this tale of the Siberia of Siberias is no fictional adventure."

—Stephen Chang, *Spectator Magazine*

"We survivors of the Hitler regime ... must tell our stories for as long as possible if a recurrence is to be avoided in the future. Bardach's book is surely an important contribution against forgetting.... This outstanding description of the past at the same time represents hope for a better future."

—Simon Wiesenthal

"An enthralling record of often dreadful experiences in what Solzhenitsyn has called 'the pole of cold and cruelty' of Stalin's labor camp system: a saga of human endurance."

—Robert Conquest, author of *The Great Terror* and *The Harvest of Sorrow*

"An extraordinary story of human brutality, human kindness, and human ability to survive under the most inhuman conditions imaginable."

—Richard Pipes, Professor of Russian History, Harvard University

"After several generations, Janusz Bardach has opened another window into the tragic world first explored by Arthur Koestler in *Darkness at Noon*. This is a worthy and affirmative book."

—James A. McPherson, Pulitzer Prize–winning author of *Elbow Room*

Surviving Freedom

Surviving

AFTER THE GULAG

Freedom

JANUSZ BARDACH AND

KATHLEEN GLEESON

[signature: Kathleen Gleeson]

UNIVERSITY OF CALIFORNIA PRESS

Berkeley   Los Angeles   London

University of California Press
Berkeley and Los Angeles, California

University of California Press, Ltd.
London, England

Title page photograph: Janusz Bardach in 1955 (from the
author's collection).

Grateful acknowledgment is made for use of the quotation
from *The Reawakening* by Primo Levi, published by and
reprinted with permission of Simon & Schuster; also titled
The Truce by Primo Levi, published by Bodley Head and
reprinted by permission of The Random House Group Ltd.

Library of Congress Cataloging-in-Publication Data

Bardach, Janusz.
  Surviving freedom : after the Gulag / Janusz Bardach and
Kathleen Gleeson.
    p. cm.
  ISBN 0-520-23735-8 (Cloth : alk. paper)
    1. Bardach, Janusz.   2. Jews, Polish—Soviet Union—
Biography.   3. Jews—Soviet Union—Biography.
  4. Political prisoners—Soviet Union—Biography.
  5. Plastic surgeons—Soviet Union—Biography.
 I. Gleeson, Kathleen.   II. Title.

  DS135.R9 B275 2003
  947.085'092—dc21

                                   2002152219

Manufactured in the United States of America
12 11 10 09 08 07 06 05 04 03
10 9 8 7 6 5 4 3 2 1

The paper used in this publication meets the minimum re-
quirements of ANSI/NISO Z39 0.48–1992 (R 1997) (*Permanence
of Paper*).

For Juliusz Bardach and Ewa Bardach

And to the memory of Elena Laneyeva Bardach

Janusz Bardach died of cancer in August 2002, before *Surviving Freedom: After the Gulag* was published. He was eighty-three. Although he regretted that he wouldn't see the book in print, it was more important to him to have completed the project and moved on to the next—we were writing a book of stories about his medical career at the time of his death.

Working with Janusz for ten years, I never ceased to be in awe of his strength and spirit. He was larger-than-life, a heroic figure whose life and personality encompassed extremes. He was born into a well-to-do family, then spent eight years living the impoverished life of a prisoner and civilian in the Soviet Union. He knew the despair of loss and atrocity and the pride of reaching world-renowned status in his field. He had an enormous capacity for work and for play—he'd sit hunched over his desk for eight hours a day writing the pages of this book, and that same evening he'd host friends or visiting international writers on his back porch with a bottle of Polish vodka. His energy was endless, and his love of life undiminished by loss and hardship.

Janusz's tenacious, joyful spirit lives on in those who knew him, and I hope that anyone who meets him in his books will come away feeling strengthened and inspired. It was a tremendous pleasure and privilege to help Janusz document his extraordinary life.

KATHLEEN GLEESON

And how much had we lost in those twenty months? What should we find at home? How much of ourselves had been eroded, extinguished? Were we returning richer or poorer, stronger or emptier? We did not know; but we knew that on the thresholds of our homes, for good or ill, a trial awaited us, and we anticipated it with fear. We felt in our veins the poison of Auschwitz, flowing together with our thin blood; where should we find the strength to begin our lives again...?

Primo Levi, *The Reawakening*

CONTENTS

Maps and photos follow pages xviii and 118, respectively

PREFACE

In 1941, as a Red Army soldier fighting the Nazis on the Belorussian front, I was arrested, court-martialed, and sentenced to ten years of hard labor. I was twenty-two years old and had committed no crime. I was one of millions swept up in the reign of terror that Stalin perpetrated on his own people between 1925 and 1953.

When I look back, I try to pinpoint the hour my life changed, the moment that my peaceful, provincial life ended and my tumultuous journey began. Was it the morning in 1940 when I left my family and hometown to join the Red Army? The moment of my arrest one year later? The evening I dug my grave and slept in it? My court-martial, when the guilty verdict was read and I was sentenced to die? When did the relinquishing begin, not of the freedoms, such as what I would eat and where I would sleep, but of the self? Spirit, drive, audacity, largesse—qualities I possessed before I became a prisoner—did I lose them or did they help me survive?

In the same vein, I've tried to reflect on the transition from prisoner back to citizen, from labor camp to freedom. This has been a difficult task. Being taken out of normal life is relatively easy to document. Loss of family, home, friends; illness, violence, starvation—all are extraordinary. But as tragic as it is to leave home, it is equally anguishing to come back and rebuild a life. The struggle for physical survival may be torturous but usually it is well defined, which makes it a concrete enterprise, something that can be put into words. But the struggle to get back to a normal life is a murky, indefinite process, one that few survivors have written about.

In my previous book, *Man Is Wolf to Man: Surviving the Gulag*, I wrote about my experiences as a labor camp prisoner and tried to give a glimpse into life and death in that abysmal and peregrine world. The following is a brief account of my arrest and incarceration.

. . .

On September 1, 1939, Nazi Germany invaded Poland from the west, and on September 17, the Soviet Union invaded Poland from the east. The secret Ribbentrop-Molotov Pact divided Poland between the two countries along the Bug River. My hometown, Wlodzimierz-Wolynski, in eastern Poland, became part of Soviet-occupied territory until June 22, 1941, when Nazi Germany invaded the Soviet Union. The Soviets liberated the town from the Nazis in July 1944, and at the end of World War II, they incorporated it, along with the eastern part of Poland, into the Soviet Union.

In July 1940, I was drafted into the Red Army. One year later, I was arrested on the front line. The circumstances of my arrest reveal the atmosphere of terror and paranoia that prevailed in the Stalinist Soviet Union. From childhood every Soviet citizen was taught the tenets of Marxism-Leninism and indoctrinated to inform on anyone, including parents and friends, who was critical of the regime. These children grew into adults who were suspicious of everyone, who watched every word that they and others said, who informed on others and in turn were informed on, and who were singled out, interrogated, and arrested or harassed to the point of ruin.

In the Red Army I found myself in a very strange environment. Raised in prewar, capitalist, democratic Poland, I enjoyed talking openly about current affairs and political leaders, and I didn't change my behavior when I was in the Red Army. Looking back, I can see how nervous I must have made my fellow Soviet soldiers. I found it difficult to keep critical comments to myself, and equally difficult to obey orders. My bourgeois upbringing singled me out further among my peers. I found the Red Army to be a frighteningly primitive environment, intolerant of weakness and suspicious of individual thought, drive, and talent.

One day when I was talking about politics, my bunk mate pulled me aside and told me angrily, "These subjects are off limits to everyone, especially to you." I was slow to realize that because I was a foreigner, I was not to be trusted, and because I spoke my mind freely, I was under suspicion of being an "enemy of the people"—the most dangerous label given to anyone who didn't conform to Soviet society. I had no idea that a cloud of suspicion surrounded me, no idea that anyone was informing on me, no idea it would take only one mistake to ignite that suspicion.

I made that inevitable mistake shortly after Germany declared war on the Soviet Union and my battalion was mobilized to the Belorussian front line. My commander had ordered me to drive my T-34 tank across a river to establish a safe passage for other tanks when my tank tipped to the side and sank with the hatch open. The tracks got stuck in the mud and I couldn't drive the tank out. The commander berated me severely and ordered me and my tank mate, Vladimir Nikitin, to stay with the tank until it could be pulled out of the river. Nazi troops were passing nearby, and if they discovered the tank we were to destroy it.

During the two days Nikitin and I stayed with the tank, I told him how worried I was about my family living in Nazi-occupied territory, and I talked at length about how much I wanted to go back to Poland to be with them. His written testimonial of our conversations, along with the tank accident itself—labeled sabotage—was the basis of the guilty verdict at my court-martial.

The morning after the tank was retrieved from the river, I was walking in the woods when two officers of the NKVD—Narodny Kommissariat Vnutrennikh Dyel, or People's Commissariat for Internal Affairs, later known as the KGB—pulled me off the path and into a thicket. Without saying a word, they stripped me of my gun, ripped the epaulets and buttons with the red star off my tunic, tied my hands behind my back, blindfolded me, and led me to a truck a short distance away. They drove me to a clearing deep in the forest and told me to dig my own grave. At the court-martial the next morning I was sentenced to be executed, but through the first of many fortuitous twists of fate the sentence was commuted to ten years of hard labor.

It took eight months to get from one prison to another, from one labor camp to another, before I reached my final destination in Kolyma in northeastern Siberia, the Siberia of Siberias, a wilderness rich in gold and populated by thousands and thousands of guards and prisoners. In the close confinement of the packed cattle cars, I lived with hunger and thirst, filth and lice, sickness and death. Dysentery and typhus ravaged the transport. It took only two weeks before I woke up next to my first corpse. His name was Anatoly, and his body, along with hundreds of others, was thrown off the train into a ditch to rot and be scavenged. As the days passed, savagery broke out among prisoners who only days before seemed to be friends. They fought each other for a crumb of bread or sip of water, ready to bite or beat anyone who got in their way. Others cried and begged. The daily ration of three hundred grams of dark, clay-like bread and half a piece of salt herring was not enough to live on, but not little enough to die on. I tried to hold my ground. I tried not to think about home. Very quickly I was transformed from an outspoken, gregarious person into a wary, isolated prisoner.

The first labor camp I went to before reaching Kolyma was called Burepolom, literally meaning "the place where one reaches the edge." We worked from six in the morning until six in the evening cutting down trees and digging out roots to build a road in the taiga, and we ate only twice a day: bread and coarse oatmeal in the morning, and bread and watery soup after roll call in the evening. Starvation accelerated the natural selection of prisoners; the dead were dead before they died. I could see it in their eyes as life ebbed away from them. And if the conditions weren't enough to kill a person, the commander of the camp took care of it every night at roll call when he randomly selected political prisoners to torture and shoot, appointing himself to continue the purges begun by Stalin.

The Soviets referred to Kolyma, a territory larger than Texas, as an island because no cars or trains could go there. The only means of transportation to Kolyma was by ship, going north through the Sea of Okhotsk from Buchta Nakhodka or Vladivostock. In the gold mines of Kolyma, half-starved and wearing ragged clothing, working in temperatures as low as fifty degrees below zero, I came close to the edge. But as I felt myself unraveling, another twist of fate pulled me out of the mines and landed me in a job as an orderly on the tuberculosis ward in the central hospital for prisoners. There, I found people with inextinguishable humanity who helped me when I fell sick with TB. They were prisoners with terms as long as mine, as filthy, hungry, and exhausted as I was, who found the strength to be compassionate when survival was difficult for everyone. I got to know many political prisoners, and I got to know many criminals. I found it easy to establish a common language with both groups of people, and I changed my prejudice against criminals because I learned that not every criminal was a criminal only.

In 1944, as the Red Army forced the Nazis to retreat and liberated many cities, I thought more and more about the fate of my family. I sent a letter to a cousin in Moscow asking her if she'd had any news about them, and through her I found out my brother had survived the war. He'd become an officer in the Polish army organized in the Soviet Union. Through his connections, he obtained my early release from the labor camps in 1945.

Although this book may read as a sequel to *Man Is Wolf to Man: Surviving the Gulag,* it did not arise out of the same spirit. I wrote this book not only to tell a story but to explore a question I have asked myself and been asked throughout my life: How did I rebuild my life after losing so much?

Poland, 1939. Janusz's hometown, Wlodzimierz–Wolynski, is located just ten kilometers from the Bug River. (All maps adapted from U.S. government sources.)

Poland after World War II. Vladimir-Volynsk is now in the Ukrainian Soviet republic, ten kilometers from the Polish border.

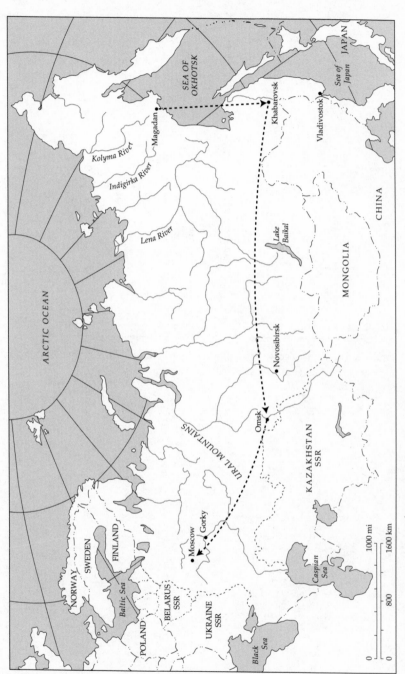

Janusz's trip by plane from Magadan to Moscow, March 1946.

Janusz's trip from Moscow to Vladimir-Volynsk, June 1946, and from Moscow to Warsaw and Lodz, July 1947.

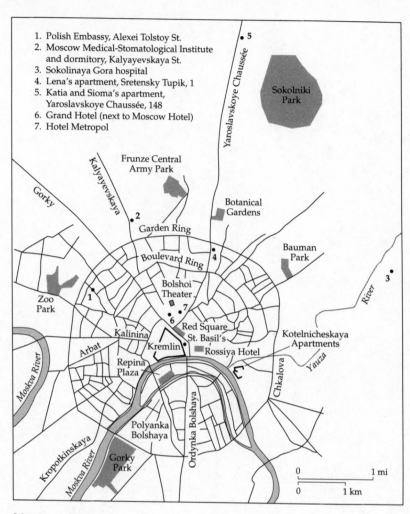

1. Polish Embassy, Alexei Tolstoy St.
2. Moscow Medical-Stomatological Institute and dormitory, Kalyayevskaya St.
3. Sokolinaya Gora hospital
4. Lena's apartment, Sretensky Tupik, 1
5. Katia and Sioma's apartment, Yaroslavskoye Chaussée, 148
6. Grand Hotel (next to Moscow Hotel)
7. Hotel Metropol

Moscow, 1950.

PROLOGUE

On May 9, 1945, the war with Nazi Germany ended and we prisoners working in the central hospital in Kolyma hoped for a general amnesty. My best friend and mentor, Dr. Nikolai Rafaelovich Piasetsky, had already been released and was living in Magadan, the capital of Kolyma. My brother Julek, a colonel in the Polish army, had informed me through our correspondence that he was working to secure my early release. The summer dragged on. Only a few other prisoners had been liberated, and my spirits plummeted. Then in late August I was called to the Office of Registration and Distribution, which oversaw prisoners working in the camp hospital. The NKVD officer in charge handed me a document to sign and told me I was free. It was six years before my term would have expired.

I pounded down the dirt path to the barracks to say goodbye to my close friends. Ivan was the camp cook, and Hela and Maria Ivanovna worked with me on the TB ward. It was a bittersweet parting. They wished me good luck, and in my heart I wished them to survive. In less than an hour I packed a suitcase with my belongings, retrieved from the camp repository the rubles that Julek had sent me, and walked up to the guardhouse. A guard we called the Bloodhound came up to the window. He was a Mongolian, as were most of the guards, with large, yellow teeth, a square face, and black porcine eyes. He was greatly feared among us prisoners for his quick temper. Standing outside the window, my prisoner's habits were still there—I was ready to turn out my pockets, open my jacket, and lift my tunic and pant legs—but the Bloodhound opened the gate and waved me through.

Standing on the dirt road with the watchtowers, guardhouse, and barbed wire behind me, I didn't know where to go or what to do. I was twenty-six years old; I had no money, no education, and no pro-

1

fession; I was fourteen thousand miles away from home; and I didn't know if my parents, wife, and sister were dead or alive. In the few letters he'd sent to me, Julek hadn't said anything about them.

Shallow gray clouds churned above and the swallows flew low to the ground, a sign it was going to rain. I walked over to the hamlet where free workers lived. Several white wooden houses with blue trim lined the dirt road that led to the Kolyma highway. Although I knew the six-kilometer highway intimately, having shoveled it and walked it hundreds of times while hauling wood during my imprisonment, I looked down it now as if for the first time. On one side of the road the taiga came right up to the houses. On the other, hills covered with dense shrubs melded into the gray horizon. There was no grass around the houses, not even planks of wood thrown down over the mud for a sidewalk. Mongrels roamed the area, but not a person was in sight.

In the cafeteria for free workers, Luba, the cook and a prisoner I'd known for a long time, introduced me to an agronomist who rented me a room. It was a spartan room with a wardrobe, military cot, and small table and chair. The conditions in the house were also spartan. There was no bathroom, toilet, or hot water. The outhouse was in the backyard, and the bathhouse, which served the free men and women working in the hospital, wasn't open. I went to bed sweaty and stinking and pulled the wool blanket over my shoulders. I lay in bed smelling the fresh linens and listening to the coyotes howling in the taiga. I heard no human sounds, which I'd gotten used to hearing constantly. For so many years I'd fallen asleep the moment I lay down, nestling into the arguing and fighting around me. In the dark room the silence loomed larger, opening into a vast nothingness. I lay awake wondering what I'd do with my life. I wanted to forget these war years and pick up where I'd left off. In my youth I dreamed of being an explorer of unknown lands, a writer with a wild imagination, a fighter for social justice. I thought I was destined to live an extraordinary life. As a prisoner my dreams were untamed by reason. I dreamed of everything possible and impossible, but the core of every dream was to be free. Although I lived the life of a slave, I dreamed as a free man about a world I'd lost but hadn't forgotten and wanted back.

The next seven months were a kind of purgatory, a life outside of life, because although I was no longer a prisoner, I couldn't leave Kolyma:

the ship going to Vladivostock was booked one year in advance. I went back to the camp hospital and worked for a brief time as a *feldsher*, a medical assistant, until I came up with an idea for my own business. The hospital was in need of a protein supplement, and I figured out a way to make one from reindeer blood spilled when the Eskimo tribes thinned out the reindeer herds. With the help of a prisoner who was an experienced chemist, I collected the blood and we enriched it with citric acid and alcohol. We called the product Hematogen and sold it to the camp hospital. Before long we expanded our business and sold the product to other hospitals in the region.

Traveling by dog- or reindeer-pulled sledge to faraway Eskimo villages made me feel free and adventurous in the vast wilderness of blue and white space. These trips took my mind off the thoughts of what had happened to my family and made me think this could be my home forever. But when I returned and went back to my room in the agronomist's house I became deeply depressed.

In March 1946, my friend Nikolai Raphaelovich bribed a pilot to take me in a transport plane carrying gold to Khabarovsk, the capital of a huge territory called Khabarovsky Krai on the Amur River in eastern Siberia. I appeared at the airport with my suitcase, and the pilot whisked me onto the plane. He cleared a little space for me amid the cargo of gold and told me to get lost as soon as the plane landed because he wasn't allowed to fly passengers. Wearing a deerskin hat and coat as well as pants, boots, and long mittens, I thought I was well dressed to ride in the back of the plane, but I nearly froze to death. For four years I'd survived one of the coldest places on earth, and now, on my way home, I was certain I'd die in the airplane. For five hours I fought the sleepiness that comes with hypothermia and forced myself to rub my hands and face and stamp my feet. When the plane finally landed I was so stiff, cold, and exhausted that I could barely walk.

In Khabarovsk I spent several days waiting in line to buy a plane ticket to Moscow. I became quite friendly with the people standing next to me. At the end of each day we signed our names to a list marking our places in line, and the next day we took up the same positions and continued sharing our travelers' tales. After getting the ticket, I went to the black market and sold my reindeer attire. With the money from the sale I bought a watch and leather jacket, which I thought would look sharp in Moscow. The watch had a life of its own, speeding up or slowing down at random, but I didn't care. I treasured it because it was one of the things I had missed most when I was a prisoner.

Sitting in the airplane on my way to Moscow, my head filled with the droning of the engines and propellers, I wondered how to begin my incipient life. I dreamed of making a home with Taubcia, getting an education, and leaving eastern Europe, perhaps even leaving the continent, and settling in a big city somewhere, maybe in Palestine, Argentina, or Brazil. But first I had to find my cousin Katia in Moscow, track down Julek, and find out what had become of my home.

1

VIEW FROM THE EMBASSY WINDOW

On a gray, cold, gloomy afternoon in March 1946, I arrived at the Moscow-Vnukovo airport. No one was waiting for me. No one knew I was coming. For several hours I trod the Moscow streets in spitting rain and snow looking for my cousin Katia's apartment. Sleet soaked through my leather shoes and unlined leather jacket, making me shiver and my teeth chatter. It was still winter in Moscow, and the Muscovites wore sheepskin coats or long military coats without insignia. I headed down Gorky Street, passing armed militiamen on street corners and in front of prominent buildings. Raindrops poised on my eyelashes fragmented the glow of the street lamps and the beams of car headlights. The gray day darkened as evening approached, making me feel even more lost. I'd never been in such a big city, never seen so many traffic lights. Cars honked and gears shifted. Pedestrians wove in and out of the traffic, jumped on moving streetcars, and hung out the doors by one arm. I didn't know what direction to take, and I was afraid to cross the street, afraid the green light would turn red before I'd reached the other side. I walked into the middle of a group of pedestrians so a car wouldn't hit me.

With a long way to go to find my cousin's apartment, I followed a shopkeeper's advice and jumped on a streetcar, which he said would take me to Yaroslavskoye Chaussée. I tried to stay near the door, but at every stop the influx of tired, irritable passengers pushed me deeper inside the car. Men and women alike fought for space near the doors. I clung to a pole near a window so that I could at least look out and see the street signs, but the haggard herd of Muscovites, their arms loaded with parcels, boots dripping and noses running, blocked my view. The windows fogged over. I asked a young woman standing next to me where the stop was for Yaroslavskoye Chaussée, and she told me I was on the wrong streetcar. Confused and afraid of getting more lost, I got off at the next stop and walked the rest of the way to Katia's building, asking passersby for directions.

To my astonishment, 148 Yaroslavskoye Chaussée wasn't a house but a massive, gray-slab, U-shaped building that stretched two blocks. I didn't know the apartment number, so I climbed the six flights of stairs in the three wings and checked the names on the doors.

I knocked softly on the wooden door and a gruff voice answered, "Who is it?"

"It's Janusz, Katia's cousin," I said.

Katia's husband Sioma opened the door and shook my hand warmly. He was stooped and balding, with heavy, black-framed glasses. Katia came to the door. I'd never met her, and I was surprised by her curly white hair and deeply lined face. "Thank God you're here," she said.

Although Katia was my first cousin, she'd spent all her life in the Soviet Union, while I'd grown up in Poland. In his letters to me, Julek had said to find Katia in Moscow when I was released and that she would know how to find him. Katia held my hand and stared at my face in amazement. The apartment was small and plain. The china figurines on the credenza reminded me of home. "Katia," Sioma said in a husky voice. "Let Janusz go and wash up, then we'll have dinner. I'll call Julek to let him know you're here."

"Julek?" I said. "Is he in Moscow?"

"He's been here since January. He was promoted to colonel and appointed the military attaché in the Polish embassy."

Sioma picked up the phone and dialed. He told Julek I had arrived and handed me the receiver.

"I'll be right over to pick you up. Welcome back," Julek said. Although his voice sounded fuller and more confident, the slight nasal tone was unmistakable.

In the bathroom I filled the short iron tub with hot water and got in, sitting with my knees drawn to my chest. I hadn't expected to meet Julek so soon, and I couldn't believe he was a colonel. He'd always preferred libraries to the soccer field and literary journals to dancing. I couldn't believe he'd changed so dramatically as to become a military man of such high rank.

I opened my suitcase and put on a dry but crumpled shirt and pants. I remained barefoot, and Sioma put my boots on the radiator to dry. Finely cut herring cleaned of the skin and garnished with chopped onions and sour cream sat on the table. A scoop of yellow butter lay in a dish next to a loaf of tangy-smelling dark bread. Plates of bacon, dry sausage, and an oily white fish I'd never seen before were spread out on the table.

There was a soft knock at the door and Sioma got up to answer it. A balding, square-shouldered Polish officer appeared. It had been over seven years since I'd seen Julek, and I hardly recognized him. Gone were his hunched-over shoulders, shuffling walk, soft hands, and hesitant manner. We embraced each other, but the hug was short and shy. "You haven't changed much," he said, half-surprised and rather absently, as he studied my face and looked at my arms and chest. I wanted to hug him again, feel him close, ask him about the family, but the invisible arm that had always kept me back was still there. Under the left breast pocket of his green military jacket were many ribbons, and on the epaulets, the rank of colonel. He was the last person I would've guessed would be courageous enough on the battlefield to become a colonel, and smart and experienced enough of a politician to become the military attaché.

We all took a piece of herring, the most popular appetizer in Russia and Poland, and Sioma filled our glasses with Moskovskaya vodka. "The herring likes to swim," Sioma said, just like my father used to say. "To your arrival and our meeting." We clinked glasses. I sniffed the crust of dark bread and drank the shot.

Katia served the pieces of white fish. "Beluga," she said in response to my puzzled look. The delicate, oily meat melted in my mouth. I licked the fishbones clean but kept from chewing on them. I soaked up the oil on the plate with the bread.

Katia sat next to me. "Eat, eat. There'll be borscht afterwards."

Julek teased the beluga meat from its bones. Between bites he gestured delicately with his knife and droned on about his job. "You have no idea how many Polish citizens were deported before and during the war. Now they want to repatriate to Poland, but many of them are still in prison or in the camps or in exile. They have no homes to return to, no money, no family. They're sick and poorly clothed. You can't imagine what it takes. It's exhausting." Julek paused and looked at me. "But you, too, must be tired."

"No. I've been waiting six years for this moment."

Julek went back to his beluga and spoke to Sioma. "My position is difficult. I have to deal with the Soviet authorities in the Department of Foreign Affairs in the Ministry of Defense. It's hard to track down the Polish citizens because they're so dispersed across the country, and for many of them there isn't enough documentation to prove their Polish citizenship."

"Julek," I interrupted. The words rose up from my chest and formed in my throat. "What happened to the family?"

Julek lowered his head and looked at me from beneath his heavy brows. "They're gone."

My mind went blank and something inside me froze. I stared at the red, gold, and blue ribbons on Julek's breast pocket, no longer listening, not wanting to hear about his new family, the embassy, Moscow. I wanted only to sleep.

It was past midnight when Julek's driver took us to the embassy. It was a long, silent drive except for when Julek turned around and asked if I had my luggage with me or if I'd left anything at Katia's place. In the darkness of the back seat I closed my eyes and felt the same distance that had always existed between us.

After seven years of living such different lives, I was afraid that we'd grown farther apart than we were before. Five years older and intellectually superior to me, Julek had barely acknowledged my presence at home. In contrast to me he was shy, introverted, and self-absorbed. With his serious, studious ways, he captured most of my mother's attention, while I was left on my own. My parents considered him to be the successor in the long line of scholars on my mother's side of the family, whereas I was considered the intellectual lightweight. Both he and my mother read leftist literary and political journals, and Julek talked easily with our parents' friends, who visited frequently. Julek had few friends, while I was the leader of several different packs.

Growing up, I felt that I had a fuller and more interesting life than Julek. I had dear, close friends and a beloved girlfriend, and I was my father's favorite son. He liked my humor, athletic ability, and even my rebelliousness. He bought me a boat, kayak, bicycle, horse, and finally, a rarity in Wlodzimierz-Wolynski, a motorcycle. He supported my passion for raising pigeons, not objecting to this shady trade popular on the seedy side of town. We walked together on Farna Street on Sundays, and I was his only companion for nighttime fishing escapades and card playing at the Jewish club.

I never saw Julek burst with anger and never heard him raise his voice, while I was well known for my temper. I was proud of Julek's achievements and tried to congratulate him when he came home for visits, but he always brushed me off. When I went to his wedding in 1938, he didn't even bother to introduce me to his bride.

We checked in at the embassy gate. Julek led me inside, past the guards and attendants, who all looked at me suspiciously. We climbed three flights of stairs, past a ballroom with enormous golden tapestries and oil paintings. On the third floor Julek remarked, "Embassy officials and staff live here. There are also some offices and guestrooms. One of them is prepared for you." We walked down an L-shaped corridor. Julek unlocked one of the doors and turned on the light. An ornate crystal chandelier hung from the high ceiling. Across the room was a large bay window, and in the corner was an ordinary iron bed covered with a green military-style blanket. I pushed my wooden suitcase under it.

"Can we sit down and talk?" I asked. "Tell me what happened to them. What do you know?"

Julek stepped toward the door. "You've had a hard day. I'm tired, too. Let's rest. We can talk tomorrow." He opened the door and stood in the doorway. "Sleep well. I hope you'll be comfortable." The door clicked shut.

I wanted to scream in Julek's face—how could he tell me that everyone left at home was dead, murdered, and then walk out? Was he so ashamed of me? I yanked my suitcase out from under the bed and threw it against the floor, spilling its contents. I threw everything that had meant so much to me only days before into all corners of the room: my comb and pocket knife, a windproof lighter, a safety razor, a metal bracelet made for me by a patient on the psychiatric ward, and a tiny gold nugget. I took off my watch, my most cherished possession, and smashed it on the nightstand. It was the first thing I'd bought in freedom. It hadn't mattered to me that it was unreliable, suddenly stopping or speeding up, turning hours into minutes or minutes into hours. I smashed it again and again against the nightstand, stomped on it, and kicked it under the bed.

Lying in bed I smelled the freshness and cleanliness of the sheets, but the memories of my parents, my wife, Taubcia, and my sister, Rachel, turned into scenes of their deaths. For all those years I carried with me their faces, voices, and movements, but now that was gone. Sounds of bombing, shooting, screaming filled my head. I heard Taubcia crying my name. How could Julek tell me that everyone left at home was dead and then walk away?

For the next several days I wanted to do nothing but sleep. Images of prisons and gold mines loomed in my mind, while the faces of my family faded away. Rolling on the firm mattress, I remembered lying curled up in my filthy rags on the prison floor. I remembered the nights when I couldn't fall asleep due to the bitter Arctic cold and the sucking, piercing hunger. I showered two or three times a day in steaming hot water but still couldn't rid myself of the feeling of filth and lice.

In the mornings I didn't want to leave my warm bed. Some days I ignored the knock at the door—either Julek or his maid, Zoya—calling me for breakfast. I lay with my eyes closed and daydreamed about Taubcia, my first great love, whom I married before leaving for the Red Army; my parents, whom I loved but had not yet gotten to know as people; and my younger sister, who liked to keep her little secrets from me. I dreamed of the desk in my bedroom, the chair I liked to sit on, the paintings my mother had hung—one called *Golden Fall* and the other a stormy sea. I awakened feeling lonely and confused, wanting to walk next door to my parents' bedroom. Most nights I dreamed I was back in the camps. Some nights I dreamed of Zina, a woman I'd fallen in love with and left behind in the camp hospital in Kolyma.

Day after day I got up, showered, and without breakfast, resumed my place at the window, parting the red velvet curtains to begin another day. The gray clouds sagged. Sleet drizzled. Slush accumulated. I cried often.

Several days after my arrival Julek rushed through the papers to change my citizenship back to Polish. It had been changed to Soviet when the Soviets occupied my hometown in September 1939. Julek got two witnesses to attest to my prewar citizenship, and in thirty minutes I had a Polish passport in my pocket and had changed from an ex-convict to a respected foreigner. The Soviet authorities and the Soviet people, like the tsarist authorities and the Russian people before the October Revolution, had a special regard for foreigners, especially for those whose homelands now belonged to the new Soviet bloc. As the result of the Yalta and Potsdam conferences, Poland, Hungary, Czechoslovakia, Romania, Bulgaria, Yugoslavia, and Albania, as well as the Soviet-occupied part of Germany, now fell under Soviet dominance.

I wanted Julek to prepare two other documents, one that said I had graduated from the gymnasium in Wlodzimierz-Wolynski in 1938, which was true, and another saying I had been a second-year medical student at Warsaw University before the war, which wasn't. Julek dictated the two documents, and the witnesses signed them. He also took me to his tailor and had him alter one of his military uniforms to fit me and make me look like an officer without rank. The Polish uniform differed from the Soviet one, and so I was recognized as a foreigner wherever I went.

When I first arrived in Moscow Julek told the ambassador, Professor Henryk Raabe, as well as Consul Piotr Motruk and the first secretary of the embassy, Aleksander Juszkiewicz, that I'd been in Kolyma. But he said I should keep my past secret from everyone else in the embassy, and especially from Soviet citizens. After some deliberation we concocted two stories about my life during the war, one for Poles, the other for Soviets.

The story I told people in the embassy was straightforward and partially true. In the summer of 1940, I was drafted into the Red Army and attended the tank academy in Orel. I was a heavy tank driver and mechanic and when the war with Germany began on June 22, 1941, I was sent to the front line in Belorus. At that point I changed my story, because it was there on the front line that I was arrested. For Poles the story continued that I was transferred to a working military battalion comprised of former Polish citizens serving in the Red Army. Poles were considered to be politically unreliable and were therefore removed from the front. My battalion was sent to Siberia, near the Chinese border. It moved frequently from place to place, and we worked odd jobs until the end of the war.

I couldn't tell this story to Soviet citizens, however, because it could be easily checked out. I told them that I joined the Polish army that was organized in the Soviet Union by General Zygmunt Berling, like Julek had. I had attained the rank of captain. Armed with these two stories, I felt safer, and Julek reassured me that no one would bother to check my past. He said that many Poles who had spent the war in the Soviet Union had experiences similar to mine in the Soviet camps, and many of them had become high Party and government officials.

In his peculiar way Julek tried to show me closeness and hospitality. He invited me to parties and receptions, and I ate with him and his wife Halina in their apartment. Twenty-three-year-old Halina was a streetcar conductor in Lodz when Julek met her after the war and invited her to his apartment. Three months later she was pregnant, and they got married. She wore heavy red lipstick, matching rouge, and her brown hair freshly coiffured. She put herself in the leading role at dinner, gossiping about upcoming social events and shopping trips to the special stores for diplomats. She demanded gold and diamond jewelry, new dresses for parties and receptions, new shoes and hats for every dress, and new sports jackets and pants for every picnic. She chattered endlessly. She talked about the squabbles for influence and prestige among the diplomats' wives. She was offended if at receptions she was not chosen to stand high enough in the order of the receiving line or not seated at the appropriate rank of her husband. It was important who and of what rank the person was who talked to her at cocktail parties. With gusto she delivered kitchen-style gossip about the latest sex scandals among the diplomats, their wives, and the embassy staff, and she dissected the sex life of their maid, Zoya, who was fornicating with Julek's driver, Fyodor. It was impossible to have a serious conversation with Julek at the dinner table, because no matter what he or I started to discuss, if it wasn't of interest to Halina, and most of the topics were not, she interrupted us in a mocking tone and made a face like a child excluded from playing with the older kids.

I was amazed by how quickly and easily Halina had assumed her new role, as if she'd been born in a palace and surrounded since childhood by servants and governesses. She lied that she'd been raised among the Polish nobility. There were others like her in the embassy, men as well as women, poorly educated, coarse in their manners, and narrow in their thinking, who had assumed their embassy posts due only to their affiliation with the Communist Party. The war scattered and displaced people like a throw of the dice. There was no predicting how people would end up: aristocrats were now cleaning streets; streetcar conductors became diplomats' wives; prewar Polish entrepreneurs and executives became clerks, if they were lucky, or populated the labor camps, while peasants and workers became Party or state officials. The war resulted in strange couplings as people tried to reestablish themselves in a rapidly changing and changed world.

From time to time I joined Julek and Halina at diplomatic receptions and private dinners, but I never sat with them. The seating assignment followed the protocol of placement according to diplomatic rank, and since Julek was the third highest ranking diplomat, he and Halina sat at the head of the table, while I sat at the end with the clerks and secretaries, if they were invited. Children, vacations, and most of all, shopping were the main topics of conversation at these dinners because everyone was afraid of saying something that could be interpreted as criticism of the Stalinist or Polish regimes or the leaders of either country.

What impressed me most at the dinners was the food. I watched the leftovers on other people's plates, wanting to grab everything, pack it, and feed the hungry. I wanted to steal the bread from the table, put it into my pocket, and chew on it at night. The sucking, piercing, nauseating feeling of hunger still frightened me. I woke up at night, my jaws stiff and aching from chewing in my sleep. As a child my parents taught me that throwing away food was the greatest sin because there were so many starving people in the world, and I felt guilty eating salmon, beefsteak, and lamb chops. I should be sharing it with people who were starving, but how? Whenever I looked at my plate I thought about how many people could be saved with what I was eating, and these thoughts upset me more, making me feel that I didn't deserve what I had and that I was taking away from those who needed it most. Before long I turned down most of Julek's dinner invitations.

At times I worried that Julek, in his highly sensitive post, didn't realize how the Soviet system worked or how closely he was watched. But Julek had learned a lot about the Soviet system during the war, especially how NKVD informers permeated society. During one dinner conversation in his apartment, he cut me off in mid-sentence with a finger to his lip, looked emphatically at the chandelier, and pointed to his ear. Whenever he wanted to talk to me he invited me for a walk outside the building, explaining, "One room in the ambassador's office is searched every day for bugs, and all important conferences take place in this room. At the restaurants the tables reserved for foreigners are bugged. The restrooms are bugged—even your room is bugged. The maids, janitors, chauffeurs, and Soviet secretaries work for the NKVD, and they report on everything."

One evening Julek invited me and several friends to dinner at an open-air restaurant. Two years after the formation of the eastern bloc, everyone in the embassy was concerned about the future of Poland. No one knew if the Communist Party would prevail in Poland, and this uncertainty generated heated discussions about the upcoming elections, which I thought were bogus. "None of you understand the system Poland is now under," I said. "You still believe the multi-party system will continue. Well, I believe it will vanish before you know it. Six months or a year from now, the Communist Party will be the only one in power."

"But many political parties still exist just like they did before the war. The vast majority of Poles want a western-style democracy," Julek said.

I was surprised by how naïve Julek's views were of Poland's fate. Educated by seasoned politicians and diplomats in the camps, I read the political situation differently. "Julek, it's only a matter of time before all eastern European countries, including Poland, are sovietized. I guarantee you, the Communist Party will rule single-handedly in all of them. These countries will follow the example of the Soviet Union; all other political parties will be banned, and members of non-communist parties will be treated as harshly as the political prisoners in the camps were treated." Although I didn't say it, I was afraid that the Polish Socialist Party, of which Julek was a prominent member, would be the first party to be dissolved, and Julek might suffer as well.

"Poland and the Soviet Union are not the same," Julek fired back. "Your vision is blurred. You don't know the situation in Poland. We have a good partnership with the Communist Party. It doesn't dominate politics in Poland."

"But it will."

I saw Julek nearly every day, but I didn't have much of a chance to talk to him. When I dropped by his office he was busy, and in the evening we often had to go to receptions or entertain diplomats at home. I felt unsettled in our relationship, and I waited for Julek to seek me out.

One afternoon he stopped by my room with his coat in hand. "I'm taking the afternoon off," he said. "Let's take a walk." We went to a nearby park called Clear Ponds. It was still chilly, and we found a bench to sit on next to the pond. "I'm sorry it took me so long to find time to talk to you. I'd like to hear about what you went through, and I'll tell you what happened to me during the war."

I told him how I'd been arrested, court-martialed, and sentenced to be executed, and how the sentence was commuted; about the cattle cars, transit prisons, ship to Kolyma; how I'd dug for gold in the permafrost and how I landed a job at the central hospital. I didn't tell him how I tried to escape, got caught in the woods, and was beaten nearly to death, nor about the horrors of the camp in Burepolom, nor about my bout with tuberculosis. I wanted to spare him the worst of what I'd been through, and I didn't want him to pity me.

We sat silently. Julek watched the ducks swimming in the pond. He began to tell me what happened to him, his first wife, Fruma, and the family. "Before the Nazi invasion I was living in Lvov with Fruma and working as an accountant. When the war started I was enlisted into the Red Army and assigned to guard a cargo train. When the train stopped in Kharkov I went to visit our uncle Fischel, our father's younger brother, and I never went back to the train. I got civilian clothes and went to Uzbekistan. I moved from one place to another to keep from being tracked down and found work as an accountant and as a teacher. In 1943 I joined the newly organized Polish army under General Berling. I became a political officer, and my military career took off quickly, as happens during war. I'm sure it was a surprise to you to see me in uniform." There was a long pause. "You know, I was in Wlodzimierz-Wolynski two days after it was liberated. That's when I found out that everyone had been killed. It happened in 1942 when the ghetto was liquidated. They were shot in the Piatydnie forest."

My eyes locked onto a mallard swimming in the pond. His shiny green back grew in my field of vision so that I no longer noticed the female ducks swimming in circles or the trees towering over the pond or Julek sitting next to me on the bench.

"Do you want to know anything else?" Julek asked.

"No." I got up and walked to the edge of the pond. The mallard dipped into the water, and I searched for where he would come up. He popped up and chewed on some grass.

Julek joined me at the edge of the pond. "I know it's not easy," he said.

"Did any of our friends survive?" I asked. Julek listed several names, and I vividly pictured every person as he talked: Ruchcia Singer and her daughter Chumcia, who lived on the hill across the street from us and across from the Polish gymnasium. She and her husband, Izak, owned the largest and most popular textile store in town. Nuchem Spielberg, our next-door neighbor and one of our best friends. He and his two brothers owned large estates with dense forests and sawmills near the village of Turia. Zelman Wasser, an old bachelor, who, along with his brother, owned a printing shop located on the first floor of our building. Grisha and Itzhak Greenberg, two brothers who graduated from the Jewish gymnasium ahead of me. Baybak Gomulka, the most admired soccer player in the Jewish sport club Amatorzy.

As Julek told me about other survivors, an unending sadness shrouded my head and heart. "Maybe someone in the family survived. Maybe someone is looking for us. Maybe everything would be different if I had been with them."

"Maybe yes," Julek said, buttoning his jacket. "Or maybe you would be with them in the Piatydnie forest."

Back in my room I lay on my bed and cried with my face against the pillow. It had been six years since I'd said goodbye to my parents, Rachel, and Taubcia, whom I'd married only six weeks before I left for the Red Army. Six years ago and the day was sunny and warm, with skies clear and blue. Pansies, lilacs, and lilies of the valley were blooming in our garden, creating the mixture of smells I liked the most. That morning in July 1940 was as peaceful and idyllic as all the mornings before the war and before the Soviets occupied our hometown. As with every morning for as long as I could remember, my father went to the kiosk across the street to get the newspaper and cigarettes. Taubcia and Rachel made breakfast, and my mother, still weak after having part of her colon removed due to advanced cancer, set the table. At noon I was supposed to report to the train station, and I hugged and kissed everyone and asked them not to go with me to the station. It would break my heart to see my mother, Taubcia, and Rachel crying on the platform. But I couldn't convince them to stay home, and we all went together. It wasn't until I was on the train standing at the open window and saw my mother hugging Taubcia and Rachel and all of them waving goodbye that I felt a spasm in my throat and tears streaming down my face. As the train moved slowly I watched them getting smaller and farther away from me until the sharp turn, when they disappeared completely. I believed I would see them again soon. Everyone promised they would visit me wherever I was stationed. But only my father was able to make a short visit. The war with Germany broke out one year later.

Lying in bed, turning from one side to the other, I couldn't find any peace of mind. I couldn't stop asking why they were murdered and why I survived, and I berated myself for not going back to them when I'd had the chance to desert the Red Army. When I'd had my tank accident in the river and was left to watch the tank for a couple of days, I toyed with the idea of deserting. Although we were in Nazi-occupied territory, I believed I could find my way home. If I'd been in Wlodzimierz-Wolynski I could've convinced my family to go into hiding. I had many Polish, Ukrainian, and Jewish friends, and I could've found shelter for us. I wouldn't have waited to be led to mass slaughter. I had not taken the chance and deserted, though, because I was too afraid of being recognized in my Red Army uniform by the Nazis or Ukrainian police. Now I regretted it.

I tried to block out memories of my family, but everything reminded me of them: the color of a coat, the smell of an Egyptian cigarette, the sound of a girl laughing. I tried to recall my mother's face, Taubcia's smile, but my memory was fuzzy. I could picture the eyes but not the mouth, one expression but not another. But the terrifying images that came in nightmares and intrusive thoughts were more vivid than reality.

In the camps I'd seen prisoners dying and lying dead, corpses stacked like pieces of wood, naked bodies thrown in mass graves. I always thought I could be one of them, and I despaired that my family would never be able to find me. I never thought it might be the other way around. Although I went through the motions of a normal day, I couldn't live a normal life, which added to my despair. I'd lost years in the camps sleeping, eating, working, dreaming not the way normal people do. I could fall asleep at any time and any place, but I didn't sleep soundly because I was alert that someone could steal my boots or that I could be beaten, robbed, or raped. I ate like an animal,

chewing on anything chewable. I didn't taste anything but swal-
lowed quickly, wanting to fill myself, afraid that a bite, a fallen crumb
might be taken away. I worked not only because I was ordered to
work but because I wanted to eat. Not fulfilling the work norm meant
smaller rations, which would make me hungrier and weaker. Over
there the sun was cooler, the winds gustier, the moon smaller, despair
deeper. In the camps I never worried about my sanity, but in Moscow
I thought I was going crazy.

For many lonely days and sleepless nights I remained detached
from embassy life, feeling I didn't belong there but to the world I'd
left behind in my hometown. Although embassy circles welcomed
me, I turned down many invitations. Instead, while Julek and Halina
were out for the evening, I took vodka from their liquor cabinet and
sat drinking at their dining room table. The same questions kept
tramping through my mind: How could I go on all alone and do
something meaningful with my life? Did I want to continue living
when everyone else was dead? Did life mean anything when spent in
solitude, when there was no one to share it with? The one conviction
that emerged repeatedly from these drunken sessions was that the
only way to deal with my past, to say goodbye to my family and my
happy years at home, was to go back to Wlodzimierz-Wolynski and
see for myself what had become of the house where we lived; what
had become of my garden, school, streets, river, all the places of my
happy, carefree years where my parents, grandmother, sister, and
Taubcia lived, suffered, and perished. I needed to know why I was
spared, why Julek and I deserved better than everyone else in the
family; why our father, warm and vivacious, with so many close Polish and Ukrainian friends, dawdled away the time and didn't go into
hiding. I couldn't imagine that with his connections he couldn't find
shelter, as so many of our friends had done. Perhaps our mother was
too ill, or our grandmother too old to travel and live in the poor conditions imposed by hiding. But then why didn't Taubcia, Rachel, and
Fruma go into hiding? They were young and strong. They could've
survived the deprivations. Maybe they decided not to leave my
parents, not to separate from each other, and to meet their fate together, whatever it was going to be. Perhaps they did try to escape the
ghetto. I would never know.

I kept my feelings inside, not revealing them to Julek or anyone
else. I didn't think Julek could fully understand what I was going

through. I'd been in Moscow three months, and he'd been questioning me about what I was going to do with my life. I had no idea, and
our conversations left me feeling anxious and depressed. I needed his
help to get a permit to travel to Wlodzimierz-Wolynski, which was
now in the Ukraine Soviet republic, in a restricted military zone only
twelve kilometers from the new Polish-Soviet border, but I wasn't
sure how to approach him or how he would react.

Julek tried to spend more time talking to me about politics, problems in the embassy, and my future. One day he invited me into his
study and took out two glasses, a bottle of cognac, and a purple velvet bag. He poured the cognac and made a toast to my future. Julek
was relaxed when he was in his study. The wall-to-wall bookshelves
and leather sofa and armchairs suited him much better than the political portraits and flags hanging in his office. Built into the bookcase
were a liquor cabinet and a tall shelf on which Julek displayed one of
my mother's beloved statues. She had bought the three-foot statue on
a trip to Rome. Professor Filarsky, our math professor and our parents' dear friend, had kept it for them during the war and had given
it to Julek when he was in Wlodzimierz-Wolynski.

Julek swirled the cognac in his glass. "I'd like to invite you to move
in with Halina and me. We have an extra room. I think you'll be comfortable here," he said.

I was stunned. I'd buried the hurt I felt when Julek put me in the
guestroom, but now it came rushing back. Wanting to remove the
thorn stuck inside me, I said, "Julek, why didn't you invite me to stay
with you when I arrived?"

"You know, Janusz, we'd been apart for over seven years. You
were wild when we were growing up. I had no idea what the prisons
and camps had done to you. I saw how the war changed people, and
I thought it was best if we had our own quarters at first. I didn't mean
to hurt you. I should've known you'd be able to take care of yourself
and wouldn't lose your heart and decency."

I knew he didn't want to hurt me and felt grateful to him for his
offer, but his words contributed to a growing feeling of self-doubt. I
knew my experiences had changed me and set me apart from normal
life, and Julek's putting me in a guestroom had confirmed that feeling of difference.

Julek opened the velvet bag and took out several dozen gold coins,
tsarist rubles. "Papa hid these in a place in the wall in his office. He

bricked over the opening and painted it. After I got married he showed me where the hole was. When I was home after the war, I retrieved the coins. Half of them are yours." The face of Nicholas II was etched on one side and a two-headed eagle on the other. I felt their weight and ran my finger over the grooved edges. Julek got a dark suit and coat from his wardrobe. They were our father's. Julek said that Professor Filarsky had kept them. "I think you should have them," Julek said. He laid them out on the couch. It was my father's most elegant suit, a black pinstriped one that he wore when he and my mother went out. The coat had a white fur collar that I loved to press my face against when hugging my father. These pieces of clothing reminded me the most of my father, a high-spirited bon vivant, always joyful and smiling.

"Professor Filarsky refused to take any gifts I offered. He said he tried to convince our parents to go into hiding in the country and that he was ready to arrange it, but Papa declined the offer. Some high-ranking Gestapo men who were his patients allowed the family to remain in the flat while other Jews were forced into the ghetto. Papa believed this was a sign the family would be left alone.

"Other people in town also offered to find shelter for the family, as well as to keep some of our parents' things. Dr. Kuzmicki bought some furniture from them. Papa was short of money. He'd been extorted frequently by a few Poles and Ukrainians who told him you'd been captured by the Nazis and that they could deliver parcels to you or even get you out by bribing the German or Ukrainian guards. They played the same scheme over and over. Papa always paid."

I couldn't bear to hear of my father's desperation. He relied on me. He confided in me. He would have done anything to find me and bring me home. "Who were the extortionists?"

"We can't find and punish everyone who hurt our family," Julek said with a sigh. "Let's not talk about this anymore. I made peace with what happened, and I'm going on with my life. I wish you would do the same."

"Julek, I do nothing day after day except think about our family. I've tried to decide what to do with my life, but I need to go back to Wlodzimierz-Wolynski first. Will you please help me get a permit?"

"But why do you want to go back? No one is there. Our friends are gone. But there are plenty of people who cooperated with the Nazis; if they find out you're searching for information, they might try to hurt you. Besides, it's in a highly restricted military zone and you probably won't be allowed to go."

"I don't think you know what it means to me. We've lived different lives for so many years that you don't understand how I think. Right now nothing is more important to me than going back home. If you really want me to get on with my life, you'll help me get a permit. When I get back, I'll tell you what I want to do."

"But you'll be too late to apply to an institute or university."

"Julek, I'm not capable of doing anything until I go back. You've been back. You're living a full life. I have nothing and no one. The only people who meant anything to me have all been murdered. I need to go back."

"Okay. If you think this is what you need to do, I'll help you get the permit, but then promise me you'll get on with your life."

2

WAITING FOR TOMORROW

Julek extended the writing board from his desk and handed me the application form from OVIR, the Office of Visas and Registration of Foreigners, which I had to fill out to get a permit to visit Wlodzimierz-Wolynski. I scanned the sections, subsections, fine print, and detailed questions. The first four pages requested information about myself; the last four pages requested information about my parents, siblings, and other relatives. I had to sign each page at the bottom, swearing that all statements I made were true. Underneath the space for the signature, in bold letters, was the customary warning that false information would be punished with a prison term.

I looked the application over twice and put it back on Julek's desk. "I can't fill this out. If I lie I'll be arrested again, if I write the truth, I won't get the permit," I said.

The radio was blaring in Julek's office. Whenever I came to his office to talk, Julek turned it on, and he kept it on most of the time in his apartment so the listening devices wouldn't pick up our conversations. Julek's tired look told me he was not in the mood for reassuring me. "Everyone here lives with application forms and documents," he said, "and you, too, must learn to live with them. They're a part of everyday life here, and it's the same way in Poland. Fill out what you know, then together we'll think about how to fill out the rest."

I filled in the spaces for my name, age, and date and place of birth. But the next question, nationality, stopped me. Being Jewish was considered to be a nationality in the Soviet Union, but Julek's secretary, a Jew who had survived the war in Poland by passing as a Pole, told me bluntly that it was better not to advertise my Jewishness because anti-Semitism raged now as much as ever in Poland and the Soviet

Union. But I wanted to honor my family and not run away from who I was, so I wrote "Jewish."

Purpose of trip: "To find the graves where my family is buried and reclaim any family possessions."

Current and previous addresses: "Polish embassy; 1941–1946—various locations in the far east."

I filled out the section on my education, the names of schools, and dates attended without any problems. But the question about membership in political groups and organizations stumped me. Before the war I had belonged to a Jewish leftist youth organization, Hashomer Hacair, and an underground anti-fascist organization under the auspices of the Polish Communist Party. I wanted to boast of my prewar, pro-Soviet, anti-fascist activities, but membership in any prewar political parties could be interpreted by the NKVD as anti-Soviet—the Polish Communist Party was disbanded in 1938 and its leadership, which had been invited to Moscow, was arrested and executed. The Jewish far-left party, Bund, met the same fate. Julek insisted that I leave out my experiences and simply state that I didn't belong to any political organizations. I followed his advice.

Military service: "Tank academy in Orel 1940–41. Driver and mechanic of T-34. Sent to the front line in June 1941."

Profession: "None."

Occupation, dates, locations: "July 1941–March 1946, various manual jobs in the far east."

Foreign languages: "Russian, Polish, Ukrainian, French, and German."

Criminal record: I closed the application. How could I avoid writing about my court-martial? How would they let me go to a restricted zone? How would I ever be able to do anything in life, go anywhere, make a future for myself?

"Julek," I said, "I have a record. I can't hide it. There will be other applications, other documents, and they'll all have the same question."

"If you run away from this question now, you'll be running away forever. You aren't a Soviet citizen any longer. You're a foreigner with good ties and the protection of the Polish embassy. Your criminal past no longer matters. Just leave it blank."

"But the instructions are to fill out every answer."

"Leave it. If you write no, you're lying. Leave it empty. Perhaps you forgot to fill it out. Let them interpret it."

The last section in my part of the application required that I give the personal data of relatives and friends living abroad, especially those with whom I'd maintained contact, and the personal data of relatives living in the Soviet Union. "List only our relatives living in the Soviet Union," Julek said. "You have no contact with anyone living abroad, so don't write down anything. The less you write, the better."

Section two requested information about my parents and siblings. What difference did it make where my father lived and was educated, or whether he served in any army? What difference did it make what political parties he and my mother belonged to? Why did I have to write that my mother was born and lived in Odessa, about her family who still lived there, or why she moved to Poland with my father? Even more absurd, they wanted information dating back before the October Revolution. I wrote, "Father, Mark—deceased. Mother, Ottylia—deceased. Sister, Rachel—deceased. Wife, Taubcia—deceased."

As soon as Julek had submitted the application, I panicked. I had broken the number-one rule I had learned in Kolyma: to be inconspicuous, never to draw attention to myself, especially from the NKVD. Although Julek assured me that no matter what the authorities knew—that I had been a prisoner or that I had lied on the application—as a Polish citizen, with a Polish passport and living in the Polish embassy, I was safe.

With Julek's reassurances I should have felt secure in the embassy, but I was plagued with fear of the NKVD. Less than three months after returning from Kolyma, I still expected my freedom to be taken away from me. I imagined I was under special surveillance by the NKVD, and at night I locked my door and left the key in the lock. I was convinced that my belongings were searched every day, so I put two small pieces of paper between my pants and shirts and checked them at night to see if they'd been displaced. They never were, but I kept doing it anyway. Whenever I went out, the militiaman guarding the gate noted the time of day, and I was sure that as soon as I left he dispatched a civilian-clothed NKVD official to follow me. I was frightened of every person in uniform, especially people in authority, such as the militia at the gate taking note of my comings and goings or the NKVD. I was afraid to talk openly to people, sure that they

could see the fear in my eyes or anger in my manner and would suspect me of something. My health was good, but I was still terrified of
a recurrence of TB. I was afraid of feeling hungry, of my stomach
growling and sucking, of cramping pain that couldn't be relieved by
anything. I was afraid of filth and lice, and I was terrified of becoming homeless. I felt ashamed of the irrationality of my fears and was
afraid to tell anyone about them.

I nagged Julek about getting the permit, but he remained unper-
turbed, telling me to be patient, that Soviet bureaucracy was slow and
the permit would come, but patience had never come easy to me. For
as long as I remember I was in motion, quick to act and react, unfa-
miliar with idle time. Time without action, of which I had plenty in
the embassy, had a disturbing effect on me. My thoughts stretched
across the empty hours, and I wore deep trails in them. I fell into the
hollows left by the people I'd lost. I crawled into the empty spaces
where my youthful dreams used to be and despaired over the arid life
I was living. I tried to distract myself by reading, but the embassy library had only a few Polish and Russian classics along with contem-
porary Polish and Soviet novels, and I couldn't concentrate on any of
the books for more than a few pages. The descriptions of nature were
lengthy and boring; the plots developed at a snail's pace; dialogues
went on for pages. I wanted to read books I'd liked in my youth—adventure stories, westerns, detective novels—but they'd been banned
in the Soviet Union as "decadent bourgeois literature," and the embassy didn't have them.

It took less than half an hour to read the two main daily newspapers, *Pravda,* the newspaper of the Central Committee of the Communist Party, and *Izvestia,* which represented the views of the Soviet
government. They were only four to six pages long, and there wasn't
a single ad. The front page always featured a photograph of Stalin in
various settings: attending a state dinner for General de Gaulle; shaking the hand of the first secretary of the Communist Party of Mongo-
lia; greeting school children from Tbilisi; discussing the progress of
coal mining with leading engineers and miners; recognizing outstanding milkmaids from the famous *sovkhoz* (agricultural collective)
in the Crimea; discussing genetics with the academician Lysenko.
The first page also featured daily letters from the Soviet people in
which they expressed their love and devotion to Stalin, and promised
to increase production in industry and agriculture. The important

resolutions of the Central Committee and Soviet government were also published.

The inside pages were nearly impossible to read. The texts of speeches given by various Party, government, industrial, and agricultural leaders were reprinted in full, and every speech followed the same formula: the beginning and end paid homage to Stalin, the Creator of All Victories, the Greatest Friend of Humanity, and the Leader of the International Proletariat. There was never a hint that anything bad happened in the country. There were no reports of crime; no reports of train, airplane, or automobile accidents. There were never floods, fires, or droughts. According to the newspapers, everyone was happy living in the new paradise on earth.

One day a letter arrived from OVIR. I expected it to be the permit, but it was a notice to show up in two weeks for an interview with an NKVD officer. Frightened, I went to Julek's office and read the note to him. "They're going to ask about my past, unless they already know about it. I never should have applied for the visa."

"Janusz, you must shed your prisoner's skin. You'll never have a normal life, never have a decent job, never make anything of yourself if you don't learn to control your paranoia. An interview is standard procedure for anyone going into a restricted zone. They'll ask you the same questions that were in the application. You just give them the same answers."

One year after the war, it was a time of dreaming and forgetting. Everyone's past lay in ruins; all one could do was try to let go and construct something new. I envied those who could forget the past and what happened to their families, but I couldn't forget even for an hour. Uncertain of the future, I lived more in the past and didn't dare dream of being happy. When I was young, I couldn't wait for tomorrow. Now, I lived in yesterday's world, which I imagined might still exist somewhere. During the day I sat on a bench in the park watching old men play chess or wandered the streets near the embassy. I saw no joy or hope in anyone's eyes, no future and no past, just the toilsome, interminable present. The Muscovites moved from home to work to the markets, as busy as ants, with no time to think or dream about a different life, and I was terrified of becoming like them.

I had one close friend, Silek Shternfeld. He was a classmate from the

Jewish gymnasium, and he survived the war in the Soviet Union. A smiling, olive-skinned young man with high cheekbones, he attended the Moscow Theatrical Institute and sang in a choir of revelers. I ran into him when he was singing in a concert at the Association of Polish Patriots. He was thinner than the last time I'd seen him, but his beard stubble was still dark and heavy, and his hair black and curly. His parents had been deported to Siberia and died there. Silek was alone. He introduced me to his circle of friends, all Jews from Wolyn, the region where we'd grown up, and all of whom had survived Nazi occupation either in hiding or in the Soviet Union. They, too, had lost their homes and family members. They, too, struggled with their grief and fought to create meaningful lives for themselves. Silek's dream was to perform on stage and direct plays. He talked about emigrating to the west. He dreamed of Broadway, even Hollywood. Many of his friends were studying, a few were working, and a few were making big money on the black market, dealing in gold and diamonds. I envied their apparent joie de vivre, determination to succeed, and the largesse of those who could pay for all of us to have a good time.

It appeared that Silek and his friends had made peace with the past. No one talked about the war, ghettos, concentration camps, or lost loved ones. It was simply a time of young people enjoying themselves, carefree and happy with their companions, drinking, eating, laughing, and toasting one another. I enjoyed myself until the conversation drifted into dreams of the future. Then pleasurable moments disintegrated into memories I wanted to forget.

One evening Silek and I walked on Nikitsky Boulevard toward Pushkin Square. The streetcars and buses were running at longer intervals. A homeless woman dressed in rags asked us for money to buy the last drink of the day. Two military men across from us drank from the same bottle and boasted about the battles they had been in. Silek pointed at them and said, "See how people live here? They drink from early morning until late at night, and do you know why? You have to be drunk to live this life. Staying sober is dangerous. It makes you wonder about too many things and ask too many questions for which there are no answers."

On the morning of the interview I got up early and walked to the metro. It was the morning rush hour, and everyone was in a hurry to get to work. During the war being fifteen minutes late to work was considered sabotage and was punishable by three years in prison, and although the law was no longer in effect, everyone was still afraid of arriving late. One person looked like the next, poorly clothed and preoccupied, scuttling along the pavement with his head hanging as if not wanting to see something he shouldn't. Lines of shoppers, mostly old women or women who worked the evening shift, stood in line with their empty *avoski*, net shopping bags, already worn out from waiting for the stores to open.

The beggars had already taken up their positions around the cafés, kiosks, and department stores. Most of them were amputees, veterans of the war, which Stalin called the "Great Patriotic War." Dressed in military coats with colored medals, the invalids rolled across the streets on wooden boards that had four small steel wheels. Sitting only inches above the pavement, they held onto small blocks of wood to propel themselves along and loudly harassed pedestrians as they walked by. If a person refused to give money, the beggar unleashed a litany of curses and sometimes chased him down. A young blind invalid, probably my age, his jacket covered with medals, played an accordion and sang at the entrance of a large department store, entertaining the crowd waiting in line. He sang "Katyusha," the most popular war song in the country. His clear baritone voice expressed the yearning and loss that still filled people's hearts, and everyone joined in, stirred by a feeling of camaraderie and patriotism. His friend, who was missing an arm, held out a military cap and walked around in a circle asking for donations. The placard on his chest read, "I fought for you in the Great Patriotic War. Now I need your help."

In contrast to the sad street, the yard in front of the red-brick mansion housing OVIR was as colorful as a coral reef, with ebony-hued Africans draped in red, purple, and yellow dashikis with gold embroidering, Indian women in airy saris with red dots on their foreheads, Indian men in white shirts and pants, and a group of Chinese students in blue uniforms. Blond Germans and Swedes towered over everyone, and olive-skinned Italians, Greeks, and Albanians talked louder and gestured more than anyone else. It was a joyous, almost festive atmosphere, because the young people were returning home for vacation after studying at Soviet universities and institutes. The Soviet government provided stipends and a free education to students from the eastern bloc as well as capitalist countries, hoping to sway them toward Soviet ideology.

For nearly four hours I waited, occasionally checking the list to see how far down my name was. When a young officer displaying the pomp and arrogance of a high-ranking NKVD official bellowed my name, I roused from my torpor, put on my jacket to hide the sweat stains on my shirt, and walked into the office, burrowing inside myself to a place of calm alertness.

The NKVD major seated me in front of his desk, which was stacked with files. He seemed bored but officious, and his wavy gray hair had not been recently washed. "Comrade Bardach," he said, "I see that you've come here to ask for a permit to travel to a military restricted zone."

I had trouble looking in the major's eyes. Like all prisoners I had learned to avoid eye contact with the prison guards. A guard had once pulled my work partner out of line and beaten him because my partner had stared at him when he went through the gate. The guards wanted to be provoked, and they considered staring to be a challenge.

"We asked you to come because we'd like to hear from you personally what your purpose is in traveling to Vladimir-Volynsk. You wrote that your family was murdered by the Nazis. What exactly would be your purpose in returning?"

"I want to find out where they're buried," I said.

"Do you intend to see anyone in particular?"

"I may meet some of my old Polish and Ukrainian friends, but I don't know who's left, and I don't know what they did during the war. They could've fought with the Soviet partisans, or they could've been Nazi collaborators. Maybe they served in the police force guarding the ghetto." Unable to think of anything more to say, I did what everyone else did when speaking, writing, or giving an interview— gave a short speech praising Stalin and the Soviet Union. In the Red Army I had learned all the wooden formulas for speeches demonstrating devotion to the Party, its leadership, and especially to Comrade Stalin, and I said, "It wasn't only the Nazis who persecuted and murdered Jews. The Ukrainian police, Russian traitors from Vlasov's army, and other Polish partisans did the same. Everyone in the Nazi-occupied territories was free to kill Jews. Only in the Soviet Union were Jews safe. Thanks to the genius of Comrade Stalin, Hitler is dead, Nazism destroyed, and Germany on its knees, divided."

My speech had little effect on the officer. He leaned toward me and with his arms folded on the desk he said, "I must warn you that you're planning to travel to a highly restricted zone in dangerous territory. Ukrainian nationalists are still fighting with the local police and army units. Many of them have families in nearby villages and are hiding out in the forests and swamps. They know the terrain. They know the roads and people. You think you're going back to your hometown, but it isn't your hometown anymore. There are no more Jews. Be reasonable and think this over."

"But I can't postpone the trip. I can't begin my studies until I go back and take care of my dead family."

"If you insist on going now, I'll issue the permit. But you must sign a document that says you were warned about the dangers, and you must report to the local NKVD immediately upon your arrival. Keep them informed about where you're staying, and don't leave the city limits. You'll be informed when the permit is issued."

I rushed to the embassy and told Julek the good news. I also told him about the major's warnings but that I was sure the dangers were exaggerated. Julek looked worried. "What the major said is true. You don't read about it in the Polish or Soviet newspapers, but remnants of Bendera's nationalist Ukrainian gangs are still active in the area. They're fighting both the Soviet and Polish army and police. Maybe this will change your mind."

I listened to Julek like I listened to the major at OVIR, thinking they were trying to sway me from my decision. I needed to go, and I wasn't afraid of any danger because none of the dangers could be compared to the dangers my family had endured. But I wondered, would going back to Wlodzimierz-Wolynski heal me or hurt me further? Did I really want to find out everything that had happened to my parents, Rachel, Taubcia, and Julek's wife, Fruma, beyond what Julek had told me? Did I want to find out how frightened they had lived every minute of every hour? I didn't know if I could remain the same person I was now, or if knowing would fill me with hatred and vengeance. I worried about my mental state and tried to find the seam in my sadness where sanity met insanity.

At night I lay awake with my eyes closed, my mind racing from one image to another. I dozed and awakened, fell asleep and dreamed. My mother is sitting at the head of the table, wrapped in her white mohair shawl. As she looks around, the shawl slips from her shoulders to the floor. No one notices that the shawl is on the floor and she is shivering in her short-sleeved summer dress. It's snowing outside. The stove is burning, but the room is ice cold. Everyone else sitting at the table is dressed in heavy winter clothing, but no one moves to pick up Mother's shawl. I try to get up from my chair but can't, and the chair moves away, farther and farther away. I am paralyzed in the way that one is in a dream, and I can't get to her no matter how hard I try. From a distance I see my father, Rachel, and Taubcia on my side of the table and our close friends Sioma, Lenia, Ojcer, and Bristiger on the other side. They all look strange. Then there is no more food on the table, and then there is no table anymore.

The men, wrapped in black-and-white-striped fringed prayer shawls, with yarmulkes on their heads, are in the room praying in a language I can't understand. I cannot hear the prayer, but I know they are praying to the Jewish God to save the Jews from hatred, misery, torture, and death. I am far away from them, but I pray in my heart the same prayer without words. They don't talk to each other. They don't look at each other. They simply bend over and pray with no sound or movement. I leave them to rush to help my mother, but she's already covered with the mohair shawl. I cannot see her face, but I know she is my mother. I search the room and every room in the house to find her, Taubcia, and Rachel, but they've vanished without saying goodbye.

I didn't know what I was looking for. A note, a letter, a photograph, a book, anything they'd touched and held in their hands, anything they'd left behind hoping that maybe someone who survived would find it. Maybe Taubcia had written a letter to me and hidden it somewhere. I would go through the attic and cellar and look everywhere in the house for something she might have hidden.

Trying to escape the gnawing pain and sadness, I imagined the places where we all lived happily together. I daydreamed that walking the familiar streets, I might suddenly meet Taubcia and Rachel wandering around looking for me, just as I was looking for them. I thought I had the strength to go back and face what I would find in Wlodzimierz-Wolynski. I believed that whatever I found would bring me close to them.

If I'd waited another six or twelve months I doubt I ever would have gone back. Normal life would have dampened the courage it took to face the truth. Perhaps I would have found some other way to deal with the loss, although I can't say what that way might have been. Perhaps I would have moved back to Poland or emigrated somewhere else.

Lying on the bunk in the sleeping car, I couldn't fall asleep. I lay with my eyes closed and listened to the words I heard in the rhythmic clicking of the wheels as they jumped the spaces between the rails. These were the same words I heard after I'd fallen in love with Taubcia whenever I went on a trip, leaving her at home. "Love you, love you, love you. Miss you, miss you, miss you. See you, see you, see you." In the middle of the night I got up and went to the corridor. I stood at the open window hearing melodies in the wind as it passed between the electrical wires.

3

JOURNEY TO THE PAST

On the train from Lvov to Wlodzimierz-Wolynski the clicking of the wheels changed its rhythm, and the words I heard were not words of love and hope but despair. The wind howling through the telephone wires reminded me of Billy, my German shepherd, and the way he howled when he contracted rabies. To keep him from being shot I lied to my parents that I saw him drinking water and eating his food, despite the fact that for several days he had had severe rabies hydrophobia. I also hid the wound where he'd bitten my hand when I tried to feed him. A few days later my father saw Billy convulsing and shot him, and rabies was diagnosed, but I still kept it a secret that he'd bitten me. Only after my lymph nodes had swollen and I could barely walk did I tell my parents. The treatment, twenty injections in the stomach, lasted three weeks, but I mourned Billy for many years to come. He was my first friend to die a violent death.

As the train slowed down outside of towns and villages, the heavy jolts and sudden stops seemed to be warning me there was still time to get off the train and turn back without visiting the place where everyone was buried but no one knew where. The names of the stations—Sokal, Manievicze, Ivanicze, Janievicze—were now written in Cyrillic. A team of well-fed, glistening horses trotted obediently alongside the train. The driver cracked the whip and shouted "Vio! Vio!" and the horses lifted their heads, whinnied, and trotted faster. Burned-out cars and trucks, their frames broken and twisted, littered the roadside and told me more than anything else that a war had been here.

The train stopped in Ivanicze. From my window I followed the train tracks as they narrowed and disappeared in the forest. The tracks led to Poryck, a shtetl about an hour away from Ivanicze, and they brought back long-forgotten memories of the trips I took there with my father. The town didn't have a dentist, and my father used to practice there for two days every other week. His office was in the home of Dr. Klepinin, the town's only physician. We used to take a horse-drawn red and yellow wooden trolley that ran on narrow rails from Ivanicze to Poryck. I was fourteen the first time my father invited me to go with him.

I admired the coachman, who addressed nearly everyone by first or last name depending on their age and status. His long gray beard, long gray hair, and straight military posture made me think he'd been a high-ranking officer in the tsarist army fighting the Bolsheviks. He was respectful and ready to help the women and children get on the trolley, and he helped the men load the luggage. I sensed a dignity in this old man, who seemed to have been the coachman of this trolley forever. No one knew when he had come to Poryck or where he was from; Dr. Klepinin didn't even know his last name. When he sat proudly on the high seat at the front of the trolley and smacked the horse with a whip, he reminded me of the coachman of a stage coach in the Wild West. His Polish had a heavy Russian accent, and he addressed the horse, Vasia, lovingly in Russian, shouting "Vio, Vasia! Vio! Davay! Davay!"

Sometimes he asked me to sit with him and let me hold the reins and whip, which made me proud and happy. I thought he singled me out because I always addressed him as Mr. Alexei, while everyone else called him Alexei only. Then I found out that he favored me because we both shared a love for horses. I talked on and on with him about my horse, Lady, which my father had given to me for my fourteenth birthday. The seven kilometers from Ivanicze to Poryck snaked through dense forests and swamps where I was certain the trolley would be ambushed. I imagined that Alexei was armed and that he would valiantly protect us.

While my father saw patients, I usually sat in the living room with Dr. Klepinin, who never talked to me, and his adopted son, Volodia, who was five years older than I, chain-smoked, and drank vodka with his father. Short and muscular, his face covered with pimples, he talked to people with both hands stuffed in his pockets, something my father forbade me to do because it was a sign of disrespect. Volodia never looked in people's eyes when talking to them, while my father demanded that I stand up straight with my chin up and eyes looking ahead, not down at the floor or pavement. Volodia had been kicked out of school for bad behavior. I was always nervous in the presence of the rotund Dr. Klepinin, whose face looked like a blood vessel waiting to burst. I didn't care very much for the Klepinin family or the village of Poryck, but I loved the trips because I could spend such a long time alone with my father.

The time we spent together on the train and trolley and the walks we took in the countryside made me feel we were there for each other, that we understood each other. At times we hardly talked, and I sensed he had a lot on his mind. I didn't suspect that he could be in any kind of trouble. I didn't realize how the growing anti-Semitism, escalating every year after 1935, affected Jewish merchants and professionals, my father among them. I believed he was immune to worldly troubles. In the evenings we walked in the empty marketplace, past clay and wooden houses without electricity or running water. Sometimes in the middle of the street I'd take his rough hand and hold it against my cheek, smelling the soap he washed with, which I also liked to use.

Twenty kilometers away from my hometown, I could no longer stand still at the window, so I walked back and forth between the cars. In the corridor connections, the wind rushed, the wheels clicked, and the railroad ties blurred beneath my feet. I wished the train were taking me back to Moscow, to Julek, with whom I argued but felt safe.

As a boy I thought the station at Wlodzimierz-Wolynski was a grand junction, a major stop for trains from all over Poland, while in reality the local trains stopped for only a few minutes, and the express trains didn't stop at all. The international express train BERLIN-MOSCOW both fascinated and disturbed me. I spent many hours trying to figure out what the two cities had in common, how the first socialist country in the world could possibly have a liaison with Hitler's murderous regime. I imagined Moscow, the capital of the new society, to be a city of brotherhood, equality, and unrestricted freedom, which appealed greatly to my adolescent craving for social justice. But when I thought of Berlin I imagined frenzied crowds throwing their right arms forward and shouting with all their might, "Heil Hitler! Heil Hitler! Heil Hitler!" The first time I ever saw a real Nazi was on a field trip to Danzig in 1936, when I was in the Polish gymnasium. Until the age of sixteen I attended the Polish gymnasium, rather than the Jewish one, because it was located right across the street from our house. I was one of the few Jews in my class, and my parents didn't want me to go on the field trip, but I insisted. I'd been bullied by anti-Semites throughout childhood, and I wanted to see the Nazis for myself. When I was young and had to change in the locker room I felt ashamed of being Jewish because of my circumcised penis. When I was older I was angry and fought back. The class excursion to Danzig was the first time I felt scared.

Danzig had been declared a free city after World War I and was supposed to be ruled by the high commissioner of the League of Nations. But the German flag flapped from the balcony of the train station, and red flags bearing swastikas hung in the adjacent windows. People wore swastika pins on their lapels and swastika armbands. The red, yellow, and black German flag hung in the front window of every bus and trolley. In the old city, Sturmabteilung troops marched straight-legged to the bombastic national anthem, singing "Deutschland, Deutschland über alles." They acted as if they owned the streets and ruled the city. None of my classmates or teachers seemed disturbed by the Germans' intimidating presence, but I felt that Nazism was real and close and dangerous.

The first thing I saw telling me I was home was the grove of birch trees that marked the city limits. Whenever I returned from a trip, I looked for the slender white trunks on the horizon. They were a reassuring sight, telling me that although I'd been away, my hometown was still there, unchanged, waiting for me. I looked for individual trees I'd come to know by the shape of their trunks and position of their branches but couldn't find them. The train eased across an open field green with tall grass and weeds. I looked for my uncle's grain warehouse, trying to remember the layout of the railroad yard. I remembered my uncle Josif.

He was a short, stocky man with bushy eyebrows and large, callused hands. When he greeted me he squeezed my hand until I yelped. His oldest son, Moses, was five years older than I. A great ladies' man, Moses married an American Jewish girl from Baltimore. She wasn't as pretty as the other girls he courted, but she got him an affidavit and a ticket to go to the United States several months before the war started. I liked him because he taught me to play blackjack, took me boating, introduced me to his girlfriends, and walked with me on Farna Street, where we "polished the pavement and ruined our shoes," as my father used to say.

The train braked sharply, and not until it pulled up to the yellow-brick train station did I realize that all the warehouses and buildings for workers had been burned to the ground. Armed NKVD border patrols spread themselves out along the platform, shouting "Documents!" I gave a patrol my passport and permit.

"What language is this in?"

"Polish," I answered.

He handed back the documents. "You must register in town with the NKVD."

I took back the passport and permit and walked over to the last platform, the same place I stood on my birthday on July 28, 1940, when my parents, Rachel, and Taubcia saw me off for the Red Army. I put my suitcase down on the faded green bench. No train was waiting, and so I sat and watched a border patrol interrogate a man wearing a light gray suit. On the morning I left six years earlier, Taubcia held my hand tightly as we waited for the train, making an effort to be strong and make me strong. She didn't cry until the final moment, when we kissed goodbye. Rachel, mature as always, hugged Taubcia. At the last minute my father put down my suitcase and gave me more money. His large brown eyes had lost the joyful, energetic spark I'd grown up with. He was sad to be losing his companion, the person he relied on during increasingly difficult times. He was worried about being left alone with four women in the household to take care of, two of whom, my mother and grandmother, were very sick. The four of them looked like orphans standing huddled together on the platform. Many of their friends had been deported or arrested, or had departed for other countries. Julek had gone into hiding in Lvov. He'd been an active member of the Polish Socialist Party before the war and had been publicly denounced as an enemy of the people. He was in great danger of being arrested. I wasn't sure how my family would fare under Soviet occupation. Despite the Ribbentrop-Molotov pact, signed in secret in 1939, and the non-aggression agreement between Germany and the Soviet Union, no one in my family or among our friends believed peace between the two regimes would last.

I was one of few recruits to be seen off by family. Most of the other recruits were Ukrainians from the surrounding villages, and their families were busy working in the fields. I felt embarrassed and tried to play down my departure to temper everyone's emotions. Sensitive about standing out in a non-Jewish crowd, I knew that the emotional goodbye could result in cruel taunting and a basis for making me an outcast later among my fellow soldiers. I had begged my family not to see me off, but they wouldn't listen. Now I was grateful that they hadn't. My father promised to visit me in three months, after boot camp, and Taubcia and Rachel promised to visit me at Christmas.

Taubcia's letters came regularly to the tank academy in Orel where I was stationed, and she kept me posted about events at home. She said my mother wanted to leave Wlodzimierz-Wolynski and move to Odessa, where she had been born and raised and had many relatives and friends. Taubcia and Rachel supported her. Most of their friends had also left town, and they both were ready to leave. Taubcia had just graduated from the gymnasium and talked about starting at the university in Lvov or Kiev; Rachel, sixteen, was thinking about attending the university after gymnasium. This would leave my father to take care of my mother and grandmother, and I was worried about his being alone. I thought it would be safest for them to move farther away from the German border, even though the Red Army was in the process of building new fortifications on the Bug River, only ten kilometers away. But my father was hesitant. He was worried about traveling with his frail mother and my mother, who was still weak and uncomfortable after surgery. He'd worked hard all his life to give my family the life we had, and he was unsure about abandoning his practice to begin a new life in a big city. If I hadn't been forced into the Red Army, I believe we would have moved to Odessa or another city farther inside the Soviet Union. I could have convinced my father to relocate, and with my help he might have felt more confident about the move.

I followed the stench of stale beer and cabbage soup into the train station. Rough, raw voices rolled out of the restaurant, which was now a filthy Soviet beer hall. Before the war this had been one of the most fashionable restaurants in town, with crystal chandeliers and red velvet curtains. Everyone in town had been proud of the train station. It had been meticulously kept. The tile floor was designed in a colorful mosaic fanning out in all directions, and the station personnel had worn crisp navy blue uniforms with gold buttons. I stood at the counter and ordered a beer. Flies buzzed around spilled beer and sugar, and a group of drunken men played cards at a table in the corner. They cursed and spit on the floor and slapped the cards down hard. Empty vodka and beer bottles piled up on the floor next to them. I tossed back the beer and went out into the train station. Taking a deep breath, I pushed open the heavy oak doors and stepped onto the plaza.

Nothing could have prepared me for the desolation of this once lively place, the departure point for the dreams that had led me into the world. There were no families gathered to see someone off, no excited children dressed in their Sunday clothes. Only a few swaggering military men waited on the curb. There was no grass and no *droshki*, horse-drawn carts. No smell of manure. No coachmen lounging on the plaza drinking vodka and playing cards. There was a taxi stand but no taxis, flowerbeds but no flowers. Not a single tree was in sight—all the magnificent chestnut trees shading the plaza and lining Kolejowa Street had been chopped down. I crossed the plaza and walked from stump to stump in the sweltering heat. Each tree had been crudely cut, and ants and termites had eaten through the rough wood. Weeds had taken root. The jagged, chipped stumps reminded me of the trees I'd cut down in the Siberian taiga. Like other prisoners, I didn't care if the stumps were cut evenly, and I sensed that the Jews from the ghetto who cut down the chestnut trees on Kolejowa Street paid no attention to how the stumps would look either.

I walked downtown under the pounding sun. The pedestrians wore the same gray clothes and the same worried expressions I saw on every face in every Soviet city. Shoppers spilled out of the stores and into the street clutching *avoski*. They waited in unmoving lines to buy items declared *deficitnye*—extremely scarce. Before the war nearly every store belonged to a Jew and nearly everyone on the street was Jewish, but I saw no Jews now. Looking closely at the faces of the people I passed, a few looked familiar but I didn't dare approach them, having no idea what they'd done during the war. I tried to decipher their faces, separate the killers from those who risked their lives to save a Jew. How many of them were informers, guards, extortionists, blackmailers, murderers? How many of them had I known in the past? How many of them had been in my home? How many of them went on living normal lives oblivious to the fate of those corralled in the ghetto and murdered, forgetting that some of them used to be their friends, forgetting that all of them were human?

I walked aimlessly through the streets shorn of their trees. Traveling to Wlodzimierz-Wolynski, I had hoped that someone in my family was alive, and I wished it would be Taubcia. I began to doubt Julek's claim that no one had survived. He wasn't there when the ghetto was liquidated, he'd only heard the story second-hand. Perhaps Taubcia had survived far away and hadn't returned yet. All those years, thousands and thousands of miles away, I lived for Taubcia, my first love. I missed her more than anyone else in the family. We met when I transferred from the Polish to the Jewish gymnasium, when she was fourteen and I, sixteen. She had blond hair, a round face, and green eyes. Like most girls of the time she was quiet and a little shy. But beneath her reticence she was strong-willed, and she wanted to explore life for herself, which often put her at odds with her parents, especially after she began to date me. Where I was quick and impulsive, Taubcia was patient and thoughtful. She was much more mature than I, and she more than anyone else taught me to control my temper and stop my immature behavior. At first she thought it was funny when I would suddenly stop while walking down Farna Street and pretend I'd lost a diamond ring. She'd laugh when I searched the pavement and passersby stopped to help. Then we'd join my friends on the corner laughing. But soon she became annoyed with this trick, along with everything else I did to show off, such as "accidentally" splashing people while kayaking and parading my horse through the middle of town. I had no sense of how immature my behavior was. My parents had tried to correct me, but I had never listened to their reprimands. I felt drunk with freedom, and in my new, expanding world, I wanted more and more of it. But Taubcia's repeated criticisms finally made me aware of how my behavior affected other people. I wanted to please her, I respected her opinion, and in time, I calmed down.

I walked toward Taubcia's house on Kolejowa Street. I could hardly believe it was the same town I'd grown up in and where I knew every house, store, street, and alley. Two years after liberation, the debris and rubble left by the Nazis still remained. The damaged buildings had been either patched over with concrete or boarded up. I walked quickly past many lots until I came to Litwaks' Hotel. The giant, faded white letters—"OTEL"—painted on the only remaining wall of the building brought back vivid memories of the years before the war and hurt me more than the blasted brick and mortar lying next to me. I kicked aside pieces of brick and wood until I found the red-brick footpath leading to the back of the hotel. I followed the fragments until I kicked something hard. It was the iron shoe scraper, rusted but still intact, that sat next to what used to be the back door. I remembered the doorbell, its scratchy ring, and the green-painted door frame. At the beginning of our relationship, when Taubcia's parents forbade her to date me, we met secretly in Bronka Litwak's room at the back of the hotel, which was owned by Bronka's parents. She was Taubcia's best friend. I used to announce my arrival with a secret code—two short rings and one long ring. Bronka and Taubcia would then come to the door, and the three of us would talk in Bronka's room. I stepped over what used to be the threshold of the house. Now I could find the living room and, looking east, Bronka's room. I walked four steps forward and several steps to the right. I looked out at the pond, trying to remember the view of it from Bronka's window. Grasses stretched across it and scraps of lumber lay on its banks. I squatted in the spot where Taubcia and I used to sit and closed my eyes again for a long while.

I walked to Taubcia's home, only six houses away. The house looked just as it had six years before, with its red shutters and wraparound veranda. I knocked at the kitchen door. A young woman with a long dark braid lying over her shoulder greeted me suspiciously. The house smelled of garlic and sauerkraut. A baby cried in the background. The woman didn't invite me inside but stood at the door wiping her hands on her apron.

"What do you want?" she asked in Russian.

"I used to know the people who lived here before the war," I said. Tacked up on the dirty walls were reproductions of typical Soviet landscape paintings—a deer in the woods, a brown bear up on its hind legs. A portrait of Stalin hung in the living room.

"Are you looking for someone in particular?" the woman asked.

"The Stern family used to live here. Do you know anyone by this name?"

"I don't know anything about the previous owners except that they were Jewish. The home was empty when it was assigned to us. We have papers from the city council."

I looked past the woman into the dining room. Taubcia's parents and brother had been sitting at their long dining room table the last time we saw them. It was the night of the deportations during the fall of 1939. The Soviets had occupied the town for two months, and now they were cleaning the city of suspicious elements, mostly Jewish refugees flooding in from Nazi-occupied territory. They also were going after local land and property owners, who were considered enemies of the people. Taubcia's father was a merchant and homeowner. I'd been tipped off by a friend about the deportations, and that evening I went to Taubcia's home and urged her family to come into hiding with my family for the night in our neighbor's underground shelter. Her parents refused to leave the house. Only Taubcia joined me.

Early the next morning, after a night of brutal searches, arrests, and deportations, Taubcia and I went to her house. A neighbor, Madame Lishner, met us in the street. She told us that Taubcia's parents and brother had been deported at dawn.

Taubcia moved in with my family and shared Rachel's bedroom. She'd spent so much time in our home during the years we dated that my parents already considered her a member of the family. She confided in my mother more than her own, and after my mother got sick, she and Rachel ran the household.

After that day I felt even more responsible for Taubcia. Not only did I love her but I needed to protect her, take care of her, be everything she had lost. I tried to comfort her in the only way I knew how: by trying to convince her that everything would be all right, that although her family had been deported they were alive and we would find out where they were. Taubcia would ask over and over, more to herself than to anyone else, "Where are they? What's happening to them?" and I would try to answer, but I only ended up feeling frustrated, and she, more alone and frightened. By evening I'd driven her away so that only my mother could comfort her, hugging and kissing her, letting her cry until she couldn't anymore.

Taubcia and I matured quickly, finding that our youthful dreams of social justice in the Soviet Union didn't fit the fate of our parents and friends. My father and uncle, who owned the building we lived in, were also considered to be capitalists and therefore were also listed as enemies of the people. Even though the building had been nationalized immediately after Soviet occupation, I worried that they too might be arrested and deported.

We received a letter from Taubcia's parents posted from a small village in Siberia. Then I left for the Red Army. I don't know if Taubcia ever heard from them again.

I left Taubcia's house and wandered far away down Lucka Street, toward Shulman's mill. I examined every house, yard, fence, and tree and thought of every Jew who had once lived there. I found the houses almost unbearable to look at. Unlike the buildings that had been destroyed, which now existed only in memory, the worn and weary houses, like the faded letters on Litwaks' Hotel, reminded me of the life that had been destroyed, and I wished I'd never come back.

I wouldn't have recognized the ghetto if Julek hadn't told me where it was. It included one side of Farna Street, the side I never liked to walk on because it seemed to me it was always in the shade. The commercial center on Market and Warszawska Streets, where most of the Jewish stores were located, formed the other boundaries of the ghetto. I walked through the empty streets, past the ruins of the Jewish school Tarbut and the big synagogue. The entire area had been left in ruins. I tried to imagine my friends crowded into the shops and shacks without running water, surrounded by sewage and corpses, waiting for death but clinging to life until the last moment. In the ghetto there was one sentence for everyone; the only difference was timing. The selections were left in the hands of the Jewish police and administration, the Judenrat, so the Nazis and Ukrainian police could watch Jews sending their kin to their death. Even my worst days in the labor camps weren't as bad as life in the ghetto. Although the labor, hunger, cold, filth, and disease decimated prisoners, everyone knew that if he survived his term, he would be free.

The emptiness of the ghetto reached farther toward Kielczszyzna, the poorest Jewish quarter. I had many close friends from the area. I met them in the soccer club and in the leftist organizations I belonged to, and I was drawn to them because of the hard lives they led. Sometimes I was ashamed of the privileged life my parents had made for us, and I believed that my friends from Kielczszyzna were stronger, wiser, and more experienced in life than I. I prided myself on being friends with people from different walks of life. I felt that by getting to know them I gained insight into the world outside of Wlodzimierz-Wolynski.

Before the war Kielczszyzna was an area of short, unpaved streets and alleys. Kitchen scraps and raw sewage filled the gutters and smelled from a mile away. There were no sidewalks, just boards thrown down alongside the road. They bounced up and down when walked on, and mud splashed beneath them when it rained. The destruction of the ramshackle tenements in Kielczszyzna hurt me more than the bombed-out buildings I'd seen in town, because I knew how hard my friends' families had struggled to make ends meet. Most of the men had worked as coachmen, porters, or unskilled laborers. They earned the few possessions they had, and it seemed that not only the tenements had been destroyed but all their years of hardship and toil.

My best friend, Chaim Ochs, had lived in Kielczszyzna. He and his family lived in a two-room house with clay walls and a hard-packed dirt floor. When I went to visit him I would find his three younger sisters sitting in the doorway playing games and singing songs. They each had only one nice dress to wear on special occasions, and so they sat outside in filthy, threadbare coats that had been handed down. Their stockings were worn and their shoes had holes in them, but their mother made sure their dark hair was freshly combed and braided. I once saved Chaim's youngest sister from drowning in the Luga River, and to show his gratitude Chaim became my devoted friend and bodyguard. Although he wasn't much taller than I, he was strong and had a reputation as a fearsome street fighter. As anti-Semitism became more dangerous, he escorted me to school at the Polish gymnasium, and later took special care of Taubcia and Rachel.

Chaim had never been to school but worked with his father, hauling farm goods to the mills and markets. His father owned a wagon and two Belgian horses, which were the family's most valuable possessions. The first few times Chaim came to our home he was extremely shy and felt painfully out of place. He didn't know the proper way to greet people, converse, or handle a knife and fork. I thought he might stop coming to my home altogether, but he wanted to learn. My mother took a special liking to him and taught him table manners, as well as how to read and write. I thought that if anyone had survived the ghetto liquidation, it would've been Chaim. He wouldn't have denied the danger; he was so fearless that he would have acted. Years later I found out that he did try to act. He planned to escape with a group of young people and had even acquired guns, but he was informed on and was shot.

In the open gutters and alleys, down bombed streets, and in the ruins of the main synagogue and the emptiness of the burned-down houses, I smelled death and destruction. I had always wondered why the main synagogue was built amid such poverty. Was it a symbol that God was closest to the poor who needed him most, or was it because it symbolized hope and a promise that life would get better? I had never been comforted by religion, and the loss of my family and my experiences in the camps hadn't changed this. We were taught in school that Jews were the Chosen People, living under the grace of the Jewish God who promised a better life, but how could such a God abandon his people and let them be slaughtered? I didn't believe I needed to be religious to be a good Jew, and all my life I had considered myself a good person and a good Jew.

At that moment I felt more Jewish than ever and wanted to pray for my family and friends, but I didn't know the prayers, so I prayed without words. I couldn't make peace with God, because the more I thought about it the more certain I felt that it wasn't God who failed his people but heinous, sadistic, and murderous people who destroyed the Jews. I left God out of it. I didn't ask him for anything, and I didn't thank him for saving my life.

4

THE HOUSE ON THE HILL

Lying on the thin mattress in the Bristol Hotel, I closed my eyes, hoping to drop into a deep, forgetful sleep. Mosquitoes buzzed around the hotel room, and the sticky night air clung to my aching body. I didn't want to think anymore. I didn't want to be hurt by one more memory. I tried counting forward and backward in all the languages I knew, but my mother's voice kept intruding: "Where are you? We need you." Her voice was calm and steady. I tried to remember my father, but his face was contorted. Taubcia and Rachel cried out my name. I couldn't recall Rachel's smile or the exact shade of Taubcia's green eyes.

In Moscow I'd begun taking Luminal to sleep, and when the hands on the clock slid past midnight I got up and took a pill. The Luminal slowed and stretched my thoughts, dissolving their connections. I lay awake and dreamed at the same time. In the middle of the night someone knocked at the door, and I sprang out of bed. In prison I slept like this. I'd fall asleep as soon as I found a place to lie down but slept vigilantly, afraid of being robbed, raped, beaten, killed. Like an animal, I woke up alert and ready to respond. The pounding continued. I expected to see an NKVD officer who had come to tell me that something had happened to Julek or that something was wrong with my visa. I put my hand on the lock, ready to turn it, and asked gruffly, "Who is it?"

A slurred voice responded. "Open the door, you dog's prick." I opened the door and stared at a flabby, pale-chested man standing in his underwear. "Who are you?" he asked, glancing inside my room. Then he slapped himself on the forehead and said, "What an idiot I am. This isn't my room. Sorry." He extended his hand and drunkenly bowed again and again.

46

Unable to sleep, I put on my pants and sat on the windowsill. I could see the old movie theater and the small park where all the trees had been cut down. The silhouette of the Roman Catholic cathedral was on the horizon. Just before dawn I lay down and fell asleep. I awakened a few hours later in the sunny, stifling room. I got up and went to look for a newspaper and cigarettes on Farna Street.

I sat down on a bench and watched people scuttling off to work. Most of the workers were Soviet—Ukrainians and Russians who'd relocated after the war. I could tell by their drab clothing and purposeful gait. Before the war people used to linger while walking down Farna Street. They stopped to talk to friends or bought something in a shop before going to work. But not a single storefront on Farna Street was the same as it had been before the war. Lerners' clothing store, where my father, Julek, and I bought our clothes, had been turned into a food store. The privately owned shops had been replaced by nationalized stores. Second-floor apartments had been gutted. Storefronts were boarded up.

I don't know how long I had been sitting with the unread newspaper on my lap when I recognized a tall, lanky, blond-haired woman. Her name was Miriam Tabak, and she'd been in Julek's class. Her father was a carpenter, and I played soccer with her younger brother, Moyshe. I wouldn't have recognized her if it hadn't been for her rounded shoulders and slightly stooped walk. Her blond hair was cut to the chin, and her face appeared longer and more angular. I leapt off the bench and ran across the street to meet her. "Miriam!" I shouted. She looked around and clutched her bag to her chest. I called her name once more, and when she saw me she ran into the street to meet me, cutting across the path of several pedestrians. We hugged each other like family members, even though I'd barely known her before the war. Miriam's eyes darted left and right.

"I work in the pharmacy in your grandfather's building. Moyshe and I still live in our old house on Kowelska Street," she said, grabbing my arm tightly. "Come back to the pharmacy with me." Her beige jacket slipped off her arm and onto the street, and I bent down to pick it up. I noticed she wore the same bulky black shoes as most Soviet women, and a pair of mended black tights.

Miriam found two stools in the back of the pharmacy. She told me that a Polish friend arranged for her and Moyshe to escape from the ghetto and that for over two years she and Moyshe hid in the cellar in her friend's home in the village. Her parents didn't dare to leave the ghetto, afraid of the hardships imposed by a life in hiding. Miriam got up to check the counter for customers.

"How's Moyshe?" I asked.

Miriam began to cry. "He's not well. I have to lock him in the house whenever I go out. He's still frightened, and he doesn't want to see anyone but me. He won't go to a doctor. I don't know what to do. I want to live like everyone else, but I can't leave him."

The bell on the pharmacy door rang, and Miriam dried her eyes and hurried to the counter. When she came back she sat down and resumed talking. "Tell me what I can do to save Moyshe. He can't stop talking about the war. He's tried to kill himself, and I don't have anyone—." I took Miriam in my arms and held her tightly, unable to find any words to ease her pain.

When I left the pharmacy I promised to visit her again before I left, and she smiled with a smile that reminded me of how much she had been admired for her beauty and charm.

Throughout my life, whenever I met a person who survived the war in hiding, I thought about Moyshe. I regretted that I didn't go to see him that day. Perhaps my presence would have triggered good memories from the past and helped him get back into the real world. Moyshe was one of the last people I would've thought would become psychotic under the duress of hiding. He was one of the smartest students in class, the toughest in school, and the most athletic on the soccer field.

I often wondered why some people were able to persevere under the conditions of hiding, while others became chronically depressed, even psychotic. Everyone who survived in hiding lived with the fear of being discovered and killed. In addition, there was the fear that something bad would happen to the hosts, leaving the survivors to starve to death in the darkness of their shelter. Poles and Ukrainians who hid Jews sacrificed a great deal emotionally and financially and endangered not only themselves but their families.

Hiding places were often shared with strangers, and tensions ran high and fights erupted with little or no provocation. After years in hiding, most survivors suffered from a mental disorder. Paranoia and depression were the most common afflictions. Phobias—avoiding other people, open spaces, close quarters, or anything that reminded them of their years in hiding—were rampant. Survivors tried to go on with their lives in a number of ways. Some people spent many years in psychotherapy trying to regain mental stability and a feeling of inner safety. Others never talked about their past, not even to their own children. A few became so ill that they spent most of their time in psychiatric hospitals or in total isolation.

Most of the survivors I knew tried to start new lives after the war. They studied, worked, married. These people did much more than survive; they regained their dignity, security, and self-assurance. Some of them talked and wrote about their years in hiding. But others, after a period of living seemingly normal lives, became depressed and withdrawn, evidence that they had never recovered from the years under Nazi occupation.

I walked down Uscilugska Street toward the "house on the hill," the name our family and friends gave to our light gray house, the place I lived from the time my family moved from Odessa when I was an infant until I was sixteen years old. With its barn, stable, yard, and garden of fruit trees, the house on the hill was the only home I ever wanted to have, and while we lived there life was good and I thought the goodness would last forever. After my family moved downtown I returned frequently to the house on the hill, like the two cats that returned to live in the barn there.

Walking to the house on the hill, I felt its presence in my bones before I saw it. I felt it as I tore moss and weeds from the stone wall at the bottom of the hill, and I felt it as I opened the gray, weathered gate and walked up the red-brick footpath. The house appeared as it always had but without the apple and cherry trees around it—they'd been chopped to the ground. The porch still had four frosted window panes and one transparent pane, which my father had replaced when a bird slammed into the window. On each corner of the house there were downspouts with wooden barrels underneath to collect rainwater, which my mother considered very special for washing hair and delicate clothing. I imagined that fish, frogs, and eels lived in the barrels, and I spent hours trying to catch them.

It was just a small, wooden house, half the size I remembered, with a cluttered veranda and broken gray shutters. My father used to close those shutters every evening, and if I heard the squeaking and banging I came running home so that I could walk around the outside of the house with him, especially when it was dark or the weather was bad, so he wouldn't be alone.

I walked over to the sun-scorched yard between the house and barn, where I played with the two dear friends of my youth, Billy and Lady. My father gave me Billy when I was eight years old. Our handyman, Ignatz, said that Billy was half German shepherd and half wolf, and I believed him. Billy's muzzle was long, black, and narrow. His palate was black, and he had large black spots on his tongue. He had a black saddle, dark brown legs, and a light brown underbelly. His dark brown ears cocked forward when he was alarmed, and his bark sounded like a half bark, half howl. He acknowledged only my father, who trained him; Marynia, our Russian maid, who fed him; and me, who ran with him in the garden and spoiled him with bones.

For my fourteenth birthday my father gave me Lady. She was a retired racehorse, and Ignatz taught me how to wash, brush, and saddle her. She was dark brown, with white socks and a white star on her forehead, and she had a mind of her own. She taught me that if I rode out one way I had to return the same way or she would throw me off and go back alone. I felt a special sentiment for these two animals because they were my friends only. I felt responsible for them. I used to talk to them, thinking they understood me, because Ignatz told me that the only way to develop a close connection with animals was by talking to them, and I did everything Ignatz told me. The barn and backyard were my private kingdom, and Billy, on a long chain, made sure no strangers entered.

No one had played in the yard in a long time. I couldn't find the outlines of the makeshift soccer field or the circle Billy had worn into the ground, and I came back and sat down on the front porch. Looking at the windows of my parents' bedroom, at the peeling paint, broken shutters, boarded-up kitchen entrance, and rotting roof, I couldn't stop crying. I cried because everyone I loved was gone and I would never see them again. I cried because I didn't know where to lay flowers. I cried because I didn't know what to do with my life when no one was with me for whom I would like to live.

I didn't hear the man and heavy-set woman walking up the footpath, and I was startled when I caught sight of them out of the corner of my eye. I wiped my face with my handkerchief and stood to shake their hands. "I'm sorry to be on your property," I said, and introduced my-self. "I lived here with my family before the war."

The man wore a Soviet military uniform with the insignia of the engineering service and introduced himself as Vitali Semyonovich Glebov and his wife as Ariadna Nikoleyevna. He paused awkwardly for a moment, then put down one of the *avoski* he was carrying and opened the door. "Please, come inside," he said. "A guest in the house is like God in the house."

In the dining room, Ariadna offered me a chair at the round din-ing table. Vitali brought out a bottle of vodka and three glasses, while Ariadna chopped up onions and herring and placed them in a glass bowl. I told them about my family and said I was living with my brother in Moscow. Vitali poured vodka in the glasses and said, "Let's drink to the memory of your family. May they rest in peace." We drank our shots and remained quiet for a moment. I felt that these two people, childless and in their forties, would honor the memory and spirit of my family. "When did you move here?" I asked.

"The house was assigned to us two months ago," Ariadna said.

"Do you know who lived here during the war?"

"A Ukrainian family," Vitali said. "The man and his brother-in-law were in the Ukrainian police during the war. They're awaiting trial along with seven others."

"Do you know who?" I asked, hoping it wasn't anyone I'd been friends with before the war.

"I don't know the names, but there are plenty of these people around. We're trying to track them down, but they've got hiding places with people in nearby villages." Vitali poured another shot of vodka and said, "Let's drink to their being found and hanged." We clinked glasses. Vitali gulped his shot forcefully.

"You're welcome to look around the house," Ariadna said. "I'm afraid we don't have much furniture. We live a simple life here."

I got up and went from the dining room into what used to be my parents' bedroom. Sunlight shone through the long lace curtains. A double bed and two nightstands were pushed against a wall. When I was growing up my parents had two beds pushed next to each other and nightstands with ceramic knobs and reading lamps. Until I was seven I slept on a loveseat at the foot of their bed, separated from them by a tall curved footboard and gauze curtains.

This room had been my mother's sanctuary, and it brought back memories of the time we spent there together when I was young, the time when I was closest to her. I was a highly energetic child, exploring everything, unable to sit still for longer than thirty seconds. I wanted to be part of every conversation and every activity, and I'm sure I exhausted my mother, who was quiet and reflective. The bedroom was filled with her books, paintings, journals, jewelry, and perfumes. Our closest moments were when I was sick with bronchitis, which happened frequently, and during these spells she kept me next to her in my father's bed, where I could cuddle up to her, feeling safe and loved. I liked it so much that I often faked being sick, sending my father to the couch and me to his bed. I loved my mother's touch, the smell of her powdered skin, her sparkling gray eyes and bobbed auburn hair. I thought there was no woman in the world more beautiful and better than she. She'd been severely burned in childhood, and scars spread like vines across her left arm and leg. I thought they still hurt, and I used to stroke and kiss them. The ritual existed only between the two of us, and even on her bad days she smiled when I did it, but sometimes she cried bitterly and held me tightly. It took years before I understood her sadness. After she married my father and moved to Wlodzimierz-Wolynski, she never stopped longing for Odessa, her birthplace, her "house on the hill." She missed the lively intellectual life in Odessa, the operas, theaters, art galleries, and philharmonics. She missed her family and friends who remained there after the Revolution. For several years she applied for a visa to visit her family, and the visa was finally granted in 1928. I was nine and Julek fourteen when she took the two of us for a two-month summer vacation.

I'll never forget my first border crossing at Shepetovka. The Soviet border guards, dressed in green uniforms and with rifles slung over their shoulders, gruffly ordered us to show our passports and visas. They searched through our suitcases. They snatched our pillows away from us and ripped them open, scattering the white feathers on the filthy floor. One young officer ordered my mother to follow him to a back room for a personal search. She came back a long time later, crying, her hair and clothing disheveled, and she cried for a long time after we reboarded the train. Because she was now a Polish citizen, she had undergone a customary body search to make sure she wasn't smuggling weapons, currency, or anti-Soviet literature.

We stayed in a spacious dacha on the Black Sea that belonged to my mother's older brother, Marcel, a professor of neurology at the medical school in Odessa. His wife, Rosa, was a famous painter, and her portraits were exhibited at galleries and museums in the Soviet Union and abroad. She painted my mother's and Julek's portraits while we were there, but I couldn't sit still long enough for her to paint mine.

Although close in age to my two cousins, Nathan and Misha, I didn't become friendly with them, finding them too bookish and well behaved. But I fell in love with the Black Sea and its sand and rock beaches, seahorses, starfish, jellyfish, and palm trees lining the boardwalk. On the beach I played with the *bezprizorniki*, children orphaned during the war, who lived on the beach in shacks made out of tin and cardboard. The long-haired, darkly tanned *bezprizorniki* were excellent swimmers and divers, and they showed off their skills to beachgoers for coins thrown into the sea. They walked the beach begging for food and money. My mother brought a sack of food for them every day, and they took to her with their eyes wide open, pleading for warmth and affection. I was happy not to be an orphan, and in those moments I loved my mother even more. In Odessa my mother seemed to be a different person, more vivacious, energetic, joyous, and talkative. I had never seen her laughing, singing, dancing, and enjoying herself the way she did that summer.

In Wlodzimierz-Wolynski my mother attracted a mixed group of friends who came frequently to our home for dinner and late-night discussions. She would sit at the head of the table, pouring Russian tea into tall glasses from a silver samovar. She created an atmosphere in which people were judged not by their appearance but by their compassion, intellectual prowess, and depth of feeling. From my mother I learned the value of ideas, ideals, and integrity, as well as the respect that I owe to others and myself. She didn't consider herself a leader, yet she was the one who brought people together at our long dining room table or on the veranda to talk about art, literature, and, predominantly as time went on, politics. I regret that I couldn't appreciate her intellectual qualities when I was young. At first I didn't understand her, then I couldn't express my feelings for her, and then it was too late.

I walked through my parents' room into what used to be Julek's bedroom. It overlooked my mother's flower garden, which was now choked with weeds. I shared the room with Julek from the time I was seven until he left for the university when I was thirteen. Julek behaved like a crown prince when we were growing up. He considered me a great nuisance and frequently kicked me out of the room. All I heard from him was that I was in his way, he had homework to do, and that I must leave him alone.

I was in my early teens when I began to distance myself from my family. I wanted to meet different people and participate in every activity. As a twelve- and thirteen-year-old I wanted to be completely independent, and it made me angry when my parents wanted to accompany me in town. Initially I argued with them, but then I just left on my own without telling them where I was going or how long I'd be gone. My parents tried to control my behavior, but all I wanted was to be out of any control. I was convinced that I was mature enough to take care of myself. My main desire at that time was to stand out, to be in some way smarter, better, stronger than others.

My first experience with anti-Semitism was when I started going to the Polish gymnasium at ten years of age. Until then I hadn't realized that people were discriminated against on account of their religion. I thought that being Jewish was no different from being Polish, Russian, or Ukrainian, and I didn't care if my friends were Christians or Jews. I was neither proud nor ashamed of being Jewish. The anti-Semitic remarks made at school both surprised and humiliated me. At first I tried to gain the respect of my tormenters. I was a good soccer player, and I was pleased when the same boys who ridiculed me wanted to be on my team. I thought it was a sign that we were friends. But in the locker room I became another "fucking Jew."

Real trouble with my parents began when I was in my mid-teens and started hanging out with a group of older Jewish teenagers my parents didn't like. Being with them, I had a sense of belonging and freedom. I began to defy my parents by staying out all night, fighting with the anti-Semitic boys who harassed me, and skipping school and spending the day on the riverbank. When I got Lady I rode to the river every day so everyone could see me horseback riding. I jumped Lady over bushes and greeted my friends with wild shouts. Lady did a great deal to satisfy my longing for unrestricted freedom. The wind on my face, the speed and strength of the horse moving beneath me, and the expanding horizon made me feel free. I dreamed about faraway lands and adventures and became engulfed in my own imaginary world. But at the same time the real world was becoming more and more dangerous.

The same year my father gave me Lady, the year I turned fourteen, Hitler came to power in Germany. At first Hitler was perceived by the Polish press and our friends as a political lightweight, a bombastic buffoon. There were many caricatures and jokes about him, and no one took him seriously. My father, uncle, and their friends predicted that Hitler's career would be short-lived and that the German Jews weren't in any danger despite the anti-Semitic slogans. The policy of the Polish government, headed by Josef Pilsudski, who led independent Poland after World War I, reaffirmed the notion that Hitler and Nazism were only temporary political aberrations. Pilsudski refused to have a close alliance with Nazi Germany and repeatedly declined to meet Hitler in person. He signed non-aggression treaties with both the Soviet Union and Germany, hoping to prevent aggression from either side. But in 1935, Pilsudski died and Poland became friendly with Nazi Germany and hostile toward the Soviet Union. State-supported anti-Semitism became widespread. Some of my classmates wore green ribbons, a symbol of anti-Semitism, and they actively picketed Jewish businesses with placards that read "Don't buy from a Jew," "Jews to Palestine," and "Poland for Poles." The Jewish community in Poland was deeply saddened by Pilsudski's death because he was considered to be a friend and protector of Jews.

The year Pilsudski died was my worst in the Polish gymnasium. I was sixteen, and I was doing very poorly in school. I was harassed daily by my anti-Semitic classmates, and I started skipping school to avoid confrontations. When I couldn't avoid fights, I fought back aggressively, not minding getting hurt because I needed to feel I could deal with the growing dangers on my own. I didn't want to study physics, chemistry, or math because I didn't like the subjects, didn't understand them, and didn't want to put any effort into learning them. Considering myself an atheist, I stopped going to Jewish religion classes. I became argumentative and rebellious at home and lazy and uncaring in school. Twice I was called to the principal for causing fights and was threatened with suspension. But the worst was when my parents were called to meet with the principal. My mother was upset and ashamed when she found out I'd been skipping school and spending time with people she didn't want me to associate with, and before long only my father went to see the principal. At times he was angry when he came home, but he loved me deeply, and I sensed that in some way he was proud that I stood up to the anti-Semites.

Not long after Pilsudski's death events in Germany became frightening: in September Hitler signed the Nuremberg Laws, which denied civil rights to German Jews. A campaign of open harassment, humiliation, and violence toward Jews began. We could hardly believe that in the middle of the twentieth century in a highly civilized European country, Jews were being beaten, tortured, and killed and their property confiscated. We couldn't understand why France and England, the great European powers, and the League of Nations in Geneva wouldn't intervene to stop the brutality.

On July 18, 1936, civil war erupted in Spain when the Spanish fascists, called Falangists and led by General Franco, rebelled against the legitimate democratic leftist government. Many young people from Europe and the United States went to Spain to fight in the International Brigade against the fascists. My friend Moniek Korn and I decided to join the International Brigade, but my parents forbade me to enlist. They had never liked Moniek, believing him to be a bad influence on me. They also said I was too young and lacked experience on my own. I was furious, thinking they didn't have faith in me. It never crossed my mind that they were simply afraid I'd be killed in Spain. The next day, instead of going to school, I ran away from home. I left my satchel with my books in the barn, took my backpack and hunting knife, and rode Lady toward Uscilug, twelve kilometers away from Wlodzimierz-Wolynski. The weather was nasty, and when I reached Uscilug I was wet, cold, hungry, and angry—I was still angry at my parents for having treated me like a child, but I was also mad at myself for running away in such terrible weather.

I went to the estate of my friend Janek Jochenson. Neither he nor his family was home, but the housemaid knew me and let me in. The next day she kept asking me why I wanted to stay when no one was around. On the third day, no longer angry, I rode back home. In town I ran into a classmate who told me the police had been out looking for me, and this news prepared me somewhat for what to expect at home. When I came through the kitchen door my father smacked me, my mother cried, and no one would talk to me, not even Marynia. I still regretted not being able to go to Spain.

Not long after this incident, I came home late one night and found my parents waiting for me in the dining room. My mother was knitting, and my father was smoking an Egyptian cigarette. "You have a busy life," my father said calmly. "Your mother and I have decided that as of today you must take responsibility for it. You're seventeen, and you may come and go as you wish, but we expect you to think twice about what you're doing and with whom you're doing it."

"There are some obligations we want you to fulfill," my mother said. Her voice was gentler than it had been in a long time. "We've decided you should transfer to the Jewish gymnasium. We hope there won't be any more fighting and that you'll do better in school. I'd also like you to pay more attention to Rachel. Take her with you to the river and teach her to swim, row, kayak, whatever you do. Take her to the woods. Teach her how to mushroom hunt. She admires you, and you should pay attention to her. The last thing I want is for you to remember that if you need anything, you can talk to us. But we aren't going to ask you any more questions."

This talk with my parents marked a turning point in my life. It was the best way to deal with me, because it meant I no longer had anyone or anything to rebel against. Never before had I realized that I had to be responsible for what I did. Elated by the new arrangement, I hugged and kissed my parents.

I believed that my father understood better than my mother or anyone else why I had changed so drastically. I believed he would help me if I got into real trouble no matter how angry or disappointed he might be. I knew he believed it was a difficult time for me and that I would grow out of it. I also overheard him tell his brother that he wasn't worried about my future because I was street smart, but he worried a great deal about Julek's. With my mother it was different. She loved me and worried about me, but she could hardly understand or tolerate my defiant behavior.

Waking up from dreams of the past, I touched the walls and windows and ran my hand over the tile wood-burning stove. Walking carefully across the floor, I found that the same two planks still squeaked like before, and the door to my parents' room didn't shut tightly. I wasn't sure what my parents thought of me after we parted. I wanted to ask for forgiveness from them, especially my mother, who may have died thinking I wasn't a good son. I wanted to thank my father and tell him how grateful I was for the life he let me live. I would have given anything to see them again and tell them that all throughout those six years I wanted to return home and do everything I could to save them, or at least be with them until the last moment.

I walked back through the dining room and into the kitchen. I didn't stop to take one last look around the room but continued out the door and into the yard. I raised my arms high overhead and waded through the sharp grass and nettles over to the barn. Billy's doghouse was gone, probably taken apart and used for firewood during the war, and my pigeons were gone, too. They'd probably been eaten. I'd raised over one hundred of them. I built houses for them in the hayloft, where they multiplied and raised their young. I studied their habits, observed the way the parents took care of the chicks, and marveled at their amazing sense of direction. I spent hours every day up in the hayloft, counting them, identifying them, and flying them out to attract and bring back other pigeons. When we moved to the apartment on Farna Street I regretted having to leave the pigeons with the new owners.

The shingles on the barn were rotted and broken and the whole roof sagged in the middle. One side of the barn door was missing, and broken chairs and filthy mattresses and box springs were piled in a corner. I leaned against the frame, my strength draining from me. I had hoped that visiting the house on the hill would bring back memories of the times when all of us lived happily together and no lives were threatened. I had hoped that in my hometown, close to the graves of my family, I would find a way to deal with my sorrow and despair. I had hoped that for a little while I would feel I was back at home. When I was growing up, home was a place that existed, had always existed, and would always exist. As a child I believed that every place in town was my home and that everyone in town was my friend. But the emptiness spilling out of the house, barn, and garden made me aware that there was no place from which I could escape into my childhood and forget the years of terror and death.

5

FARNA STREET

Visiting the house on the hill didn't help me feel any better prepared to face the future. I still needed to go to the apartment we lived in on Farna Street, even though there were no happy memories for me to recover there. From almost the day we moved in it brought nothing but death and destruction to my family, and I held it as accountable for our suffering as I held the house on the hill accountable for my happiness.

The apartment on Farna Street was a step up in life for my parents. Modern, spacious, it had indoor plumbing and was located in the heart of the city. But shortly after we moved there in 1936 our lives began to change. Sickness, suffering, and death greeted us on Farna Street, and fear wedged its way into our lives. These were the years of the Great Terror, which threatened our relatives in the Soviet Union, and the years of rising fascism and anti-Semitism, which erupted in Germany and spread across Poland, reaching our small town on the eastern border. Our apartment on Farna Street did not turn out to be the cultural salon my mother wanted it to be but a meeting place where family and friends gathered to grieve and worry. I was afraid to see the last place my family lived, but I wanted to fulfill the promise I'd made six years earlier to come back.

Located on the corner of Farna and Kowelska streets was the Roman Catholic cathedral. It was an imposing building, with old stained-glass windows depicting saints and trumpeting angels. It was surrounded by a tall iron fence. Throngs of people used to gather there on Sundays and holidays. The fence was gone, along with the crosses on its three towers. Tacked up on the entrance door, a handwritten poster announced movies from 4:00 to 6:00 p.m. and dancing after 7:00 p.m. A sign above the door read "Cultural and Social Club of the Komsomol"—the communist youth organization. On the opposite corner, where Kaufmans' pharmacy had been, a typical Soviet-style concrete-slab building now stood. Next to the pharmacy had been the Tepper photography studio. The owner's daughter, Niunia, had been my classmate. The windows of the second story were boarded up, and on the ground level there was now a shoe repair shop. I had a glimpse beyond the building into what had once been the liveliest commercial part of the city, but all I saw was a peasants' market without a single store. It had been only six years since I had left town, but I could hardly recognize the street.

Walking tall amid the dreary Soviet crowd was a man with wavy brown hair and a green Polish uniform. It was Jenka Karkushevsky, a friend from the Polish gymnasium. I shouted his name and ran over to greet him. He hugged me forcefully, nearly crushing my ribs. "You're in the Polish army?" I asked.

"The same army as your brother," he said. He held me at arm's length and looked me over. "I heard you were alive. You don't know how happy I am to see you." People were passing us and staring, but we paid no attention. For a moment we didn't know what to say to each other. We'd been classmates in the gymnasium for six years, and at times we had been good friends, especially when we played on the riverbank. Jenka's family had lived in the quarter called Bialobrzegi, "white shores," named for the chalky white soil in the area. His father had two boats and Jenka had a kayak, and we used to take trips together. His mother was Ukrainian and his father was Polish. He was one of the classmates who never harassed me.

"So what happened to you during all these years? You look good, healthy, and looking at your uniform, you must also be a military man."

"I have a long story to tell," I said.

"I do too. So let's sit down somewhere and talk. What brings you here? How long are you staying?" he asked.

"Just for three days. I leave tomorrow. I wanted to see what was left of our town." Jenka nodded and was quiet for a moment. We continued walking down Farna Street. "So where should we go?" I asked.

"There's only one place in town where we can get a decent meal," Jenka said. "My parents' house."

"I don't want to go all the way to Bialobrzegi. I'm heading to our old apartment on Farna Street. Isn't there another restaurant around here?"

"The only one I know of is in your building. By the way, will you try to get your building back from the city?"

"Jenka, I haven't thought about it. It isn't something that was on my mind."

"It's your property. If you want it back, I can be of help." Seeing that I wasn't interested in the subject, Jenka dropped it.

As we got closer to the building, I saw the iron balcony on the second floor and the driveway that led to the backyard, where my father's patients tied up their horses and wagons. Our two-story building took up half a block. We passed the fourteenth-century water tower in the city square, which used to house the Tomb of the Unknown Soldier. However, instead of two Polish soldiers standing guard and keeping the flame, two drunken old men joked and laughed with a kiosk vendor. The tomb was gone, and weeds had overtaken the square.

Strzecha, the name meaning "thatched roof," had been the most fashionable restaurant in the city. It took up most of the ground floor in our building. It featured a five-piece band that played every evening, and in the summer, when the windows in my room were open, I listened to tangos and romantic English waltzes as I fell asleep. I imagined myself gliding gracefully with a beautiful dancer on the shining parquet floor, everyone admiring and applauding us. Strzecha's elegant signboard had been replaced with a sign that read "Café-Restaurant" in Cyrillic. Inside, the café resembled the bar at the train station.

We took a table near a window facing the backyard. I could see the outhouses toward the back, each with a little heart-shaped hole high up on the door, and the stairs leading to our kitchen. My father's office and waiting room were right above us. We ordered lunch and half a bottle of Moskovskaya vodka. Next to us a group of elderly Ukrainian men talked about wild boars attacking cattle and ruining the fields. At another table two sad young women were drinking tea and whispering to each other.

The waitress smiled flirtatiously, impressed by our foreign uniforms. Jenka poured two glasses of vodka and raised his glass for a toast. "To old friends," he said. I drank with him, feeling strangely in-

timate and distanced at the same time. "I'm sorry about your family,"
Jenka said. "There aren't many people around anymore. It's a different town. I live in Poland, but my parents are still here. I'm visiting
them."

We talked about our friends—those who'd died, those who'd survived. He knew from his parents about many things that had happened during the war.

"Jenka, there's one thing I want you to tell me. Julek was here right
after the war, and he found out that some local people, maybe even
our classmates, extorted money from my father. They told him they
could find out what happened to me. Do you know who they were?"

Jenka chewed on a toothpick. His gray eyes were hard. "You don't
need to know all the horrible things that happened here. My father
talks on and on about the informers, blackmailers, and murderers. I
have to ask him to stop talking because I can't listen to it anymore.
Knowing who did what isn't going to bring your family back, and it
isn't going to make you feel better. I know who extorted money from
your father. They aren't here anymore. The NKVD took care of
them."

I didn't ask Jenka any more questions. He was right: knowing who
hurt my family wouldn't do me any good. I hadn't come to
Wlodzimierz-Wolynski to seek out the killers.

When we finished eating I told Jenka I needed to go upstairs to see
our apartment one last time. "Janusz, there's nothing left for you to
see," he said. "It's a Soviet office now. Why don't you come and have
dinner with me and my parents?"

"Jenka, I need to go. I'll come and see you in the evening." I got up
from the table and Jenka stood and embraced me warmly, both of us
knowing we wouldn't see each other again.

I went outside to the front entrance of our apartment and climbed
the staircase to the spacious first-floor landing. The walls were dingy
and cracked; the plaster, chipped. The smooth oak railing I used to
slide down was gone, replaced with a rusty iron bar. The door
straight ahead led to my grandparents' apartment, the one to the
right led to my uncle's, and the one to the left was ours. On the center door was a large signboard reading "Otdel Narodnovo Prosves-
chenya," Department of Public Education, and below that the names
of the sections of the department. There was no trace of the engraved
brass plate bearing my father's name and professional title. All the

things that had happened while we lived in the flat flashed through my mind. In hindsight, they fell into a kind of fateful order.

The events that marked the end of our worry-free lives affected my parents, who for many years had been sending money and food parcels to their relatives living in the Soviet Union. Suddenly they wrote to my mother and told her to stop sending anything. The letters were very short and superficial. Then in August 1936, shocking news came from Moscow: Grigory Zinoviev and Lev Kamenev, both Politburo members, and fourteen other old Bolsheviks in high Party and government positions were tried for treason. They confessed to being traitors and saboteurs plotting to kill Stalin and the Party leadership. No one knew what to believe: the signed confessions in the open trial or the comments from the BBC and Polish press claiming that the accused had been tortured and their families threatened. My friends and I in the leftist organization argued about whether Stalin was a murderer or defender of communism. I couldn't decide what to believe, but my mother was sure that the confessions had been forced by torture.

My family was so concerned with the Moscow trials and the fate of our relatives living in the Soviet Union that we paid little attention to another political event taking place: a pact signed on October 25, 1936, by Hitler and Mussolini creating the fascist Berlin-Rome Axis. A year earlier Mussolini had invaded and annexed Abyssinia, but it had taken place so far away from Poland that it didn't resonate in our home or with my friends.

A few months later tragedy hit closer to home when my grandfather died suddenly in his sleep. It was the first death in the family I experienced, and I remember the commotion in the early morning and my parents going back and forth between the flats. While we were still mourning my grandfather, my aunt Sabina became sick with pemphigus, an incurable skin disease. Large, painful blisters formed all over her body and lined her mouth, and within weeks she could no longer eat. My father and uncle took her to see doctors in Lvov, Warsaw, and Vienna, but no one knew how to treat the disease. Eventually no longer able to swallow liquids, she was starving to death and begged my father to give her some medicine to put her to sleep. My grandfather's death saddened me, but my aunt's death terrified me with its prolonged suffering and unbearable pain. Her sickness made me aware of the limitations of medicine and of my own mortality. We buried her next to my grandfather in the Jewish cemetery.

The Moscow trials continued. In September 1937, a new group of high Party and government officials were tried as enemies of the people and executed. Among them were members of the Politburo and Central Committee, the highest military commanders, and even the chief of the NKVD, Genrikh Yagoda. The years 1937–1938 were the time of the Great Terror, also known as Yezhovshchina, after the new NKVD chief, Nikolai Yezhov. News from Moscow was getting scarier every day. The underground organization I belonged to was in turmoil; we were stunned that so many old Bolsheviks were turning out to be traitors and enemies of the people. Rumors spread that the leadership of the Polish Communist Party had been imprisoned in Moscow and that the party had been disbanded by Stalin's order.

To the west, German Jews were being beaten, arrested, and put in concentration camps. Their property was confiscated. In Poland, Jewish businesses and professionals were boycotted, and Jewish university students were singled out and forced to stand on the left side in classrooms. Worse, some were thrown from balconies, cut with razor blades, and killed. In Wlodzimierz-Wolynski, groups of young Polish hooligans roamed the streets looking for Jews to harass and humiliate. It started out as name-calling but soon turned violent. Anti-Semites attacked older Jews. They threw stones at Jewish windows and marked doors with hate slogans and obscenities. On the river, groups of young Poles splashed Jews dressed in their holiday clothes while boating or kayaking. When few Jews were around, the Poles overturned the boat or kayak, forcing the people in it to swim to shore. The fiercest fistfights occurred on the soccer field between the Polish and Jewish teams. However, hooligans weren't the tough, fearless fighters they thought they were. They were cowardly scoundrels who were powerful only when in a group. They were students, young officials, and army officers swept up in the wave of rabid anti-Semitism spilling into the provinces from the country's capital with the full endorsement of the Polish government.

In only three years Polish anti-Semitism mutated from prejudice to humiliation to assault. The town became divided. Friends drifted apart. I lost one of my closest friends, Bubi Schön. He was the son of the local Lutheran pastor and my benchmate during my first three years in the Polish gymnasium. As children we attended each other's birthday parties and played in each other's homes. But after he spent the summer of 1935 in Germany, our friendship began to cool. In 1936, after I transferred to the Jewish gymnasium, he avoided me altogether. The last time I spoke with him was in late 1938, when I saw him on the street and he invited me for a walk.

He was tall and trim, and there was something stiff in his posture. He looked straight ahead, and there was nothing superfluous in his manner. "For some time I've wanted to talk to you," he said. "I know you think I don't like you. You probably think I've forgotten our early friendship. Well, I haven't." He didn't wait for me to respond but continued as if he were reciting the conversation from memory and didn't want to forget the words. "You know I've spent the last several summers in Germany. I can't tell you what I did there, but I want to warn you and your family to leave this country as soon as possible and go some place outside of Europe. Bad things are going to happen to Jews here."

"You mean that what's happening to Jews in Germany will also happen in Poland?"

"Let me just say I don't want you and your family to wait for what's going to happen. Trust me. I know what I'm talking about. I can't say any more."

I felt Bubi was telling the truth, but I didn't tell my parents about his warning. I didn't want them to be more frightened than they already were by the rapidly rising anti-Semitism and frequent visits of Nazi leaders to Poland. I often speculated about why Bubi warned me and what kind of person he was—if during his trips to Germany he became indoctrinated and became a Nazi, or if he remained a good person and was just making his career in the German army. I wondered if after being more than decent with me he went on and murdered other Jews, not because he hated them but because he was obeying orders. I wish I could meet him again in another time and place, ask him these questions, and listen to his side of the story.

The anti-Semitism in the streets of Wlodzimierz-Wolynski and throughout all of Poland began to affect our family. My father, who used to have three dental technicians working for him, now only had one, and I worried about what my father would do if he lost any more patients. One summer night he invited me to go fishing as we'd done since I was a child. We packed sandwiches, lemonade, and several shot bottles of vodka for him and pulled the boat out of Schlomo's marina. But instead of putting the bait on the hook and casting the line, my father said, "I'd like to talk to you about something, but I don't want your mother or anyone else in the family to know. I've got problems with the officials. I've been practicing here since 1921, but now the Board of Dental Examiners wants to see my original diploma from dental school in Kharkov. I graduated just before the Revolution in 1917, and I never received a diploma, just a certificate that I completed my studies. It's been honored ever since I began to practice. The dental school doesn't exist anymore. No documents can be found, not to mention the original diploma."

I couldn't believe what he was saying. He was highly respected in town. The mayor, city council members, and high military officers stationed in the city were his patients. I was sure that they'd intervene on his behalf.

"Papa, why is the original diploma so important? After eighteen years of practice, why can't the local authorities intervene? What about your patients in influential positions?"

He waved his hand to stop me. "It's not the diploma. The local officials are new. They won't do anything for me. They're afraid to intervene on behalf of a Jew. Someone went through my documents and found out there's no original diploma. They're looking for a good reason to harass me, and this is it. My appeals were denied. I've been offered a chance to re-take the exams, but how can I pass them when I've been out of school for twenty-five years?"

I'd never seen my father so desperate. In my eyes he had always been untouchable. "Papa," I said, "we need to emigrate from Poland and go to any other country. I'll go to work to support the family. I'm sure we'll do well, and at least we won't be harassed and treated as second-class citizens."

"Don't talk about emigration," my father said sharply. "Do you expect me to drop everything I worked for and start over from scratch? I worked very hard to make a good life for us here. I can't just walk away from it. I can't take your mother and my mother some place where I can't give them the comfort they need."

"Please, listen to me. It isn't going to get better for Jews here in Poland, only worse. Look what's going on in Germany. The same is going to happen here. If you don't want to move now, please, let me go alone. Many of my friends are leaving. I'll establish myself, and I'll bring everyone to wherever I am."

My father was quiet for a long while. He flicked the cigarette he was smoking into the river and struck a match to light a new one. "You're going to graduate next month," he said calmly, "and I'd like you to try to get into dentistry. I found a professor in Warsaw to tutor you for the exams. If this fails, I promise we'll talk again. I'm also waiting for a response to my last appeal. My lawyer tells me things may change for the better. Let's wait. Then we'll decide."

I felt I'd suddenly reached adulthood, with my father relying on my opinion and including me in the decision about what to do next, and I felt more responsible for the family than ever before. I believed I was more experienced than either my father or Julek in dealing with people. I wondered if I should tell my father what Bubi had told me, but seeing how set he was on staying in Wlodzimierz-Wolynski, and how frightened he was, I didn't want to worry him more. I wanted to make him feel confident and secure again.

At that time I was happier than ever to be in the Jewish gymnasium, surrounded by friends and sheltered from the harassment I'd experienced in the Polish gymnasium. Never again in my life would I have as many close, wonderful friends as I had during those three years in the Jewish gymnasium. Despite the growing anti-Semitism inside Poland and danger of a Nazi invasion, we continued to dream and make plans for the future. Nearly every summer day Taubcia, Rachel, and I went swimming and kayaking. We sang, told stories, and shared food with other Jewish friends as if the outside world didn't exist, unaware of how close we were to the end of our fragile tranquility. The Jewish gymnasium and my new friends gave me a strong feeling for and understanding of my Jewishness.

In 1938 I graduated from the gymnasium and made plans to attend dental school in the fall. The quota for Jews entering the university was low, between five and ten percent, and in medicine, dentistry, and pharmacy it was even lower. My father told me that the only way to get into dental school was to bribe a university or government official. The state entrance exams were only a formality and played no role in being accepted or rejected if the bribe went into the right hands. That summer I spent six weeks in Warsaw, where my father got me a tutor, the assistant and supposed bag man for Dr. Alfred Meissner, a famous professor and dean of the dental school. My father paid big money not only to the tutor but also to Dr. Meissner's brother, a colonel in the Polish army. Upon accepting the money they both guaranteed my acceptance. But I didn't get into dental school, nor did my father get his money back. I returned from Warsaw deeply wounded, ashamed, even, for my father's having been swindled, taken as a small-town Jew who knew nothing about city life, and for my having dared to try to enter a world that deemed me unfit and inferior.

I was still in Warsaw when Hitler succeeded in blackmailing and threatening England and France, and the English prime minister, Neville Chamberlain, and the French prime minister, Edouard Daladier, capitulated in Munich and allowed Hitler to annex Austria and then part of Czechoslovakia, the Sudetenland. This was a crushing defeat for European democracy and an unquestionable victory for fascism. The Nazis, elated with Hitler's success abroad, staged a violent campaign in Germany, and on November 9, 1938, the windows of stores and houses owned by Jews were smashed. Jews were beaten and killed, and thousands were arrested and sent to concentration camps. Kristallnacht was the beginning of state-sanctioned violence toward Jews, and it frightened us because it encouraged Polish anti-Semites to call openly for the expulsion of Jews from Poland to Palestine or Madagascar.

When I got back to Wlodzimierz-Wolynski I went to work in my father's office, helping the dental technician, Chaim Cukier. The months wore on. In the summer of 1939 more tragedy entered our lives when my mother was diagnosed with colon cancer. I'll never forget the late afternoon when my parents came home with Dr. Podlipski, the chief surgeon in the city's hospital. My mother came in the door crying and went to her bedroom. My father called me into the hallway. "Your mother is very sick and needs surgery," he said. His face was white and throat dry, and he could barely say another word. "Zygmunt will explain it to you."

Dr. Podlipski and I sat down in the dining room. "I won't hide anything from you. Your mother's cancer is quite advanced and she needs immediate surgery. I'm not sure if the cancer has already spread. The operation is quite debilitating. It will leave her without an anal sphincter, but there's nothing better we can do."

I could hardly breathe as Zygmunt talked. The word cancer struck me with terror. I believed it to be as deadly as the bubonic plague, cholera, and pemphigus.

"I understand how frightening this is to you, but I can't hide the seriousness of her illness. The surgery can't wait any longer."

I went to my mother and sat next to her. She was our home. She held us together. I couldn't imagine what would happen if she were gone. To help my father, I told Rachel and Taubcia, and the shattering news drew the three of us even closer together.

After surgery my mother was in pain and severely depressed, but she insisted that life go on as usual. The dinners and evenings spent around the dining room table with our friends slowly resumed, but the mood was never again light and cheerful. The Nazis bombed Poland only a few weeks later, and the Red Army occupied our town only a few weeks after that.

I opened the door to what used to be the waiting room to my father's dental office and walked in, arousing the curiosity of the clerks and typists. Taubcia and I had gotten married there. Facing my imminent departure to the Red Army, we wanted to make our bond permanent, giving each of us the comfort of knowing we would be together in three years, after I'd done my service. Standing at the doorway, I remembered the plants and chairs arranged in a semicircle in the waiting room. I remembered the *hupa* and the gold rings. I heard the smooth, reassuring voice of Rabbi Finkelhorn as he read the vows, Taubcia and I repeating the words after him, the glass smashing as I stomped on it, and everyone saying "Mazeltov." But there was no jubilation in the words, only a forced joyfulness, faint hope, concealed fear, and stifled sadness. There was no music, dancing, or singing at this wedding.

Taubcia, Rachel, and their friends prepared the meal, because, although it was a year after her surgery, my mother still hadn't recovered her strength. My father toasted us and wished us a happy life together. He announced that as a wedding gift he and my mother would give us their bedroom, which was sunny and spacious, while they moved into my room. Taubcia wore a light beige dress, and on the collar she wore a gold brooch my mother had given her. She carried three long-stemmed red roses from my father. I looked deeply in her eyes for a glint of happiness, but all I saw were tears and an innocent questioning, as if she couldn't understand why anyone would want to hurt her.

During the brief time we were together we tried to live the life of newlyweds. Taubcia decorated the room as if it were our own home. She brought some special things from her home—her parents' framed wedding photograph, which she displayed on the nightstand, her yellow and white embroidered pillowcases and towels, a small Persian rug from her bedroom, her bedside lamp, and her lucky charms—a stuffed white kitten and stuffed brown bear. It was a warm, cozy room, and we pretended it would be ours forever.

I was surprised but relieved not to see a single piece of our furniture in the room. My large oak desk was gone; my books, paintings, and the loveseat that had stood at the end of the bed were gone. I wondered when everything had been sold—or taken. Nothing from my past remained in the room except for the walls and white tile stove.

My parents' bedroom was bare except for a large heavy desk in front of the window. A young man sat in front of it while an older man scolded him in an arrogant, commanding voice. The subordinate sat on the edge of his chair, nodding and mumbling rhythmically, "Yes, sir. Yes, I understand, sir. I'm very sorry, sir." I closed my eyes. A conversation I'd had with my mother came back to me. It was one of the few times we really talked to each other.

She'd just had surgery, and I was trying to make her life easier by shopping and taking care of Rachel. One afternoon she called me into her bedroom, where she lay in bed knitting. We sat quietly for a while, and then she turned to me and said, "Do you know that many things can be said in silence? Ideas can't be communicated this way but feelings don't need a word." I'd never thought much about silence. Like solitude, I could appreciate it on occasion, but it wasn't in my nature to seek it out. I needed to talk and express my feelings. I never realized silence could be another way of communicating. "There must be a strong emotional bond between people to be silent and happy together. Most people like to talk about their thoughts and feelings, but too much talking diminishes the strength of a few words, the right words. Just remember this when you're in love. And I think you're in love right now."

That evening we talked for a long time about my future. "I know you long to see the world," my mother said. "I'm sorry you've had to spend your life in this provincial town. I know you love to travel, and you love geography. You have a wonderful imagination. Your heart is in the right place. I hope you never forget that there are always people who need you, just like there are always people who love and care about you. I don't want you to stay here all your life. Move to a city and learn about a different kind of life and culture. There is no culture here." She'd become sad and pensive, and we both sat quietly. Not a word was said about cancer, suffering, or surgery.

"What do you want here?" A sharp, insulting voice jolted me out of my dreams.

"I have no business here," I said. "I'm only visiting. I used to live in this apartment."

"Well, we work here," the older man barked. He took note of my altered Polish military uniform. "What's your name? Where are you from?"

I told him I was Polish and that I had a permit to travel here. He picked up the phone. "Fomin speaking. Director of Education. There's a foreigner here. Polish. He claims he has a permit and that he's registered with you." He turned his back to me, and I walked again through the rooms. Not a single piece of furniture, not a single painting, candelabra, rug, book, or curtain was left in the apartment. Even the kitchen had been remodeled into an office. I went into what had been my father's office, hoping to get a moment of peace and privacy. A young man stood on a ladder hanging a picture across from where my father's desk used to be. It kept tilting to the side, and two young women sitting at their desks giggled at his clumsy efforts. When they noticed me in the doorway they stopped giggling. "They can help you across the hall," the man said.

I didn't move, just stared at my father's beige leather chair with its semicircular back and armrests. My father used to sit in that chair making notes, and he'd swivel around when I came to see him and talk to me about my day. I saw him so clearly now—his bald head, white coat, pince-nez, and round, smiling face.

The man hanging the portrait twisted around and gruffly told me to leave. He began hammering again. For twenty years my father embraced me with love, joy, and friendship. It ended abruptly with bombs, terror, and murder. I stepped up close to the man and hissed in his face, "Stop hammering this wall, you fucking bastard. I grew up here. This room is a temple to me." Startled, he stopped hammering and stepped down from the ladder. He left the room, along with the two young women.

I sat down in my father's chair. It still swiveled. The leather on the armrests was cracked and faded, but I could picture my father sitting here with his sleeves rolled up and the chair hugging his stout body. I wondered how he could take care of his patients, many of whom were Nazi officers and officials, day after day, keeping his hand steady and mind clear, knowing that anyone at anytime could accuse him of error and he could be shot. I knew how determined he would've been to continue his practice, demonstrating to the Germans how valuable his services were and believing that his artful work would earn him the protection of high-ranking Gestapo officers and save him and the family.

I looked out the tall window, through the dense canopy of leaves, into the backyard. The acacia trees might have been turning brown or yellow on that morning four years earlier, but for the most part everything would have been the same. The brick footpath hadn't changed; the posts for the clothesline were still there. I made myself confront the last moments of my family's lives as witnessed by Chaim Cukier, my father's dental technician. I had run into him in the Polish embassy in Moscow when he was getting his documents to go back to Poland, and we spent an evening together talking about the past. Chaim told me that he was in the apartment when the police came to get my family. He had already told Julek the story, but when Julek and I talked at Clear Ponds, I hadn't been ready to hear the details of my family's deaths. Sitting in the restaurant with Chaim, however, I felt close to my family again, and I wanted to hear him talk about them, even if it was about their last days.

Chaim told me that on September 1, 1942, the Nazis and Ukrainian police began liquidating the ghetto in Wlodzimierz-Wolynski. Everyone slept fully dressed, ready to get up if anyone knocked at the door. My father had given everyone cyanide capsules. For an entire week, no one left the apartment. At dawn on September 7, Chaim heard heavy footsteps on the stairs, pounding at the door, and shouting in Ukrainian to open the door. He jumped out the dining room window into a large bin full of garbage in the backyard. From the bin he crawled to the outhouse and hid down inside the hole. Through a crack in the wall he saw the Ukrainian police leading my parents, grandmother, Rachel, Taubcia, and Fruma downstairs to a truck that was waiting for them. When they reached the backyard, Chaim saw my father fall to the ground, convulse several times, and lie still. At the moment my father fell, Rachel and Taubcia ran to him but were pushed back and kicked by the policemen, who ordered everyone onto the truck. Rachel, Taubcia, and Fruma pulled my mother and grandmother up onto the truck bed. The truck drove away. My father lay dead on the ground. Chaim said it was true that one of my father's patients, a high-ranking Gestapo officer, had promised my father that the family would be safe when the ghetto was liquidated. But the man had to leave for two days during the action, and while he was gone the chief of the Ukrainian police ordered his men to take my family out to the Piatydnie forest.

Chaim survived the ghetto liquidation by hiding for the next several weeks in the attic of the Holc family. When the liquidation was over he returned to our apartment and worked as a dentist, taking over my father's practice, even though he'd only been a technician. Several months later, afraid of being caught in another action, he escaped to a nearby Polish village and went into hiding at the homes of some of my father's patients. From there he joined a Polish partisans' group and worked as a dentist until the end of the war.

Leaving our apartment, I didn't want to live. I walked down Horodelska Street toward the soccer field, and as I walked I realized that the cracks in the hardened dirt under my feet had shape and form. I kneeled down and began scratching the dirt away with my fingers. I didn't know what I was looking at, but something told me that these strange-looking stones didn't belong there. I grabbed a stick and dug the dirt out of the cracks. Engraved Hebrew letters emerged. I stepped off the sidewalk and into the street, but there I found more broken tombstones. I deciphered the Hebrew names of Zilber and Gwircman and followed the broken tombstones all the way to an empty, devastated field that had been the Jewish cemetery. Not a single tombstone remained intact. Some were turned over and crushed to pieces, but most were gone, along with the red-brick wall surrounding the cemetery. I wanted to know who the people were for whom it wasn't enough to kill the living but who needed to annihilate the memory of the dead. What kind of savages used the tombstones for pavement, where they would lie under everyone's boots, to be stomped on, spit on, and forgotten forever? Newcomers to Wlodzimierz-Wolynski would never know that only six years earlier, this town had been vibrant with centuries of Jewish culture. It took only four years to erase the people and their history. Was it the local people who did such a thorough job killing the Jews and devastating the cemetery? Were they living in Jewish homes, wearing Jewish clothes and jewelry, and sleeping in Jewish beds? Would nothing disturb their well-being because no Jews, living or dead, would be around to remind them of their crimes?

I hired a driver with a horse and cart to take me to the Piatydnie forest. Six kilometers west of town on the road to Uscilug, we turned from the main road into an open field that stretched nearly to the horizon. I got out of the cart and walked into the open space. The humidity hung so thick it blurred the trees in the distance. The ground was wavy. Grass and weeds clung to the sandy soil. The waves across the expansive field were uniform, like trenches, stretching as far as I could see. I would later learn that twenty-four thousand Jews lay in this field. For a long moment I couldn't move, not knowing whether to walk in the indentations or on the ridges to avoid stepping on bones. I walked farther into the field and chose a place for my family cemetery. I collected six small rocks and built a little pyramid to mark a family plot. As I arranged the stones I composed a personal prayer vowing that I would love them always and never forget them. I took a pencil and piece of paper from my pocket and wrote their names on it and put the paper under the stones. My family cemetery was so tiny compared to the huge field of depressions and mounds. I stepped over the stones and said goodbye and promised again that I would never forget them. But I've always wondered what will happen when the last person who remembers my family dies. Will my family have passed through life in vain, unknown and forgotten forever? It frightened me to think that all the people I'd known six years earlier and I myself would be soon forgotten, no matter what kinds of lives we had lived.

I spent the rest of the day and night sitting on the riverbank. There was nothing left of Schlomo's marina. The big shed where boats and kayaks were stored in winter had been dismantled, as well as

Schlomo's main cabin. The place was an empty shore, with small piles of gravel, boards, and beams scattered around. Weeds and cattails grew densely from bank to bank. I'd come here hoping to be consoled, but nothing on the lazy flowing river overgrown with seaweed brought back any happy memories. The river was as foreign to me as the streets and stores filled with people I'd never met, the house on the hill occupied by strangers, our garden without the apple and cherry trees, the barn packed with looted Jewish furniture, our apartment on Farna Street inhabited by Russian and Ukrainian clerks, the sidewalks paved with Jewish tombstones. The only person I had was Julek, and we would remain linked forever, but he had his own family, friends, and career. I said goodbye to Wlodzimierz-Wolynski early the next morning, feeling as homeless as the war invalids on the streets in Moscow, as orphaned as the *bezprizorniki* I'd once played with on the beach in Odessa.

6

NO MAN'S LAND

I leaned my head against the cool glass and closed my eyes as the train pulled out of the Wlodzimierz-Wolynski station. I didn't want to think about anything or remember anything. I just wanted to lose myself in the wind, with the sun shining warmly on my arm and life outside disappearing as quickly as it had come.

Another train sliced through the roaring wind, and I opened my eyes to see the silver cars rush by on the adjacent tracks. It was the commuter train heading toward Wlodzimierz-Wolynski. For a moment it was hard to tell if I was moving forward or backward, and I sat as if suspended between the trains, outside of time, as if my past and future were sliding by on either side of me. But as quickly as we met the oncoming train, it was gone, and dark fields and forests blurred before my eyes.

Back in Moscow I wanted to talk to Julek about my trip and our family, but I felt that his time of anguish had passed, and I had no right to stir up his memories. I didn't want to go back to living in the embassy, a world I neither belonged to nor cared for. I was bored in the company of diplomats, where conversations were substituted for by exuberant arrays of politically correct slogans. Growing up, I imagined diplomats to be cultured, educated, refined people proudly representing their motherland. I was surprised to find that intrigues and backstabbing ruled the interaction within the diplomatic community, and that a stratified system governed the closed society of the embassy. The diplomats and their wives, only a few of whom were refined and cultured, snubbed the clerks and secretaries, the clerks and secretaries ignored the drivers and maids, and the drivers and maids, assuming the airs of their bosses, pitted themselves against each other. I was astonished to learn that some of the diplomats and officials were smuggling gold, diamonds, and foreign currency from Moscow to Warsaw and bringing back suitcases full of rubles. When Julek insisted, I went to receptions, but I felt out of place at those gatherings and aggravated by always being introduced as "the younger brother of Colonel Bardach." People asked what my plans were for the future, and although ashamed, I answered honestly, saying I had no plans. I was also ashamed to be living a life of luxury I had neither earned nor deserved. I didn't intend to stay there forever, but I had no idea what I was going to do.

During the long summer days I went to Clear Ponds and played chess with the regulars I met there. In my adolescence I had played a great deal of chess. I was fascinated by the endless combinations and amazed by how many solutions could be found to defeat my opponent. While working in the Kolyma hospital, I had played chess with experienced players and learned a great deal about opening gambits, attacks with sacrifice, and tenacious defense. I liked the challenge of the variations, especially at the endgame, when only a few pieces were left and the maneuvering and anticipation of countermoves was crucial. At Clear Ponds the regulars had their preferred benches and tables situated in the shade away from the running, screaming children and their babushkas. Most of the regulars were retired men, some of whom were quite sophisticated players. A group of kibbitzers surrounded each table. They could hardly restrain themselves from commenting on the game, but any expression of approval or disapproval was strictly forbidden, and this kept everyone quiet, whispering only to their neighbor.

For several days I was a silent kibbitzer, but one morning I asked an old man to play with me. He waited for his partner, and after checking me out he said, "One game only." It happened that I won the first game, and this opened the door for me to become a regular. At first I thought that by playing chess I was merely killing idle time, but the deep concentration involved in solving chess puzzles took my mind off the past and aroused my innate competitiveness. Thinking of my future beyond the chessboard, I wished I could design an opening gambit and attack. I had learned about tenacious defense in the labor camps, but I wasn't sure about the strategy I needed to succeed in life. Although it was only a game, winning in chess kept me from feeling like a complete failure, which was how I felt when I compared myself with Silek and with Mendel Kagan.

Mendel was a classmate and dear friend from the Jewish gymnasium. He and his parents had been deported to Siberia during the roundup of capitalists and Jewish refugees in our hometown in 1939. Both of his parents had perished there, unable to survive the harsh conditions. Mendel was now a student at the Pedagogical Institute and worked in the evenings unloading crates in a supermarket. Silek was still singing in the revelers' ensemble. When they talked about their jobs and studies, I felt a sting of envy and disappointment in myself. We were the same age but they were so much farther ahead in life than I. I felt bitter that I'd lost so many years of my life, and I feared that I'd lost my ability to study and achieve what I felt I was capable of before the war.

Although Silek and Mendel had both lost their families during the war, they were over their grief and didn't need to talk about it. However, they talked quite frequently about our summers on the river and our amorous pursuits. When I would tell them about my troubles in Kolyma, Silek would stop me. "Everyone had a bad time during the war. Stop feeling sorry for yourself. I want to see you back the way you were at home. You were the leader. You knew what you wanted. But now you're just floating. Get to a shore, wherever it is. Just do something. We have more than one past, and one of them is a very happy past. Forget about the other one."

"Get back to your old self," Mendel added. "You don't need to feel guilty or sorry for yourself."

They both were right. I needed to stop living in the past, I just had no idea how to do it. I needed to recover my strength, ambition, competitiveness, and, above all, belief in myself. As a teenager it was natural for me to be a leader. I could easily convince my friends to do things I wanted them to do, but I never stopped to think why they listened to me and trusted me. I had a very hard time in the Red Army and especially in the camps, taking orders and living according to strict rules.

For five years I had no choices and made no decisions. I listened to no voice except the barked commands of the guards. Some faceless officials in the NKVD decided when, what, and how much I ate, where I lived, where I worked, what kind of work I did, how much I had to produce, and when and where I could relieve myself. These officials decided what my final destination was and how I would get to it, how I would be dressed, and when I would be shaved and de-

loused. Breaking an order was punished harshly. As I learned to ignore the churning in my stomach, the filth, and the lice crawling over
my body, I forgot what I'd learned in the gymnasium, the ideas I believed in, books I'd read, and people I'd met. The only decision I
made for myself was to follow the compass of my instincts and survive day after day, hoping that I might be lucky and finish my term,
although I knew I would be a very different person when I got out
and wouldn't be going back to the life I'd left behind.

Julek, Katia, and Sioma urged me to study. In the camps I had
dreamed of being a doctor, and I knew I'd be a good one. Working in
the Kolyma hospital, I could give even the very sick TB patients hope
that their future was not in the morgue. Fedia, only twenty-six years
old, had come to our ward from the mines. He'd been bleeding for
several weeks; both of his lungs were infected with TB.

I held Fedia's sweating hands when he told me his story. "I
haven't even begun living, and my life is already over," he said.
"There are so many things I'd like to see, learn, and read. So many
people left to meet." With his spiking fever, he burned like a candle
and sweated profusely. He spit up blood and coughed spasmodi-
cally. His dark eyes looked even darker against his flushed cheeks.
He was losing weight, but every day I told him he was getting better and that in the spring I'd let him walk outside. He held my hand
and looked in my eyes like a little child and asked, "Please, tell me,
am I better today?" I don't know if he believed me, but I lied all the
same because it brought a smile to his face. Soon he was too weak
to walk, and I held his feverish body close to me, trying to transfer
my strength, health, and energy to him. He died quietly at night,
and I carried his body to the morgue. I missed him like a little
brother, and I missed hundreds of others who died holding my
hand, all of them believing until the last breath that they would get
better.

When I took care of the patients in Kolyma, I discovered that I enjoyed the nascent attachment of the patients who needed me. I believed that they needed not only a good doctor but a warm, compassionate person to take care of them. Although my duties were limited
to taking temperatures, measuring blood pressure, giving injections,
and distributing medications, I wanted to do more for the patients,
who never stopped hoping that something good would happen and
they would be cured. When I came onto the ward, I saw hope and ap-

prehension in their eyes, as if I were bringing them some miracle drug, not ordinary cough syrup or sleeping pills. They asked how I thought they were doing, and I lied to them to make them feel better. A few patients lost the will to live and asked me to end their suffering. It was more than disease that inspired their death wish. They were old communists who felt betrayed, their lives and struggles wasted. They had once been strong and courageous, but they had nothing to live for anymore.

Even now I wonder where I got this intuitive knowledge about people and why helping them came so easily to me. With my neophytic enthusiasm, I believed I was special, and I trusted my lucky stars that I wouldn't get infected on the open TB ward. Dr. Piasetsky and the nurses warned me to spend as little time on the ward as possible, to wear a mask, and to turn my head away from coughing, spitting patients, but I felt my mission was different from that of the doctors and nurses. My mission was to make the patients feel better by holding their hot hands, talking to them as they fell asleep, and giving them hope even if it was false. I tried to transfer to them my strength and will to live. Taking care of TB patients kept me from thinking about my own misery and pitying myself. I felt I had a purpose in life.

Tired of Julek's nagging, one morning I went to the First Medical Institute and got the application, the list of entrance exams, and the schedule of courses. The entrance exams included Marxism-Leninism, chemistry, physics, and biology. At the registration office I met a crowd of young students right out of high school. They joked and laughed loudly. They seemed to be sure of themselves and confident they would pass the exams. Determined to try to get into medical school, I bought the physics and chemistry books and sat down at Julek's dining room table to study them. I didn't know where to begin. I had a hard time remembering what I'd learned in the gymnasium. The material was completely foreign to me. I didn't know the Russian terms. Staring at the open pages, I thought that in many ways I still remained a twenty-year-old provincial boy with an impaired brain and little memory, and it became clear to me that I didn't need to apply to take the entrance exams because I had no chance of passing them. I pulled the application out of my briefcase and shredded it. I was angry with myself, and I was angry with everyone who pushed me to study. I just wanted to live a simple life with a simple job and be left alone. I didn't need the glitter and glory.

I'd finally gotten used to living in the metropolis. I'd learned to jump on and off moving streetcars, and I wasn't afraid to weave between cars on the six-lane streets. I got used to standing in long lines in stores and to irritable, hostile Muscovites preoccupied with their miserable lives. In fact, I was afraid I was becoming one of them. Without a future to dream about, I lived only in the past and present, jumping from one lonely planet to the other, depending on which one was the least painful at the moment.

In the evenings I walked the streets near the embassy, never planning where I was going or what time I'd get back. I wanted to get lost, blend in with the crowds, be left alone but be among people. I couldn't tolerate solitude because it made me feel deserted, but I didn't want to be with my friends or people from the embassy because then I felt hopeless and inferior. Diving into the underworld in Moscow, where I felt the thrill of danger, brought back my confidence. I could be mugged, beaten, even killed, but I felt safe in the confusion, where there was no pressure and no expectations.

To blend in with the crowd I wore the dark green pants and black shirt I'd bought on the black market. I turned off Gorky Street, the most crowded promenade in Moscow, and walked unknown streets and alleys, taking sudden turns, left and right, and turning again in quarters where I'd never been before. I walked and walked, taking up the gait of an *urka*, a professional criminal, stepping onto the pavement with my head lowered, eyes darting, one hand in my pocket and the other holding a cigarette.

The more disturbed my thoughts, the more I wanted to get lost in unknown neighborhoods. I told myself that if I wasn't afraid to be on dangerous streets, I didn't need to be afraid of people in uniforms. I got into dangerous situations just to practice talking to myself to calm down. I'd done the same thing as a teenager, when I intentionally got lost in the forest. I knew the direction from which I'd come and when lost, I looked for the moss growing on the tree trunks to determine which way was north. Then I could guess the direction to take to get home. But sometimes I got really lost, couldn't find my way out, and panicked, scared of being stranded overnight and attacked by wolves or wild boar. When that happened I sat down on a log and told myself not to be nervous, that I would find my way home. When I emerged from the forest and walked home in the dark, I felt more confident about handling my fears in everyday life.

Ramshackle buildings with tiny grated windows and broken front doors marked the fringes of Moscow. Feral cats yowled in the alleyways, and drunkards slept on the bare ground, covering themselves with newspapers. Fetid kitchen scraps clogged the gutters. Lampposts were scarce, and no policemen were in sight. Some people frightened me. Shadowy figures lurked between buildings, and heavily made-up women invited me into doorways. On street corners and outside taverns gangs of young, bare-chested men laughed loudly and shared a bottle, hurling insults and making catcalls as if the street belonged to them. Most pedestrians crossed the street to avoid them, but I knew their type: they had courage when in a group, especially toward women and the elderly, but when they were alone, they were cowards.

I played the role of an experienced *urka* out of the camps and was respected. When stopped or harassed, a blast of obscenities allowed me to pass without trouble. Sometimes the hoodlums even offered me a swig from their bottle. My stance, glare, tight lips, readiness to fight, and, above all, my language told them I'd stand my ground. I couldn't reach those who'd hurt my family, but I'd hit, kick, scratch, or bite anyone who tried to hurt me. I clutched a set of brass knuckles I'd picked up on the black market, and I wouldn't hesitate to use them.

In the camps I had felt an affinity with the *urki*, although I never wanted to become one of them. I told them stories, and my reputation as a storyteller gained me their respect. The *urki* fed me when I was hungry and taught me their language and rules and code of honor. They helped me survive, and I found that many of them were sensitive and compassionate. However, the old truth held that in each group, like in each society, there are good and bad people, and to survive one must learn to differentiate between them. Diving into the underworld in Moscow, I proved to myself that I could still deal with menace.

There are times in life when logical reasoning and friendly persuasion don't work, and this was one of them. I knew that Julek, Silek,

Mendel, Katia, and Sioma were perfectly right to tell me that I must start studying or working or just do something worthwhile, but it wasn't as simple as changing a coat or hat. I wanted an education. Geology was an area in which I'd had some experience, and it had fascinated me for a long time. I'd begun to think about a career in geology when still a prisoner. Most ex-convicts remained in Kolyma after serving their terms—they were prohibited from living in large cities—and knowing this, I thought that if I survived I, too, would remain in Kolyma as a civilian worker. I was attracted to the freedom of roaming through the vast northeastern territories, many of which had never been explored, and considered myself familiar with rocks and rock formations, especially those that might contain gold. Without an education I couldn't predict the richness of a vein once it was found or its direction, but I could work on a geological team. Although I eventually came to hate gold, the beauty of the subarctic landscape, with its snow-capped mountains and hills, crystal-clear streams teeming with fish, and white-water rapids, captivated me. When the taiga awakened from its winter hibernation, deer, reindeer, and jackrabbits, black and brown bears, badgers and wolves roamed the forest and open fields full of wildflowers and blue and red berries. I never saw mushrooms as large and healthy as those in Kolyma. Boulders that had formed during the Ice Age lay everywhere, even in the thickets of the taiga and on the highest mountain tops. It was wild, pristine wilderness where no human had ever walked, and it was unlike anything I had ever seen.

With these fresh memories I went to the geology department at Moscow State University and picked up the curriculum. But math, physics, and chemistry were emphasized to an even greater degree than they were in medical school, and the thought of ever having to take these subjects again frightened me to the point that I refused to consider any career that required them.

I hung out at the black market, the *tolkuchka,* meaning "push place," where, out of all the places in Moscow, I felt most at home. The *tolkuchka* reminded me of the black market in Magadan, where I had spent a lot of time after my release. At the Moscow *tolkuchka* I bought some small things that reminded me of Kolyma, such as handmade hunter's knives, pipes, and cigarette holders. I was nostalgic, and I wondered what I was nostalgic for. The camps, or perhaps Zina. I was lonely. Before long I established connections with several of the *urki* who ruled the black market and that gave me a sense of belonging.

The black market wasn't really an entity in itself but something transient, constantly in motion, where things changed hands and people changed places, appearing and disappearing at will. One never could count on meeting someone more than once. In Magadan the black market was the only place where a feeling of freedom prevailed, and I felt the same euphoric feeling on the black market in Moscow. It was bursting with energy, a social hub for all kinds of crooks, thieves, cheaters, and robbers; the downtrodden, who depended on selling things for a living; the buyers, who picked through hundreds of items before spending a ruble; and those people who visited the black market as an amusement park, not understanding its rules and not aware of the pickpockets lurking around. This was one place where I knew the rules, and I approached the *urki* in such a way that they knew I knew the rules.

That summer passed slowly, without anything to distinguish one day from the next. The summer flowers had already bloomed and faded, and the leaves were at their darkest green. The aroma of acacia was sweetly intoxicating, reminding me of the old acacia trees blooming in the garden at our house on the hill. It was a schizophrenic life, dividing my days between Clear Ponds and the *tolkuchka*, walking the streets at night, and sleeping and eating at the embassy. After weeks of hanging out on the black market, going to the university seemed less and less appealing. Why did I need a higher education? Why torture myself with trying to choose a career and prepare for the entrance exams? I could work for myself in Poland, where private enterprise flourished.

My first thought was to become a taxi driver or mechanic, jobs that seemed to promise independence and peace of mind. Driving a taxi especially appealed to me. I'd be good at it. I'd be capable of keeping the car in excellent mechanical condition, thanks to the knowledge I'd gained as a tank driver and mechanic in the Red Army, and I would get to meet new people, and, most important, be my own boss. I also hoped I'd meet someone from Wlodzimierz-Wolynski, perhaps a girl from the Jewish gymnasium, and get married. Eventually I decided that although I'd accept almost any kind of work, I was most interested in starting my own business, maybe making colorful ties, designing fashionable shirts, or opening a restaurant with a gypsy band. I'd always loved gypsy melodies, and since my young years had been fascinated with gypsies. But these dreams made little sense, since I had no money. In the meantime, Julek kept nagging me to study, reminding me that our parents had had high expectations for me. Finally I told Julek what had happened when I had tried to apply to medical school and to the university to study geology. I explained to him that I had no chance of passing any entrance exams and that I had to go back to Poland and start living on my own. He thought seriously about my plight, and finally he stopped objecting to my not going to the university. He even offered for me to live in his apartment in Lodz, and I made tentative plans to leave at the end of the summer. Lodz had become the main administrative, intellectual, and academic center of Poland because eighty percent of Warsaw had been destroyed during the war.

I was getting ready for my departure when one afternoon Julek called me to his office. "I know you're impatient and want to go to Poland," he said, "but I want you to try once more to go to the university. I've arranged for you to have an interview with the director of the Moscow Medical-Stomatological Institute. This is a courtesy extended to me by the Department of Foreign Affairs in the Ministry of Defense. It's a unique institute because after the first two years students can choose one of two tracks, medical or dental."

I was astounded. For weeks I hadn't thought about studying. I was looking forward to going back to Poland and meeting some survivors from Wlodzimierz-Wolynski who lived there. I was hesitant, but Julek said, "You have nothing to lose. Just go and have an interview. See what the man has to say."

"But I can't pass any entrance exams."

"I know," Julek said. "So you might waste another two hours."

7

LYING AND CHEATING

My interview was scheduled for 4:00 p.m., but I left the embassy early in the afternoon to spend time at Clear Ponds and rehearse the lies I intended to tell about my past medical education at Warsaw University and military service in the Polish army. Lying and cheating had become a way of life, and it came easily because it had saved my life in the gulag. Since arriving in Moscow I'd gotten used to lying about my past during the war, so another lie about my medical education seemed to me an extension of my new persona. Sitting on the bench at Clear Ponds, eating sunflower seeds, I thought less about the interview than about how the swings of fate had changed me for better or worse. I tried to clarify to myself whether I had any more principles and where I stood with them. I was well aware that I'd lost the principle of honesty with which I was raised. But my lying and cheating helped me and didn't hurt anyone else, and I had no qualms about it.

It was nearly an hour's walk to the Medical-Stomatological Institute at 18 Kalyayevskaya Street. Across the street from the institute was Butyrki Prison, one of the most notorious prisons in Moscow. The massive yellow building was surrounded by a high red-brick wall with coiled barbed wire and broken glass on top, and it spanned two full blocks. The windows were boarded three-quarters of the way up so that the prisoners inside could only see a sliver of the sky. No one walked on that side of the street. The institute itself was in a fin de siècle mansion with stained-glass windows and a semicircular tower at the corner of the building. The yard was paved over with asphalt, and no shrub, tree, or blade of grass was in sight. Two new floors had been added. Built in typical Soviet style, they were made out of plain gray concrete slabs with unadorned windows.

It wasn't true that I had nothing to lose in the interview. This was the last chance I had to attend the university, at least in Moscow. I could try to get an education in Poland, but I would likely face the same obstacles I encountered here—entrance exams and lack of documents. Julek told me that Professor Aleksander Yevdokimov, the director of the institute and chairman of the Department of Maxillofacial and Reconstructive Facial Surgery, was Stalin's personal oral surgeon and had been chief of maxillofacial and oral surgery in the Kremlin for over twenty years. The institute, Yevdokimov's brainchild, was created as a special favor for him.

I waited for nearly an hour before Professor Yevdokimov invited me into his spacious office. Everything in the room was big: the ceiling was twice as high as normal; Professor Yevdokimov towered over me; and Stalin's portrait loomed on the wall behind Yevdokimov's ebony desk. A bronze bust of Lenin was perched in the corner of the room. Yevdokimov scratched his white mustache with the stem of his glasses and said, "You're the first Pole to apply to the institute. Where are you from?"

"Wlodzimierz-Wolynski. It's now in Western Ukraine. From 1937 to 1939 I lived in Warsaw and went to medical school."

"So you know Warsaw," Yevdokimov said with a burst of enthusiasm. "I have fond memories of Warsaw. I was born there. I remember where the university was, but I don't remember the medical school. I still remember some Polish." For a moment he switched to Polish, which he spoke with a heavy accent and many grammatical errors. He strained to say how much he loved Lazienki Park, known for its ancient trees, rolling hills, palace, and concert hall. I nodded in agreement, although I'd never seen the park.

He switched back to Russian. "Where did you live in Warsaw?"

A map of the city popped into mind, and I remembered the name of a street in the Old City. "Dluga Street," I said.

"Oh, yes, the Old City. I used to go to the Royal Castle on Sundays. Did you live in Warsaw alone, or did you have family there?"

"I rented a room with a doctor's family, my father's friend."

"What does your father do?" Yevdokimov seemed accustomed to plowing into people's personal lives, the usual style in Soviet culture. It wasn't unusual to sit next to someone on the train who immediately started asking personal questions, and I'd gotten used to it, even liked it.

"My father was a dentist. He and my family were murdered by the Nazis during the war."

"I'm sorry to hear about your family," Yevdokimov said, shaking his head. "Very sorry. So many innocent people were killed. Warsaw is in ruins." He took a fountain pen from his pocket and scribbled something on a sheet of paper, then suddenly straightened up and declared, "Twenty million of our own Soviet citizens were killed during the war. Our army liberated Poland and the other eastern European countries. Soviet soldiers conquered Berlin and put the Soviet flag on top of the Reichstag. You realize that the Soviet people sacrificed the most during this war, and our victory is the greatest in the world, all due to the Greatest Genius and Greatest War Strategist of All Time, Comrade Stalin." The sudden transformation left me wondering what other personalities lurked behind Yevdokimov's friendly face. I imagined him at a Party organization meeting or at the council of professors, or perhaps this was the usual style that he employed with students and faculty. It was hard to tell.

I nodded eagerly. "Yes, sir. We all admire Comrade Stalin, and we're grateful to the Soviet army and the Soviet people for their sacrifices. The Polish people will never forget."

Yevdokimov cleared his throat. "I understand you're interested in attending the institute. I haven't had time to go through your application, but were you aware that we gave the entrance exams one month ago and the class for this year is full?"

"No sir."

He nibbled on the stem of his glasses. "I wish you had applied a month ago. I can assure you that you would've been admitted. But let me think what I can do now. I can arrange for you to take a special entrance exam sometime this week. I'll talk to the dean of admissions. Leave your phone number with my secretary, and she'll get in touch with you." Yevdokimov came out from behind his desk. "I hope to see you again soon as our student." He put his hand out to shake mine.

"I'm sorry, sir, but this isn't exactly why I came to see you. I didn't apply to be admitted to the first-year program, and I don't intend to take the entrance exams. If you'd look at my application, I'm sure you'll see the document stating that I was a second-year medical student when the war started. I thought I'd be exempt from the preliminaries. I'm sorry for the misunderstanding." A copy of the document

Julek had made for me stating that I'd studied medicine in Warsaw was attached to my application, and Yevdokimov went back to his desk to look at it.

"Why don't you tell me how you'd like to proceed with your studies." Yevdokimov sat back down and fidgeted again with his glasses.

I remained standing, feeling I could be more persuasive that way than if I were sinking into the deep leather chair. As he turned the pages of the application, I said forcefully, "I applied to be admitted to the second or third year at your institute. I don't intend to repeat my studies from the beginning. If you can't admit me to the second or third year, then I'm not interested in studying here. Next week I'll be back in Poland. I'll find a way to continue there."

"Do you by any chance have your transcripts from Warsaw?"

"Sir, I'm sure you're aware that the university was destroyed during the war. I can't get any documents from a non-existing university to verify what I'm telling you, but I guarantee you that everything I wrote in the application is true."

"At what level do you think you should start?"

"Well, I think the second year would be appropriate. The third year might be too advanced. I know the program is slightly different here and in a different language, but I'm sure I can do it." I was hoping to get out of taking the basic science courses and sail into the medical subjects, which I felt much more secure about due to my experiences in the Kolyma hospital.

Yevdokimov opened a drawer in his desk and pulled out a list of courses. He put on his round, frameless glasses. "In our institute, all the courses are obligatory. Let's go through the list to see if the courses you took in Warsaw match those in our program. How about anatomy?"

"Yes."

"What about the political sciences—Marxism-Leninism? These are very important courses in our institute, and I'm sure you didn't study them in Warsaw."

"I studied Marxism-Leninism when I was in the Red Army. I'm sure I can pass the exams."

Yevdokimov sat back and looked me directly in the eye. "Don't underestimate this subject. It's a very important one."

"Yes sir. But I assure you, I won't have trouble with these courses."

Yevdokimov moved his finger down the list. "Physics?"

"Yes."

"Histology?"

"Yes. This complemented the anatomy course."

"Biology?"

"Yes sir."

"Chemistry?"

"Of course."

Yevdokimov put down the course list with a pleased look on his face. "It sounds as if the courses match up very well. I should be able to accommodate you in the second year, but you'll still have to take the special exams in Marxism-Leninism. By the way, I was wondering, did you have both organic and inorganic chemistry?"

I didn't know there were two chemistries and wondered if they were taught in sequence or at the same time. Yevdokimov waited for my answer.

"Organic chemistry. I don't exactly remember inorganic. I think you're right that I should start at the second year."

I tried to read Yevdokimov's thoughts in the lines on his forehead, but they revealed nothing. "It's exactly as I thought," Yevdokimov said. "It's been a long time since you took the basic science courses. I don't think you remember what you studied anymore. I have an idea. You're a young man. You're beginning a new school in a new language. Why don't you begin with the first year? Just take the regular curriculum. It will be easier for you because you've already had these courses, and you won't need to take the extra exams in Marxism-Leninism. You won't have to catch up. I think this is the best course to follow." Yevdokimov stood and lumbered toward the door to let me know his mind was made up and that he'd spent enough time with me. "Come to the admissions office tomorrow," he said. "You'll need to fill out some papers. I'll inform the administrators about my decision this afternoon."

I ran back to the embassy. Julek had once said, "Papa always believed in you. He thought that after you let off your youthful steam, you'd have a good career in any field you chose." I hoped he was right. I opened the door to Julek's office. He looked up, and without asking a question came over and gave me a big hug. "We'll celebrate tonight," he said, and hugged me again.

The next morning I went to the medical bookstore and bought the books for the first year: a three-volume anatomical atlas, manuals for chemistry, physics, biology, and histology, a textbook on political economy, the first volume of Marx's *Capital*, and the *Short Course of the Communist Party of Bolsheviks*. Back at the embassy I stacked the books on the chair next to my cot and waited for the first day of classes.

On September 1, 1946, the freshman class of one hundred sixty-four students assembled in the auditorium on the second floor of the institute. Five university officials, all formally dressed in dark suits and ties, sat behind the presiding table, which was draped with a red cloth. On the blackboard behind the officials was a huge red banner that read, "Long Live Comrade Stalin, the Genius of Mankind." Only Stalin's portrait hung above the banner. A red flag with a sickle and hammer was draped down the front of the podium.

In the Soviet Union there were no colleges where one could get a general education. Immediately after finishing high school at eighteen or nineteen years of age, students began their professional training at a university or other institute of higher education. They entered the work force between the ages of twenty-two and twenty-six. The disproportionately high number of women in our class surprised me, probably because in Poland, where private practice flourished, the medical and dental professions were the domain of men. In the Soviet Union the situation was reversed: private practice didn't exist, education was free, and women dominated both professions because both were poorly paid by the government, the only employer in the state. Trolley car drivers, factory workers, and miners earned more than doctors.

I joined a small group of male students wearing green military tunics with war decorations. They talked about the war, bragging about what branch of the armed forces they'd served in and what front they'd fought on. Some of them had been demobilized only a few months before. The men appeared much older and more serious than the giggling young women scattered in small groups around the auditorium.

A tall, brown-haired man named Sasha had driven the same tank I had, the T-34, and had fought on the first Ukrainian front. "I was in the greatest tank battle in history, near Kursk," Sasha said. "The T-34 won the battle and won the war." He looked around to make sure everyone heard him.

"I also drove this tank," I said.

Sasha shook my hand. "I'm glad to have another tank driver in the class. Do you remember the feeling of breaking fences and crushing buildings? We tank drivers have to stick together."

When Yevdokimov and his entourage came on stage everyone sat and quieted down. Yevdokimov stepped up to the podium, script in hand, and silenced the students with an outstretched arm. "The faculty of the Medical-Stomatological Institute welcomes you to the beginning of the academic year," Yevdokimov thundered. "And I'm sure that all of you are proud to be starting an exciting career." Looking around at the young women and military men, I didn't see any excitement or expectation, only boredom. The Soviet students had been through dozens of these new academic year speeches since kindergarten, and I'd gotten used to them in the Red Army. On any anniversary or state holiday, the entire tank academy was assembled to listen to two hours of speeches by the presiding officers and political instructors.

"Today is another glorious day in the life of the Soviet people. In every institution of higher education across this magnificent country, we begin a new academic year to expand our horizons under the wisdom and leadership of Comrade Stalin."

Everyone exploded in applause, clapping vigorously for as long as Yevdokimov clapped.

"Only under his leadership will the medical sciences and all other areas of human endeavor flourish. Our victories are waged not only on the battlefield but in the classrooms and laboratories across the country. Thanks to the genius of our Great Leader, we can look forward to new victories and new advances toward the victory of communism throughout the world. You must never forget what you owe to the Soviet state, the Communist Party, and personally to Comrade Stalin for providing you with a free education and a bountiful life in this free and victorious country. Long live Comrade Stalin! Onward to the victory of communism!" Frenzied clapping and cheering filled the auditorium, and continued for several minutes, until Yevdokimov introduced the next speaker, Dean and Professor Vladimir Mikheyev.

The spotlight accentuated Mikheyev's finely chiseled features and canopy of white hair. As he glorified Stalin he held onto the edges of the podium and swayed back and forth. "Only under the warming sun and radiating wisdom of Comrade Stalin, the Greatest Scientist of All Time, can we proceed to new achievements and new discoveries in the medical sciences. We will strive to care for and cure the workers and peasants of our Motherland, but not as greedy doctors, as takes place in the capitalist world." The audience clapped and grumbled loudly in agreement. Mikheyev went on to list the curriculum and cite the rules and regulations governing the institute.

The next speaker was one of our classmates by the name of Spirin. The gold star of the Hero of the Soviet Union, the highest war decoration, shone brightly on the left side of his tunic. He stood proudly at the podium, taking his duty as class speaker very seriously. "The Greatest Leader of All Time, Generalissimo Stalin, led our nation with his iron will and steady hand through the perils of liberating war to historical victory. With that same wisdom he will lead us forward to the final victory of communism in the world, and to the total defeat of the capitalists and imperialists of this planet. Anytime there is another call to arms, I will be there right away, and I am sure—" Spirin stopped and looked around at the freshman class "—every one of you will follow the call to finish off once and for all the dying and decaying capitalist world."

Everyone stood and applauded vigorously, as if on command. Initially, there was just chaotic clapping, but within seconds it changed into a synchronous sound, reminding me of the steps of soldiers marching in parades. From time to time a gaunt, gray-haired woman wearing a white coat interrupted the applause. She stood at the presiding table, raised both hands over her head, and shouted, "Long live Comrade Stalin! Hooray! Hooray! Hooray!" These enthusiastic outbursts continued throughout the ceremony.

The speeches sounded as wooden as the editorials in *Pravda,* and I wondered if anyone in the audience was as appalled as I was. Given the number of people arrested and imprisoned during the Great Terror, I was sure that many students had relatives or friends who'd been arrested or maybe even executed.

Yevdokimov introduced the last speaker, Professor Vladimir Rutko, first secretary of the Party at the institute. Rutko spoke emphatically. "Millions and millions of heroic Soviet soldiers gave their lives to liberate our country and the world from the hordes of murderous fascists. Our nation paid the greatest price, losing over twenty million people, while our so-called allies watched us bleed to death. The United States and England entered the war after we, the Soviet people, had already secured victory. We can never trust the capitalists and their imperialist masters. We need to be aware that there are still enemies outside and inside our country. Now more than ever we need to watch our neighbors, our friends, and even our families. We need to unite around the Party and our leadership, and most of all we need to follow the guidance and teaching of our Great Leader, Stalin. Death to all the capitalists and imperialists in the world. Long live Comrade Stalin!"

We stomped our feet and chanted "STA-LIN, STA-LIN, STA-LIN!" My hands burned from the continuous clapping.

It seemed that I'd missed some big changes during the years I was in Kolyma. Before the war, tributes were paid to Marx, Engels, Lenin, and Stalin. Stalin was praised as Lenin's most trusted friend, comrade-in-arms, and successor. But now, in the media and on banners, in the institute and across the country, Marx, Engels, and Lenin had been pulled down from their pedestals, while Stalin was raised higher and higher, reaching God-like status. I wondered if everyone was duped or just frightened. Did everyone really believe Stalin was the greatest leader and military genius, the greatest philosopher, historian, and biological and medical scientist? The victory of the Great Patriotic War didn't lessen the fear instilled in people by the Great Terror and the war itself. During the war, being fifteen minutes late to work was punishable by a three-year sentence in the labor camps; stealing a loaf of bread or sack of potatoes resulted in a three- to five-year sentence; and political jokes and critical comments about Stalin or the Party leadership were most severely punished, resulting in ten- or twenty-five-year sentences. Suspicion spread like a virus; everyone knew someone who had been arrested without committing a crime, and therefore everyone knew how vulnerable he or she was. The Party and NKVD established special troika courts to quickly process the continuous stream of cases. A popular saying at the time was "If you were not [arrested], you will be. If you were, you'll never forget."

Classes met six days a week from 9:00 a.m. until 5:00 or 6:00 p.m. The institute's only cafeteria was always packed because the food there was cheaper than in other public eateries, and the line moved quickly because there were no food choices. No public eatery was open for breakfast except for kiosks, which began selling vodka, beer, and dark bread at dawn. A shot of vodka was a hundred grams, and the standard order was a hundred grams of vodka, a beer chaser, and bread, although everyone smelled the bread first before eating it, in order to kill the odor of the poorly distilled vodka. Kiosks were located on nearly every corner, supporting the principle that when you drink, you don't think. Cafés and restaurants were scarce in the city and opened only at midday, and the service was slow and rude unless one ordered a bottle of vodka and appetizers to start off, which told the server there would be extended libations and a chance to cheat on the bill. Good food was served only in the restaurants in hotels for foreigners, and it was extremely expensive. In the basic sciences building, where we spent most of our time during the first two years, there wasn't any food available, so everyone brought sandwiches for lunch.

The basic science courses were held in a new building at the Sokolinaya Gora hospital on the outskirts of Moscow, over an hour's commute from the embassy. Equally far away was the anatomy lab in the Sokolniki hospital. The class was divided into ten groups of sixteen students. In my group there were five men and eleven women. All the men were war veterans, and all wore military uniforms without insignia. My uniform was distinctly different from that of the Soviet students. The Polish officer's jacket had lapels, and I wore a green military shirt and green tie. The other men wore green Soviet military tunics. The news that there was a foreigner in the institute spread quickly, and I was frequently approached during breaks while walking the main halls of the basic sciences building.

The euphoria of the first days of attending class and being a student wore off quickly. Although I kept up with classes in anatomy, histology, biology, and Marxism-Leninism, when it came to physics and chemistry, I fell farther behind my peers with every class. In the evenings I laid my books out on the dining room table and did the assignments for the other courses first. Then I worked well into the night on physics and chemistry. Often I woke up with my head in the crook of my arm and obscure notes scribbled on the page. I couldn't figure out, no matter how hard I tried, what the formulas meant or how to apply them. I drank strong coffee late into the evening, but it didn't improve my comprehension of the rules of dynamics. The formulas for average linear velocity, average linear acceleration, Newton's law of universal gravitation, orbital velocity, and minimum escape velocity got mixed up in my mind when I tried to memorize them without understanding what they meant. I had problems with molecular structures, and the principles of hydrodynamics and aerodynamics were far over my head.

As the days passed my ignorance compounded. Watching my classmates take notes in lectures and seminars, I tried to do the same, but I'd never acquired the habit. I had no idea how to select essential information from the verbiage. I tried to write word by word but was too slow. I wasn't capable of listening, comprehending, and taking notes at the same time, and from then on I stopped trying to take notes and instead listened attentively, memorizing as much as I could and from time to time writing down key words that would help me recollect the essence of the lectures. The seminars were particularly painful because I was constantly confronted with how little I knew and how far ahead of me everyone else was. I felt like I was playing blind man's bluff, where I was the only one with my eyes covered and was spinning around and around, lost in time and space.

At the end of the first month our physics instructor, Olga Fedorovna, wrote a quiz on the blackboard with three story problems all related to linear velocity. I half-heartedly sketched the story problems on a sheet of paper and stared at them. The other students wrote furiously. Olga Fedorovna passed between the tables and glanced over the students' shoulders. Twice she passed by me. When I handed in my sheet, she asked me to come to her office.

When I arrived she plopped into her chair, looking old and tired. "Please, sit down," she said, pointing to another chair. "I wanted to see you because it seems you're having difficulty in my class. I'm not sure what's wrong. You seem to be attentive in the seminars, and you haven't missed any of them, but this is the third time you've turned in a blank sheet of paper for your exam. What seems to be the problem?"

Although Olga Fedorovna spoke gently and wanted to help, I felt guilty, as if I'd done something wrong.

"Is it the terminology that's giving you trouble? I know you're a foreigner. I'm sure it must be difficult studying in another language."

I wanted to confess and tell Olga Fedorovna how ignorant I was but decided it was safer to take the easy way out. "Yes, you're right, the terminology is difficult for me. I learned this material when I was in medical school in Warsaw before the war, but so many years have passed and everything in Moscow is still so new. I have no doubt that as I get better adjusted, I'll catch on."

"Well then," Olga Fedorovna said, "perhaps you need to get a language tutor. You must be having trouble in your other courses, too. It's up to you. I'm sure you're working very hard and learning something, so please, on the exams, don't hand in a blank sheet of paper. Write something, anything you remember. If you need more help, come and talk to me."

"Yes, Professor," I said. "I'll think about what you said. Thank you for taking the time to talk to me." As I left her office I decided to seek help without further delay. But I needed more than tutoring to catch up with my classmates. I needed time, time I didn't have, and therefore the only solution was to cheat as I'd done in the Polish gymnasium.

In chemistry class I sat next to Mark Pertsovsky, a highly decorated artillery officer. He'd been discharged at the rank of captain. He was tall and handsome, with dark hair which he wore slicked back. From the first days at the institute we were friends, and this friendship would last twenty-three years. During exams he knew I was copying his work, and he pushed it closer to me so I could copy without drawing the attention of the teaching assistant. He said he didn't mind if I sat next to him, but he warned me that at the end of the semester every student would be sitting alone to take the final exam and that I would be in deep trouble. He advised me to get a tutor, but he didn't offer to work with me.

Mark was the first person in my class to invite me to his apartment to meet his parents. They lived only ten minutes away from Gorky Street, which was lined with luxury hotels, theaters, and restaurants, but their street was dark, narrow, and foul-smelling. It reminded me once again of how different the façade of the Kremlin and its nearby streets were compared with the dilapidated buildings and cramped living quarters of ordinary citizens. Mark was an only child, and his parents, although somewhat uneasy having a foreigner in their home, greeted me warmly. His father was an editor in the state publishing company, and his mother, a mathematician, taught in a high school. When they realized I was Jewish they spoke more freely about recent cultural and political events, but I didn't have a feeling of open discussion. The visit seemed to bring Mark and me closer together, but we spent little time together outside the institute; I spent all my free time studying, while Mark, an outstanding student, conducted a busy love life. I lived vicariously through him as he introduced me to each new female friend and gave me regular reports on the relationship's progress.

One Sunday when visiting Katia and Sioma I told them about my difficulties. Sioma, who was a chemical engineer, asked me to drop by with my manuals to see if he could help me with chemistry and physics. The next evening I loaded up my books and took the trolley to Sioma's.

He took one look at my homework and said, "You're going to have to start at the very beginning and work hard to catch up with your peers. I think you can do it if you follow my instructions and do the homework I'm going to give you. I can spend two evenings a week and Sunday mornings tutoring you. We can start tomorrow if you'd like."

I was deeply grateful and took Sioma up on his offer. Mid-term exams were coming up, and without help, I would fail. But I had to pay a price to go through this tutoring, and the price was to reduce my sleep, because the ride from the embassy to Sioma's and back took at least an hour and a half, and I usually spent another hour or two with him.

One Sunday when Sioma was tutoring me on the basic principles of electric charge and Coulomb's law, I caught my mind wandering far away. Wlodzimierz-Wolynski. Kolyma. The cattle cars. Mother. Taubcia. Zina. "Sioma," I said, louder than I intended. "My brain doesn't work like it used to."

"What are you talking about?" Sioma said. "You're just tired. You should go home."

"Those years in Kolyma made me a mental cripple. My brain shrank. I can't understand simple things. You're wonderful to spend all this time with me, but it isn't working." I closed the book.

"Wait a minute," Sioma said. "This isn't only your problem but mine as well. Your failure is my failure, and I don't like to fail. I won't let you off so easily."

"But I don't have the ability. I'm not making any progress," I said.

"I'm only going to say it once. For four years you suffered and worked hard for no cause. Now you have a good cause, and I want you to work as hard as you did before. You've already made progress, and I'm sure that in another two or three months you'll catch up with your classmates. It isn't going to happen overnight. You can't expect to wake up tomorrow and know everything."

Sioma was right. I had to stop thinking about my limitations. Worrying about my inadequacies kept me awake at night, and the next day I was too tired to concentrate. I revived the meditation techniques I developed in Kolyma, where I taught myself to meditate while mining gold. I didn't think about anything except getting rest. I didn't hope for anything except that the next day might be better. When dead tired and depressed, I made myself relax, forgetting for a short while where I was and what was happening to me. It was like rising above the horrible reality and floating weightlessly where no one could hurt me. But I wondered if my brain had suffered any permanent damage from the prolonged pain, thirst, hunger, and exhaustion I'd been through. If so, I wondered if the damage was reversible or if I now had a lower threshold for pain.

In the camps, where everyone had a weakened body, I saw how the mind kept some prisoners alive while it led others into the abyss. I wondered how my mind gave me the will to live and maintain my dignity. A certain aura surrounded those prisoners who had the will to survive despite the abominable conditions. They walked straight, worked steadily, ate hungrily, and looked others in the eye. But the *dokhodyagi*, those who were close to death, slouched, shuffled, kept to themselves, avoided one's gaze, and lurked around the camp eating vermin and rotting food. The most unusual example of the power of the mind over the body was when prisoners who before their arrest suffered from chronic conditions such as stomach ulcers, high blood pressure, or depression recovered from these. And as they got better, their will to live strengthened.

I left Sioma that morning feeling neither encouraged nor discouraged but determined to show him that I was working hard and that if I failed, it was due to circumstances beyond my control—my damaged brain.

Every night I went through the same scenario. Sioma had told me it was important to build upon the knowledge I'd gained from our previous day's work, so I'd turn to those unsolved problems first. Even with a fresh mind I'd rarely advance much beyond where I began—or worse, I'd go back and start changing my answers—and then it would be getting late and would be time for me to start working on my class assignments. Just as with Sioma's assignments, when

I got stuck on one problem I'd go on to another, and when I got stuck on that one I'd go on to yet another. When I reached the final road-block on the class assignments, I'd take out the new assignment Sioma had given me, study his examples, and half-heartedly scrawl down a few equations. Then I'd decide I was too tired to work any longer and would go to bed for however much was left of the night. The result: a trail of unsolved problems and cryptic equations that grew longer by the day.

At this difficult time another person offered me help and friend-ship. It was my classmate Viktor Sheimberg, whose quicksilver wit and intellect entertained everyone. He was the first in class to raise his hand and answer questions; the first to complete exams; and the first to joke, laugh, and make fun of himself. His wife, Bella, had just fin-ished medical school and was in training as an internist. She was the daughter of Professor Boris Bynin, the chairman of the Department of Prosthodontics at the institute. Since 1939 he'd been chief stomatolo-gist of the Soviet Union and was a laureate of the Stalin's Prize, the highest medical-science award in the country.

Viktor lived with his family in a spacious apartment in a six-story house on the corner of Neglinnaya Street and Stoleshnikov Pereulok, in the heart of Moscow. Stoleshnikov Pereulok was famous in diplo-matic circles as a *tolkuchka* of the highest class. One could buy gold, diamonds, and furs there, items not available in any store or on the ordinary black market.

Viktor was aware of my problems with physics and chemistry, and he offered to tutor me as well as study anatomy and histology with me. I created a schedule, spending two evenings a week and Sunday morning with Sioma and the other evenings with Viktor. We became good friends, but despite long, late-night talks in which we shared our youthful convictions and experiences, I never mentioned a word about the gulag. This issue remained off-limits to everyone in the in-stitute, and I never slipped.

The course I did best in was Marxism-Leninism, the one everyone was most terrified of because of the professor. Professor Grigory Ab-garian was tall and stooped, with a drooping face and long, horsey teeth. Every day he wore the same military uniform without insignia. He had the look of a fanatic, with sunken cheeks, raven black hair falling on his forehead, beady, darting black eyes, and tight, narrow lips. During the war he had been a high-ranking political commissar in the army. His lectures included verbose adulations of Stalin and endless quotations from Lenin's and Stalin's writings. He never smiled, and he spoke Russian with a heavy Armenian accent.

The two-hour seminars on Marxism and Leninism ran twice a week, and the basic text was the *Short Course of the Communist Party of Bolsheviks*. The first three chapters of the blue and gray hardcover book covered the history of the communist movement, and the fourth chapter, written by Stalin, was devoted to dialectical and historical materialism. This was the most important chapter, and Abgarian required us to memorize the entire chapter and be able to quote from it exactly as it was written. There was no class discussion, commentary, or questions, only recitation.

He conducted class by calling on a student and asking a question. The student was to recite the answer from the book. The only comments or deviations allowed were quotes from other works by Lenin and Stalin supporting the concept or providing an explanation for the material. I picked up the material quickly and easily, having already been drilled on it in my political education classes in the Red Army. The first time I read the text I memorized the beginning of each paragraph. When I read the text the second or third time, I already knew the contents of each paragraph and what page the material was on. When Abgarian called on me I stood up—no one was allowed to answer a question sitting down—and recited the text calmly. Abgarian's hat trick was to call on another student while one student was in the middle of a quotation, to make sure the entire class was acutely attuned to the ongoing discussion. Anyone who failed to get into the rhythm of recitation had to repeat the same class with another group. The recitations went something like this:

"What constitutes the production forces of society? Bardach," Abgarian would bark.

I would stand and say, "As Comrade Stalin, in his genius work, said in chapter four of the *Short Course*, I quote: 'The instruments of production wherewith material values are produced, the people who operate the instruments of production and carry on the production of the material values thanks to a certain production experience and labor skills—all these elements jointly constitute the production forces of society.' Next paragraph. 'But the productive forces are only one aspect of production, only one aspect of the mode of production, an aspect that expresses—' "

"Enough," Abgarian would shout. "Hitterer, continue."

Misha Hitterer would begin where I left off: "The greatest philosopher of our times, Comrade Stalin, wrote the following. I quote, '. . . expresses the relation of man to the objects and forces of nature which they make use of for the production of material values. Another aspect of production, another aspect of the mode of production, is the relation of men to each other in the process of production, man's relations of production. Men carry on a struggle against nature and utilize nature for the production of material values—' "

"Enough. Asner, continue."

This would have been hilarious if it hadn't been so frightening. Everyone feared Abgarian and his class because failing Marxism-Leninism was worse than failing any other subject; the student would be considered politically unreliable and would therefore be suspected of anti-Soviet thinking or activity.

One day after Abgarian's class his secretary found me in the basement cafeteria and told me he wanted to see me immediately in his office. When I entered his office he was immersed in a phone conversation and seemed not to notice my presence. After he hung up the phone, he said gruffly, "So, I understand you're Polish. Why don't you speak Russian with an accent? Did you have some special training in Russian?"

"I was raised bilingual. My mother was from Odessa, and my parents spoke Russian at home."

"You're Jewish," he said. "How did you get a Polish first name?"

"It's just the name I have."

" 'The name you have,' " Abgarian smirked. He looked at my military jacket. "What did you do in the Polish army?"

"I drove a T-34."

"Well, I don't like or trust foreigners," he said, throwing each word in my face. "I know you Poles. I was in Poland during the war, and I didn't like how the Poles treated us. They wouldn't let us into their homes, and they wouldn't serve me in restaurants." As he picked up speed, his guttural Armenian accent crept into his voice. "Today the Poles are our allies, but don't forget you're still foreigners. You know what Comrade Stalin said about trust? 'Trust and check,' and that's what I'm going to do with you. I'll be watching you."

I was rattled by his abrasive comments, and I was especially frightened by the way he had singled me out. He could cause trouble for me in the future just to prove his point that foreigners couldn't be trusted. I tried to figure out who or what had prompted this conversation. My class performance had been flawless, and I'd passed all the exams. All I could figure was that as a professor of Marxism-Leninism, he might be the self-appointed eyes and ears of the Party, trying to prove his loyalty by detecting enemies of the people among the students.

8

GUARDIAN OF THE DEAD

It wasn't long before the sleep deprivation caused by the extra work with Sioma and Viktor and the commute to and from their apartments began to wear on me. At first I was just tired during the day, but as the fatigue accumulated I lost my ability to concentrate, and then my ability to control my fears and obsessions. Abgarian's threat loomed over me. Fear of failure in chemistry and physics led to fears of flunking out of medical school, which made me question my future, which ignited fears of illness, joblessness, and homelessness. To make matters worse, the few hours of sleep I got each night were hardly restful. Goya-like monsters with contorted faces and empty eye sockets, their limbs and bodies twisted in a mortally sinister dance, invaded my dreams. Images of corpses floating in tanks of formalin—some of the bodies cut in half, some only heads, talking to me, asking me where their bodies were—haunted me during the day. On top of everything else, the anatomy lab was taking its toll.

I don't know what I was expecting the first time I went into the anatomy lab. I'd seen hundreds of corpses and thought I'd become indifferent to them, but what I saw in the dank basement of the Sokolniki hospital was far more gruesome than what I had seen in Kolyma. Four large, waist-high cement tanks contained not only whole corpses but heads, arms, legs, and torsos floating in a brackish brown-gray fluid. Yuri Ginsburg, our instructor, used a rusted hook to grab the corpse or necessary body part and pull it out of the formalin, creating waves that made the severed heads bob up and down. The sweetish-sour stench of flesh soaked in formalin oozed out of the bodies, penetrating my hair and clothing. My eyes teared; my nose ran.

The Sokolniki hospital was one of the largest in Moscow. As such it was one of the primary repositories for the city's unclaimed corpses, which eventually ended up in our lab. The entrance to the lab was through the morgue, which had a frosted glass door with a sign that read, in large black letters, "Visitors welcome Monday–Friday, 2:00–4:00 p.m." I didn't like passing through the morgue, where dead bodies in various stages of autopsy were scattered across iron tables. It brought back the worst of the memories I was trying to forget. Also, I was superstitious. I believed that seeing a corpse was a bad omen, and the fewer I saw, the better. In the camps, where the bed of death lay everywhere, I developed rituals to break their curse. In the anatomy lab, I reduced my exposure to them by avoiding passing through the morgue and entering the lab through the iron staircase of the fire escape.

Three days a week, Ginsburg—tall and lean, with ruby lips, dark, wavy hair, and penetrating dark brown eyes, the heartthrob of all the young women—lectured to our group and demonstrated how to dissect body parts, which he fished out of the tank and heaved onto the table like bags of sand. During the war he had worked as a surgeon on the front line, and he still wore his green captain's uniform. He'd received his medical degree before the war, and in addition to working at the anatomy lab, he worked in the Department of Surgery, which elevated him even higher in our eyes.

After the first few weeks of introductory seminars, I paired up with Viktor to perform dissections. Ginsburg told us we could dissect whichever body part we wanted, and Viktor and I fished an arm out of the tank. Viktor dissected the arm while I worked on the hand. Holding the scalpel felt good; I'd used one many times in the Kolyma hospital to drain abscessed wounds. My fingers worked quickly and precisely, cutting through the brownish-gray skin, which was thick and tough, a cross between rubber and leather. Alternating forceps and hook, I undermined layer after layer of tissue, isolating the tendons and nerves, and was done with my part faster than Viktor, who was still trying to isolate the muscles and tendons of the arm.

Ginsburg and his long-legged, blond-haired assistant, Svetlana, roamed the lab, checking on our progress. I held up the dissected tissue with a pair of large, sharp hooks, demonstrating the intricate alignment of the hand ligaments and tendons. "You're doing an excellent job," Ginsburg said as he bent over and scrutinized my work. He pulled Svetlana over to see. "Look what clean work he's done, and he's just a beginner. Have you done this before?"

"I performed dissections before, when I was a medical student in Warsaw before the war."

"Well, keep up the good work," Ginsburg said in an unusually friendly tone.

Viktor put down his scalpel and looked at me for a moment. "I didn't know you were in medical school before. You never told me. What else should I know about you?"

"Nothing. That was a long time ago. I hardly remember anything except dissecting corpses." I helped Viktor finish his dissection and we both went outside for a break.

The hand I was working on belonged to a woman. It had small scars. Her fingers were long and slim, her nails dirty and broken. I thought she must have had a hard life. As I dissected the hand nerve by nerve, tendon by tendon, and bone by bone, I wondered who she was and how she lived. Was she homeless, walking the streets and sleeping in entryways? Was she mentally ill? Was anyone with her when she died? We were never told where the corpses came from or why they and not others ended up in the anatomy lab. None of them had name tags. Every corpse was a mystery, but one thing was certain: they had been lonely people, since no one had claimed them as a parent, child, relative, or friend. We mutilated them without acknowledging the fact that we were dissecting the body parts of people whose misfortune had brought their corpses to our lab. Instead we dissected the entire corpse, system by system, shredding the flesh and rinsing it down the drain until nothing was left.

At every seminar, as we moved on to new areas of the body, Ginsburg gave a brief introduction and demonstration of the dissection. He spoke in a cold, detached way, without punctuation and without looking at us, which gave me the feeling he was more comfortable working with the dead than the living. I imagined he would be equally adept at instructing us in laying bricks or repairing shoes. Sometimes I thought he enjoyed cutting the dead flesh and was proud of his proficiency.

In our next assignment Ginsburg and Svetlana gave Viktor and me a beheaded torso. The man's torso had dark, thick chest hair. His genitals had been removed and his groin was a gaping space. I was sure that another pair of students was dissecting this part of his body. Working on the beheaded torso made me want to find all the parts of his body and restore him to the person he used to be. I wanted to put him together, wash him, dress him, and bury him with his name and the dates of his birth and death etched on a tombstone in a real cemetery. I couldn't do it with his body, so I did it by imagining a legend of his life. I named him Yasha, and a quick scan of his body made me think he'd been a manual worker. His chest was muscular, and the muscles extended around the sides of his torso. He had a dark brown birthmark near his navel, a long, narrow strip with smaller markings trailing behind it like a band of islands. He had two parallel scars across his belly, reminding me of the *urki* in the camps. Some of them had similar scars, which they inflicted on themselves so they would bleed and get out of work. I didn't think Yasha could be much older than fifty, and I imagined he'd worked in a factory, moving crates or operating heavy machinery. Or perhaps he'd developed his strength mining gold and cutting down trees in the gulag. Perhaps he'd once been an engineer or professor, but fate had chosen a different life for him.

I cut through the sternum to open the ribcage and expose the lungs and heart, but not until I cut through the pericardium, dissected all the vessels leading to and from the heart, and held the heart in my hands did I realize that I couldn't slice the heart open to examine its chambers. Since my youth the heart had meant a great deal to me. I believed the heart was a special place, the location of one's emotions, the location of the soul.

I believed the soul was the source of our conscience, decency, and compassion. I believed it was the source of our emotions and creativity. I believed that when we died, everything died within us, including our souls. The heart stops beating, the blood no longer brings oxygen to the cells, and the moment the brain stops functioning and the heart doesn't beat anymore, the line is crossed and only the body remains. Those who believe in an afterlife may die easier, may be prepared to leave this world and enter another promised to them by the God in whom they believe. I respect their beliefs, but I don't share them. I don't know if we will ever be able to open the other side of our being, which is not being. We can look in the eyes of others to see ourselves. We can see our images in the mirror. But we cannot find ourselves on the other side of the mirror.

Viktor waited for me to continue the dissection, but I laid the heart back in its place in the chest, washed my hands, and went outside.

In the camps I developed strong ideas about death and corpses. In the hospital there was a well-worn path between the back door of the TB barracks and the front door of the morgue, and I walked the path frequently, carrying my patients. I watched Dr. Umansky, the pathologist in the camp hospital, perform autopsies on them, feeling I owed it to them as a symbol of the last rites, a place where I paid my respects to a person I cared for, talked to, played chess with, and lied to in order to make feel better. I watched Dr. Umansky open the ribcage and remove and slice open the heart and lungs. He opened the abdomen and did the same with the liver, kidneys, pancreas, spleen, and intestines; and finally he opened the skull, removed the brain, and sliced it into pieces. After examining the organs and taking samples of them for microscopic examination, he put them back into the chest and abdominal cavities and sutured the muscles and skin from the neck down to the pubic hair, returning the body to its original shape. He put the brain back into the skull and replaced the crown of bone above it, then sutured the scalp so that the corpse looked the same as before the autopsy. I didn't mind this procedure because there was no profanation of the dead. In my eyes the dead remained the person I knew. In the labor camps I often felt relieved when a prisoner died from his illness or finally collapsed and died at the work site. Not only his suffering but his dehumanization had finally come to an end. Although I didn't believe in an afterlife, the notion of resting in peace was profoundly meaningful to me. But the anatomy lab continued where the camps left off.

I often found myself an outsider in the lab. I had no companion on my breaks, because I was not a good companion to my classmates, who found the severed body parts irresistible props for playing crude practical jokes. The male students tossed severed body parts around the room, while the girls looked on, laughing. I found the games to be brutal and offensive, and I wondered what kind of doctors these callous and insensitive students would be. I couldn't stand the idle chatter that went on in the lab, either. The women talked about where to find lipstick and clothing, and everyone talked about where to find food. I realized it was important that they exchange this information because the stores were nearly empty. Everything was sold under the counter at an extra price or through personal connections called *blat*, which in many ways resembled a barter system, and the only way to make connections was through word of mouth. On breaks my classmates pushed aside the body parts they'd been dissecting, spread out the morning newspaper on the cement table, and unpacked their food. Talking gaily with each other, they peeled hard-boiled eggs and sliced off pieces of lard and sausage. I ate my sandwich outside even on the coldest winter days, bare-headed and without a coat, airing myself of the stench of formalin. The sandwich even reeked of it. When I finished eating, I spent the remaining time smoking and exposing my face and body to the sun and wind.

One evening Viktor and I were studying the bones he'd smuggled home in his briefcase. In my youth I had trained myself to memorize all the details from the geography atlas, and I competed with a friend who knew more than I about the names and locations of various places in faraway lands. Now I got back into the same mode, competing with Viktor, and by doing this I discovered that my memory wasn't as faulty as I had thought it was. Studying anatomy, I felt that Viktor and I were on equal footing; only when we switched to physics and chemistry did I feel inferior and doubtful. It was the first indication that perhaps my brain wasn't as damaged as I'd thought, and it made me feel optimistic.

As we were kidding around, Viktor suddenly said, "What happens to you in the anatomy lab? You seem to be tense and angry, not your usual self. You hardly even talk to me. But when we go out to a bar or when you come over here in the evening, you're a different person. Is it the stench of the place or the corpses?"

I was surprised by Viktor's comment and wanted to shrug it off, but he was right. After the anatomy lab was over, I often went out with several of the guys for drinks at the shabby bar across from the hospital. Outside the lab I felt free to talk, joke, and laugh. We stood around tall pedestals and drank from a bottle of Moskovskaya vodka, which had a strong odor of poorly distilled methyl alcohol and an unpleasant, stinging bite. The beer chasers were watery and warm, and the only food available was dark bread, hard-boiled eggs marked with fly droppings, and slimy gray sausage. The bartender, a ruddy-cheeked, redheaded elderly woman named Bella, displayed her special favor to our group by serving us extra beer on the house.

Sometimes Ginsburg joined us, and outside of the lab, I liked him. After two or three shots he loosened up and shared his war stories with us. He had a knack for spicing them up with amorous adventures with female doctors and nurses, who all competed for his attention. After the war he married one of the doctors, a wartime flame, only to find out that she had been sleeping with men from the medical battalion and that she continued to have affairs after their marriage. He was torn over what to do because he loved her deeply, and we were more than ready with advice. The heart-to-heart talks required more and more vodka and longer sessions, and we roamed from bar to bar until midnight. One evening, after many shots, Ginsburg spilled his guts, telling us his wife had left him and was now living with a professor of surgery who'd been his commander in the military. We all felt sorry for him, but at the same time we were relieved to put an end to the deliberations about how to solve his marital problems.

I wished I could be as lighthearted as Viktor and the others, but I felt some kind of loyalty to the corpses in the tanks, even though I had no idea who they were. I explained to Viktor, "The bodies in the formalin tanks were once people, and I feel sorry that they ended this way. I'm sure many of them were good people—maybe sick, maybe poor, maybe crazy, maybe simply unable to find their place in life—but for me they remain people, not just dead flesh and bones to teach students anatomy."

"I didn't know you were so idealistic," Viktor replied. "I can see your point, but I wish you could look at things the way everyone else does. It's just another course in our education. You selected this school just like I did, and you have to take this course whether you like it or not."

Unending days of leaden skies, freezing rain, and bone-chilling temperatures heralded the beginning of winter. With the increasing darkness, I spent more time in my thoughts. I wondered where my father's body ended up after he bit into the cyanide capsule and fell dead in our backyard. I had visions of his body being brutalized and thrown into the garbage pile behind the restaurant, eaten by rats and hungry dogs. I wanted to remember him only as loving, energetic, and gregarious. I wanted to remember how he opened our home to

Jewish refugees who were fleeing from the Nazi-occupied territories. He made sure everyone who stayed with us left our home well fed, well dressed, and with money. Some of the refugees stayed for over a year, and my father, working ten- to twelve-hour days, supported them and never lost his friendly disposition. This was how I wanted to remember my father, not as a corpse struck with rifle butts and kicked by the boots of the Ukrainian police. I wanted to remember my mother, Taubcia, and Rachel the way I left them, not thrown into mass graves together with thousands of other Jews and covered with dirt. They weren't buried. No one is buried in mass graves. People in mass graves are murdered and erased with nothing left to remind anyone of them.

It was on a particularly wet, windy day, one on which it took all my willpower to get up after four hours of sleep and drag myself to the hospital, that I exploded at Vasia Kozin, surprising both him and myself. "You fucking bastard, do you realize what you're doing? You scum with no feelings! It was someone's heart, you can at least respect it." Unable to concentrate and shut out the usual noise and commotion in the lab, I had looked up to see what everyone was laughing at and saw Vasia shooting baskets with a heart.

The lab fell silent. Vasia's face was red. "I didn't mean anything. It's a piece of flesh like everything else. Why are you so crazy?" I walked out before he finished talking.

Viktor came after me. "What's the problem? We're always joking around in there, you need to learn to cool off."

"I guess the war made me this way. Suddenly something boils up inside me and I can't hold my temper. Some days it seems like the war destroyed everything—my home, my family, even my mind. It destroyed everything but the bad memories. I know that sometimes I act crazy."

Death and anonymity. Bones and mass graves. Murderers erasing bodies and memories so there were no witnesses. After this incident in the lab, I tried to convince myself that like everyone else, I needed to consider the corpses as tools for learning. Death was the end point of life, but it could also contribute to the continuity of life: the living learned about life from the dead. In order to continue with my studies, I could no longer be the guardian of the dead.

9

MARCHING ON RED SQUARE

I missed the November 7 parade marking the anniversary of the October Revolution. I'd always thought it strange that the October Revolution was celebrated in November. This came about when the communists took power in October 1917. They changed from the old Greek Orthodox calendar to the Gregorian calendar, which pushed the date of the Revolution forward to November 7. But the anniversary retained the original name: the October Revolution holidays.

On the day of the parade I lay sick in the embassy guestroom with coughing and a fever, and I was terrified I had a recurrence of TB. I had moved back to the guestroom because I was afraid of infecting Julek and his family; highly contagious TB was one of the most feared of diseases. When Julek and I were growing up, it was believed that TB couldn't be cured completely, and that once contracted, the person was always contagious. Therefore, everyone who caught TB was stigmatized for life. When I returned from the camps I no longer had active TB and was no longer contagious, but I still didn't tell Julek that I'd had the disease because I was unsure of how even he would react. Lying in bed in the guestroom, I checked my temperature compulsively, looking for the characteristic pattern of a rise in the evening and a fall in the morning, and after every coughing attack I checked my handkerchief for blood. Although weak and tired, I forced myself to eat heartily and to walk outside in the fresh air, the regimen that helped cure me in the camps. The only positive thing about being sick was that it took my mind off my problems at the institute. I went to Botkin's Hospital, the special clinic for diplomats and their families, and the internist I saw there didn't think I was sick with anything more serious than bronchitis, for which he prescribed expectorants, aspirin, fluids, and rest.

When I returned to the institute a week later, the secretary told me to report to the dean of student affairs, a man the students had nick-named the Worm. He was tall and gangly, with jerky movements, thick black-framed glasses, and thinning yellow hair. He stood in the corridors and watched as students arrived for class, and he checked attendance at lectures and seminars. Although only a minor bureau-crat, everyone considered him to be dangerous, and he was greatly feared.

The Worm asked gruffly for the certificate from the doctor attest-ing that I'd been sick the day of the parade. Although I'd been absent the whole week, the Worm was interested in that day only. He brought his fist down hard on his desk and said, "As a foreigner studying in the Soviet Union, you must follow the rules just like everyone else. Marching in the parade is an obligation of every per-son in this country, citizen or foreigner. It is a tribute to the Soviet state, our great leaders, and especially our Greatest Teacher, Com-rade Stalin. It is a special honor to walk in Red Square and see Stalin, and I advise you never to miss another parade unless you're dying. I need your doctor's certificate for November 7. You're dismissed."

At break I saw Viktor in the hall and told him about the meeting. He pulled me over to the windowsill at the end of the corridor. "You'd better look out," he said. "Everyone has to participate in the parades. Because you were gone, the Worm will be watching you. Make sure you get your doctor's certificate."

The October parade was one of two grandiose parades held every year; the other was the May Day parade. Although the parades took place in every city and village, the country was really only concerned with what happened in Red Square. Everyone examined the stage closely, noting the order in which Politburo members and the invited leaders of foreign communist parties stood. Arranged by Stalin him-self, the order was the most important indicator of each Politburo member's personal standing with Stalin. Those placed closest to him were considered to be his most trusted comrades, while those rele-gated to the flanks were probably falling out of favor or were already marked to be removed in the next reshuffling of leaders. Constant un-certainty kept this elite, powerful group fearful, loyal, and vigilant about rank and status. Another important indicator of rank and sta-tus involved the military leaders. The person selected as commander-in-chief of the parade, who reported the start of the parade to Stalin, was considered to be Stalin's most powerful and trusted military ally at the time. In the October Revolution parade that I missed, the commander-in-chief was Marshal Georgi Zukov, the great hero of World War II. Zukov was greatly admired by the citizens and military staff, but Stalin felt threatened by his rising popularity and eventually demoted him to the position of commander of the military district in Georgia.

At the beginning of the second semester I felt rested and more confident. I worked just as hard as I had the first semester but worried less and began to feel I was accumulating the base of knowledge that my classmates had at the beginning of the year. But even though life at the institute was easier, I still had nightmares and sleepless nights, still had the same anxieties about being hungry, sick, homeless, and rearrested.

Preparations for the May Day parade began in early April, with posters plastered all over the institute announcing the parade and bearing slogans such as "Long Live Comrade Stalin, Leader of the Working Class of the World," "Long Live May 1, the International Holiday of the Working Class of the World," "Onward to the Victory of Communism, Onward to the Victory of the International Proletariat." On May Day I got up before daybreak to make sure I'd be at the institute by 7:00 a.m. I intended to take a bus or trolley, but they were packed and weren't even stopping at the regular stop on the Garden Ring close to the embassy. The crowd grew by the minute, with everyone in a great hurry to reach his destination before 7:00. Several older women stepped in front of an oncoming bus and raised their hands to flag it down, but the driver didn't even slow down, just swerved to the center lane and drove by, leaving a wake of loud curses and shouts. I felt sorry for the elderly people trotting nervously to their gathering places, but I was too panicked myself to help.

The front yard of the institute was swarming with students and faculty. I spotted Professor Yevdokimov's large, square frame, his thick white hair blowing in the wind. He was surrounded by top administrators and several professors, all dressed in dark suits and ties. At 7:30, the first secretary of the Party Committee announced through the bullhorn the order of the procession. Every detail of the parade, including greetings to be shouted, songs to be sung, and the formation of the marching columns, had been authorized by the District Party Committee, the Regional Party Committee, the City Party Committee, and finally the Central Committee. Party members with red armbands and buttons with Stalin's portrait on their lapels ran frantically around the yard, shouting at everyone to assemble on the street. Being chosen as an organizer was a distinction for Party members, and both Viktor and Mark had been selected. They arranged the professors and instructors, placing the tallest people in the right flank to face the central stage in Red Square. Other organizers ran around among the students, dividing everyone by class and subdividing the classes into groups. In my row of six I was placed between my friend Misha Hitterer and Kolya Bashanov. As we left the yard, each of us was given a button with Stalin's portrait.

The formation took shape on the street in front of the institute. Spirin, the gold star of Hero of the Soviet Union shimmering on his tunic, led the formation. He had the honor of carrying the Soviet flag and of being accompanied by two tall, blond female students who wore red sashes and held Stalin's portraits. In the next row four students, two men and two women, also wearing red sashes, carried the institute's monstrous emblem. It resembled a badly painted mural with images of a hammer and sickle, an industrial building, tassles of wheat sending off brilliant golden rays, and a worker, farmer, and doctor. In the next row another student carried the institute's flag. The director of the institute and the first secretary of the Party walked on either side of him. The professors formed a group behind them, and the instructors and technical personnel followed. With an air of self-importance, the organizers checked their lists and marked off the names of those present. Abgarian and his assistants, wearing red ties, red armbands, and red badges, walked from one group to the next and checked their own lists. Before we left the institute, the lists had been checked four times: by the group leader, the class president, the Party organizers, and the ideological group led by Abgarian. The organizers selected the most impressive-looking students to face the stage, and several musicians, playing accordians and guitars, led the student body, striking up patriotic songs on command. Before 9:00 the first secretary shouted through the bullhorn, "Anyone who needs to go to the toilet or get a drink of water should do so now. When the formation leaves the premises, there will be no toilet or water breaks."

Finally we began walking toward the Garden Ring, one of Moscow's main arteries, changing pace as dictated by the policemen standing on the center line of the street. When the pace accelerated, I felt as if I were in the Red Army, goose-stepping to the sergeant's shout— "One, two, three. Left. Left. Left." When the pace slowed, I was filled with the familiar lethargy of marching day after day with my brigade to the forest to cut down trees or to the gold mines, with armed guards shouting, "A step to the left or to the right will be considered an act of escape and you'll be shot without warning." The only things missing in the May Day parade were the German shepherds snarling at my heels.

As we reached the Garden Ring our column merged with several others and the march slowed to a turtle's pace. At the first stop the Party organizers checked their lists again to make sure no one had left the parade. The musicians played patriotic tunes, mostly wartime songs, and everyone sang, even myself, although I didn't have a good ear. I'd gotten used to singing in the Red Army, and I sang loudly there because the soldiers next to me were listening for the fervor in my voice the same way I was listening for the fervor in theirs. Announcements broadcast through loudspeakers informed us of the progress of the march.

On the way to Red Square the column stopped many times. During these five- to ten-minute stops we weren't allowed to leave the column or even step away from the row. During longer stops that lasted thirty minutes to an hour, we walked around but not too far. When we were standing still, the smells of sweat and warm asphalt stained with oil and urine were almost unbearable. Elderly professors sneaked into doorways to relieve themselves, and I thought I might need to join them. At one stop I dived into an open doorway with other students, hoping to urinate on the floor, but couldn't. Bystanders brought tin buckets of water and offered us drinks. Professors and students spread their handkerchiefs on the curb and sat down for a brief respite until the organizers herded us back into the columns. When a particular group passed the central stage in Red Square, cheers of "Long Live Stalin" blasted through the loudspeakers. The Party organizers waved their hands for everyone to join in, and we shouted "HOORAY! HOORAY! HOORAY!" then broke into staccato screaming, "STA-LIN! STA-LIN! STA-LIN!" I pictured Stalin on the stage, waving his hand as if blessing his children, acknowledging the enthusiastic crowds that poured non-stop into the square.

In the early afternoon we reached Petrovka Street, next to the Great Opera Theater and across from Univermag, the first and largest department store in Moscow. Unable to wait any longer, I ran into the alley behind the opera building and urinated on the back wall of the theater. The alley was packed with men and women shamelessly relieving themselves. It was the last chance to relieve myself; as much as I hated urinating in public, I didn't want to be stuck in Red Square.

The final push toward Red Square signaled that the six-hour march was coming to an end. Waving batons and barking commands, NKVD and military officers separated the marchers from the onlookers and ordered us to keep up with the column ahead of us, closing the gap between groups. The weather had been balmy in the morning and the sky blue. But during the last stop, clouds had formed and blocked out the sun. The wind picked up. It seemed it would start pouring any minute. For as far as I could see, identical portraits of Stalin bobbed up and down above the sea of shouting marchers, and I pictured them stretching all the way across the Soviet Union to Kolyma. A Party organizer gave me a little flag with Stalin's portrait and said, "This is a souvenir to remember this unique day when you, a foreigner, were honored to walk in Red Square and see Stalin himself."

We were nearly running when we reached Red Square and the first raindrops fell on my face. The military and NKVD officers kept shouting to hurry up, and reports on the progress of the march blasted continuously through the loudspeakers. Row after row and column after column responded with a deafening "Hooray!" My ears throbbed from the noise. The rain was now falling steadily. Our column was so far away from the stage that I couldn't recognize Stalin or anyone standing with him. The swift current of marchers carried me through the square and spilled me out onto a narrow street leading to the old city. As soon as we got to the street, the organizers gave their final command to disperse. I looked for shelter in the closest entryway. It was packed. I squeezed in and spotted several students from the institute. Galya, a third-year student, invited me to join her and her friends for a party at her apartment.

The three large, cheerful rooms were furnished with light birch furniture. Old paintings, some by well-known masters, and African masks hung on the walls. An antique credenza was loaded with crystal and china. Books of literature and international politics lined the walls from floor to ceiling. I'd never seen such opulence in a Moscow apartment, and I thought that Galya's parents must be very high Party or government officials.

Galya and I had met several times in the halls of the institute. The first time we met she spoke to me in broken Polish, which she'd learned from her grandmother. Several of us sat on the floor in the living room resting our feet and drinking Armenian cognac. Different versions of the war song "Katyusha," performed by the popular band of Leonid Utesov, played on the gramophone. Galya's friend Rita sat next to me, caressing her glass of vodka. She yelled to the other room, "Whoever is in charge of the music, change the record. We've heard this patriotic stuff all day. Now I want to dance."

"Wait, don't change the record," Sasha Yeluchin, Galya's classmate, yelled. The only thing I knew about him was that he'd been in the army during the war. He got up slowly and was unsteady on his feet. He grabbed the bottle of vodka and went around pouring it into empty glasses. When he filled Rita's glass he stopped and said, "I like this music. It talks to my heart. Let it play, and let's have a toast." He raised his glass, and said loudly, "The first toast is to our Great Leader, Comrade Stalin." Everyone stood up, clinked glasses with their neighbors, and gulped. Sasha sang "Katyusha," and everyone in the room joined him. One song followed another and soon the whole group was singing and drinking. Then another toast was made, and we drank and sang more.

Someone shouted at the other end of the room, "Don't be so stupid." Lova Feinberg stood and pointed at the student sitting next to him. "For as long as I remember I've been going to these parades, and I like the festive atmosphere. Don't tell me they're senseless." Lova crossed to the other side of the room and leaned against the bookcase. The other student, Tolya, trailed behind. "We had a good time and friendly talk. Why did you snap? Why are you twisting what I said? I'm as patriotic as you or more. Don't pull this shit on me."

"I don't want to fight, but I also don't want to listen to your lies. Now you're twisting what you said a minute ago," Lova said. Fima, a Party member, tried to separate Lova and Tolya. "We are having a party, not a political meeting. Let's have fun and stop arguing. You both are fine young men. You both were soldiers and you're both devoted Party members, so behave like it. Let's have a toast to the Greatest Leader in Human History, Comrade Stalin."

Front view of the main synagogue in Wlodzimierz-Wolynski in 1914, the year
it was built. Courtesy of Morris Goldstein.

Ottylia and Rachel Bardach. 1930. Author's collection.

Mark Bardach with his cousin, Fira Bardach. 1938. Author's collection.

Train Station, Vladimir-Volynsk. 1999. Courtesy of Nathaniel Deutsch.

Soviet-style tenement houses and the Roman Catholic cathedral on Farna
Street. 1999. Courtesy of Nathaniel Deutsch.

Original post office in Vladimir-Volynsk, built in 1935. 1999. Courtesy of
Nathaniel Deutsch.

State Polish gymnasium, which Janusz attended from 1930 to 1936. 1999.
Courtesy of Nathaniel Deutsch.

Building on Farna Street once owned by the Bardach family, Vladimir-Volynsk. The second floor was occupied by Janusz's family, his uncle's family, and his grandparents. On the first floor is the restaurant Friendship, formerly known as Strzecha ("thatched roof"). 1999. Courtesy of Nathaniel Deutsch.

Farna Street and Bardach family building, Vladimir-Volynsk. 1999. Courtesy of Nathaniel Deutsch.

Sidewalk paved with Jewish tombstones. Vasilyevska Street, Vladimir-Volynsk. 1999. Courtesy of Nathaniel Deutsch.

Jewish tombstones. Vasilyevska Street, Vladimir-Volynsk. 1999. Courtesy of Nathaniel Deutsch.

Sign in Ukranian announcing Piatydnie village. 1999. Courtesy of Nathaniel Deutsch.

Piatydnie forest. Trees cleared to the horizon indicate the area of mass graves where the Nazis buried over twenty-five thousand Jews in 1942–1943. Note the waves in the field marking the trenches. 1999. Courtesy of Nathaniel Deutsch.

Monument erected in the Piatydnie field in memory of the Jews killed by the Nazis. Built in the 1970s and funded by Jewish survivors of Vladimir-Volynsk. 1999. Courtesy of Nathaniel Deutsch.

Detail of monument. An inscription in Ukrainian reads, "Twenty-five thousand peace-loving Soviet citizens were murdered here in 1942–43 by the fascist occupiers." An inscription in Hebrew on the other side dedicates the monument to the Jewish victims. 1999. Courtesy of Nathaniel Deutsch.

Alexander Ivanovich Yevdokimov, director of the Moscow Medical-Stomatological Institute. 1954. Author's collection.

First-year medical students. Janusz, front row, middle; Lena Laneyeva, second row, second from left; Misha Hitterer, third row, first from left. Note military instructor in middle of second row. 1947. Author's collection.

Mark Pertsovsky, Lena Laneyeva, and Janusz. 1950. Author's collection.

Misha Hitterer and Lena Laneyeva. 1950. Author's collection.

Lena and Janusz in Lodz, Poland. 1955. Author's collection.

We clinked and drank again and sang the "Internationale." Rita sat close to me, her long, brown hair sweeping over my arm, the special smell of her Red Poppy perfume tickling my senses. I had wanted to dance, had hoped to meet a young woman I might be interested in, but the fight between Lova and Tolya had spoiled everything. I wasn't among friends. I wasn't in an atmosphere where I could relax and not have to think about what I said and did. The argument was an act for the rest of us to witness and take note of, and I was sick of these contests, sick of everyone trying to prove their devotion to Stalin and the Party. I excused myself from Rita, thanked Galya, and left.

Beginning in kindergarten, every Soviet citizen was taught to praise Stalin and the state. They were taught to tell their teachers if they heard anyone criticize Stalin or the state, including their parents, family, and friends. As children became more sophisticated, they learned another lesson as well, if their parents were brave enough to teach it, or they learned the lesson themselves: if you have doubts or criticisms about the Party or state, you must never voice them. After years of political education, the entire Soviet society acted like well-trained puppies, following Party orders and endlessly praising the Greatest Leader of All Times. From the preschool girl holding a bouquet of flowers and reciting a poem to the most senior member of the Politburo publishing sycophantic articles in *Pravda*, everyone glorified Stalin. Soviet citizens my age and younger, having no memory of tsarist times, believed the perpetual barrage of propaganda claiming that Stalin was the only one who would lead the world's working class to the victory of international communism.

The evening at Galya's brought back the ferocious loneliness I had felt when I arrived in Moscow. Becoming friends with Mark and Viktor distracted me from my deeper longings, but I needed more than friendship. I wanted to love someone and to be loved. I'd never been a loner. My young years were permeated with love from my parents, relatives, friends. Falling in love with Taubcia changed me for life. After meeting her, I walked on clouds and dreamed in beautiful shapes and colors. To me there was no one in the world more adorable than she, and that feeling only intensified until we parted in July 1940. I couldn't see, or didn't want to see, the real world outside our love until it changed and the war started. Love came to me early in life, and I longed for it even in the camps, where it was forbidden and severely punished.

Being in love with Taubcia was a natural part of my life. No sacrifices were required. But my love for Zina was born of danger. Any prisoner, man or woman, caught in a close relationship was shipped away from the hospital to do hard labor where no one thought about love. Zina and I both knew what was at risk. She happened to be more cautious and discreet than I, and she took her time before risking a relationship with me. She warned me again and again how secret our affair must be. I don't know how it had happened that I was swayed by Zina, because after leaving home all my thoughts of love were directed toward Taubcia, and later, all I could think about was survival. But in the relative safety of the hospital I longed for love as if it were the air I needed to breathe. We carried out our courtship during the brief moments we met at the pharmacy. Loving Zina brought me moments when I was able to forget that I was a prisoner with a long-term sentence. I dreamed about the future, our future, which I imagined would be in Kolyma. Zina was warm and gentle and at the same time strong and decisive. She didn't leave me when I was sick with TB. She held my hot hands, wiped sweat from my face, and kissed me when leaving the hospital room. My early release from the camp, however, was felt by both of us as a betrayal, and I felt that I'd ruined our love, which was never allowed to see the light of day. I still missed Zina. Love had as many faces as the women I loved, and no one love was the same as the other. When I lost one, I hoped there would be another.

Several days after the May Day parade, Galya invited me to go to a movie. I wasn't sure what to expect. I didn't want to spoil a budding friendship, and I had no idea how I felt about her. After the movie we ate ice cream, and Galya told me about her family. "My life story is simple," she said. "It's my parents' and grandparents' lives that are interesting. My grandparents were from Vilno, and they moved to Moscow after the Revolution. My grandfather was Jewish. He was a journalist and devoted communist. My grandmother was Polish and an accomplished pianist and music teacher. She taught me Polish and how to play the piano. My grandparents raised me. Both of my parents are in London in the foreign service. My father is the political adviser to Ambassador Maysky. My mother, half-Georgian, half-

Russian, is a journalist at the embassy. I plan to visit them this summer. Tell me about yourself," she said, cocking her head playfully. I
told her about living in the Polish embassy and that my family had
been killed by the Nazis. Galya listened carefully, and when I finished
giving her my legend, she remained attentive and receptive, wanting
to hear more. "What's Poland like? I've never been there."

"I don't know what it's like today, but when I was growing up it
was a wonderful country. It was a friendly place, at least until 1936.
It's beautiful. There are forests, mountains, lakes, and rivers. In my
town, Poles, Jews, and Ukrainians lived peacefully together." This
nostalgia for my homeland surprised me, and I stopped talking for a
moment. Then I moved on to more secure ground, telling her more
of my legend. "When the Soviets occupied Poland, I was drafted
into—"

"Never again use the word 'occupied' to refer to the Soviet army,"
Galya interrupted. "The term is 'liberated.' I don't want you to get
into trouble." Her warning fell like a hatchet in our conversation. Although I thought she meant for it to be friendly, I couldn't be sure,
and it dampened my mood for the rest of the evening.

Galya and I went out several more times, but she kept me at a distance. At the end of the evening we'd kiss passionately, but she never
invited me to stay the night. Then one day at the end of May she
asked me not to call from the embassy anymore. "We see each other
every day at the institute," she said. "I don't think it's necessary to
talk on the phone."

With this request I understood Galya. Stalin had issued a decree
forbidding relationships and marriages between Soviet citizens and
foreigners. I hadn't known how literally to take this law, because I
was with Soviet students all the time and it was hard to see the line
between friendships and relationships, but now I realized the seriousness of it. Stalin had issued the decree after an incident involving
the son of the Chilean ambassador, who was dating a Russian girl.
The NKVD wanted to find the girl for questioning. Frightened, she
asked her fiancé if she could stay with him and his parents in their
private suite in the Hotel Nationale, which, as part of the Chilean embassy, was under diplomatic immunity. The Chilean ambassador
took her in, and the NKVD guarded the suite night and day, waiting
to arrest her. The state of siege lasted so long that it infuriated the
NKVD and the foreign ministry. When it was reported to Stalin, he

became enraged and ordered the decree banning marriages between Soviets and foreigners, contradicting the basic principles of internationalism, the cornerstone of communist ideology. Later, I was told that the girl was smuggled out of the country in a trunk by a crew from the English or U.S. embassy. Stalin's decree was never published but was enforced by all state agencies.

Before the end-of-the-year exams Galya and I went for a walk in Gorky Park. I felt an icy partition between us, and after talking superficially about the upcoming exams, Galya said, "What I have to tell you isn't going to be pleasant for either one of us. We can't see each other anymore, and believe me, I'm very sorry it has to be this way. I really like you, and I like spending time with you, but there's no future for us."

There was no point discussing the matter further. I understood what she meant, and she wouldn't have felt free enough to discuss it in the open anyway. I nodded and agreed. When we came back around to the entrance of the park, she gave me a brief hug and left. I walked aimlessly in the park for another hour or so, feeling that much more had been lost than just the relationship with Galya.

10

FIRST FINAL EXAMS

There were changes in the Polish embassy. Ambassador Rabbe had been recalled to Poland, and a devoted communist by the name of Wolpe became chargé d'affaires. He didn't like the few diplomats, Julek among them, with roots in the Polish Socialist Party. Julek was notified that after summer vacation, he would be moved from the embassy to the Grand Hotel, an old, fashionable hotel right across from the Kremlin. Although the Grand Hotel was in a prime location, being removed from the embassy did not bode well for Julek.

Two rooms had been reserved for him in the hotel, and Julek invited me to stay with him. Halina and their daughter Krystyna had moved to Lodz, where Julek had been given a spacious apartment on Gdanska Street. Spending more time with Julek, I felt that he had transferred his love for the family to me, but he cut off any attempt I made to talk about them. For years I wondered if he had buried the past or if he was as haunted as I was but didn't show it. He didn't know how long he'd remain in the embassy, and his plans for the future were uncertain. He confided to me that he'd like to finish his Ph.D. dissertation. His research and writing had been interrupted by the war, and he wanted to go back to his academic career. I had little understanding of and even less interest in the area of his research: the history of law in Lithuania. I'd never been interested in any of Julek's studies, and we never discussed the subjects. But Julek was very interested in how I was doing at the institute. He asked specific questions about anatomy, histology, and chemistry, and he could hardly believe my description of Abgarian's classes. A devoted prewar socialist, Julek never liked the communists' dogmatic ways of thinking, and he found Abgarian's method of memorization and recitation absurd. Julek loved my Abgarian stories, and he told them again and again to his close friends.

With Julek's future in Moscow uncertain, I felt a great deal of pressure to do well on the exams so that I could get a Soviet stipend. Time again was a problem. Classes at the institute continued up until the first day of final exams, and so I had to prepare for class at the same time I prepared for exams.

Every day at 7:30 a.m., I rushed to Sokolinaya Gora. I went to classes all day and was back at the embassy by 6:00 p.m. I ate quickly and rushed over to Viktor's home, where we studied until 1:00 or 2:00 in the morning, preparing for the next day's classes as well as the final exams. The next day I repeated the same routine. As the days passed, I became exhausted but also exhilarated. I couldn't sleep. Lying in bed, I went over the formulas and planned out what I still needed to study. Although the pressure of finals was completely different from the pressure I'd experienced as a prisoner, I fought with the same intensity and determination. Both situations required that I focus in order to lose myself in the work and not think about the perilous consequences of failure. Many of my classmates showed severe signs of stress as finals approached. They cried, vomited, became depressed. With the pressure I put on myself to get straight A's, I felt anxious but knew how to manage it. I assumed that as long as I studied and stayed focused, I would succeed. In a way I thrived under the pressure because it sealed out the memories that continued to disturb me.

I made up a calendar of the days I had left before the exams and filled in what I had to do every hour of every day. Initially I left seven hours for sleep, but then as I calculated the time left and how much I had to do, I reduced it to six and finally to five. Every day I listed the specific subjects I had to study, and I crossed off each topic as I completed it, which made me feel organized and disciplined. I thought I was original in writing out such an elaborate schedule, but as finals week drew near, I realized that nearly every student had drawn up a calendar, some of which were more elaborate than mine.

Viktor hung his calendar and list of subjects to study on the wall next to his desk, and with great satisfaction he crossed off the topics we covered each evening. We coordinated our calendars and lists so we could proceed at the same pace, and I trusted that with Viktor's experience and intelligence, he would help me get the highest grades possible. Sitting across the desk from each other in Viktor's study, we spread out our anatomy books and notes. We quizzed each other, jumping from one area to another to keep all the bones and structures of the body fresh in our memory. Since we both had done well in anatomy during the year, we focused on minutiae, especially on the complex bone structures of the temporal bone, maxilla, brain, and the attachments and functions of various muscles. We established one rule that I brought with me from childhood: we couldn't ask each other a question to which we ourselves didn't know the answer. We gave elaborate answers to the questions, as if sitting in the examining room. If I wasn't sure of an answer or couldn't elaborate on it enough, I looked up the material and wrote it down on a fresh sheet of paper, which imprinted it in my memory. Between 10:00 and 11:00 p.m., Viktor and I stopped to drink strong black tea or coffee. Viktor used amphetamines and he offered them to me, but I didn't want to take them.

One evening Viktor and I took a break and stood at the stove waiting for the kettle of water to boil. I was tired of sitting all day and studying things of no real interest to me. I was certain I'd never use chemistry or physics a day in my life, and the only way I could cope with the boredom was to think of the future, when I wouldn't have to deal with any of it. I had no doubts about being in the right profession; I wanted to help patients. Viktor poured tea and sat down at the kitchen table. While finishing off an apple pie, Viktor said, "We're making good progress. We've got fourteen days before the first exam. I think it's time we made our accordions."

"Accordions?"

"You know, cheat sheets. We'll keep studying as we have been, but just to be on the safe side, we'll make up an accordion for each subject." Viktor took a thin strip of paper and proudly explained how to make one. "We'll fold the paper like an accordion and write down notes on each fold to remind us of facts and formulas. Then we'll attach the paper to a long rubber band and sew it into the lining of our coat sleeves. When you need to check an answer, you just pull the paper down and hold it in the palm of your hand. For me it's a source of security in case I'm not sure of something." I was used to copying my benchmate's exercises, but I'd never hidden a crib sheet up my sleeve. Only once had I been part of an elaborate cheating scheme, and that was unwittingly, during final exams in the Polish gymnasium.

In the gymnasium, the written exams took place in a large conference room on the second floor of the local bank, and each student was seated at a small desk. On the first day we translated a section of Ovid's text. Latin was one of the subjects that interested me, and I was very good at it. While reading the text I felt something poking into the sole of my shoe. At first it was a light touch and I thought I'd imagined it. But then I felt it again, harder, and again, and when I moved my foot away, I saw a thin brown stick moving upward along my pant leg. At the end of the stick was a little metal tube with a rolled-up piece of paper. When I saw the stick moving upward, I wanted to run to the head table and report to our Latin professor that something extraordinary was happening. Instead I glanced around to make sure no one was looking, took off the metal tube, and unfurled the piece of paper. It read, "Write the first and last sentences of the text. The translation will be delivered to you in two parts. Send the translation to Samuel Kushelewitz." Although I was nervous, I did as I was asked and pushed the stick back down the hole and covered the hole with my foot. Half an hour later, I was poked in the foot again. The stick appeared, and I took the rolled paper out of the tube. While the professor and her assistant were talking at the head table, I passed it on to Izia Landsberg, who sat behind me. I wrote a note telling him to deliver the message to Samuel. Half an hour later I received one more shipment and sent it to the addressee. I finished my translation ahead of time, covered the hole in the floor with a chair leg, and turned in my exam.

Outside the conference room, Samuel came up to me. "Sorry," he said. "It was a bad mix-up, but you did great. I was desperate." Samuel was indeed desperate. This was his second attempt to pass the final exams and graduate from the gymnasium. Samuel was a smart guy, but the girls were in love with his sense of humor and bright blue eyes, and he had a hard time fending them off. He spent more time flattering them than studying.

That evening Samuel and his friends patched the hole under my table and drilled a new one under his.

During the three weeks preceding the exams at the institute I discovered many things I hadn't known about myself. I hadn't realized I had the capacity to study fourteen to sixteen hours a day and sleep only four or five hours a night. My memory and intellect became sharper the more I studied. I found that I enjoyed the state of exhilaration, the heightened tension, and the anticipation of confronting the examiners. But most of all I felt my old burning ambition to challenge everyone in class and prove that I could be among the best, like I used to be in Wlodzimierz-Wolynski.

My first exam was in anatomy, which I'd become interested in once I got over my anxiety with the corpses. Professor Kolesnikov, chairman of the anatomy department, sat at the head table surrounded by his associates, among them Yuri Ginsburg. I arrived for the examination half an hour early and walked up and down the halls and talked to other students, feeling calm and concentrated. At 8:30 Kolesnikov passed out three exam topics to each student. My topics were the anatomy of the liver, the anatomy of the orbit, and the attachment and functions of the muscles and tendons of the foot. We were allowed ten minutes in which to make notes that we could use during the oral exam. I volunteered to go first, without preparing notes. Yuri Ginsburg nodded approval when I sat straight in my chair with my hands folded on the desk and described the anatomical details of the liver. Professor Kolesnikov let me finish my presentation about the liver, and then he listened to my description of the bones creating the orbit. He let me skip the last question, and I got my first A.

I passed the exams in histology and biology with A's, but the next exam, Marxism-Leninism, made me nervous. The meeting with Abgarian at the beginning of the year left me with the feeling that he'd established an imperceptible surveillance to catch me saying or doing something that could be considered anti-Soviet and get me thrown out of the institute. During the year he'd stop me in the hallway and ask the same questions: "How are things in Poland?" "Have the Poles really changed?" "Have they learned to respect us?" Then he'd shake his head, as if to emphasize his dislike of Poles. Although I knew the material for Marxism-Leninism by heart, I was afraid Abgarian would still trip me up. If I showed any anxiety, he would certainly prey upon it, and if he failed me, my medical career would be over before it had begun.

With his heavy Armenian accent, Abgarian said, "Don't you need time to prepare yourself for the exam?"

"No, Comrade Professor. You taught us very well all year long. I'm ready to answer all the questions."

Abgarian smirked. I began citing my answers to his questions as we'd been taught to do in class, quoting directly from the *Short Course* without hesitation. When I asked if I should quote further, Abgarian's facial expression changed. He whispered something to his assistant, looking smugly satisfied.

"If all Poles learn the *Short Course* as well as you have, I believe they'll become our real friends." In addition to the A he scribbled in my exam book, he extended his hand and awarded me a firm handshake.

The last two days were reserved for exams in chemistry and physics. I prepared an accordion for each day, and I used it during both exams, but only to confirm that my answers were right. I felt uneasy pulling it down my sleeve, tucking it in the palm of my hand, and flipping through the folds. I felt confident during the chemistry exam but was less sure of physics, and I found myself very nervous when I went to the institute to find out my grades. Outside the registrar's office, lists of grades were posted on the walls. I looked for the beginning of the B's. "Bardach, A, B." With only one B—physics—I was certain that I'd be in the top competition for a full Soviet stipend. Otherwise I'd get a partial stipend, and the next time, I'd get straight A's. I felt I had succeeded and had regained my confidence and self-respect. I vowed never to copy off my classmates or use an accordion again. I no longer felt I'd been cheated in life or that I had to cheat back.

After I made it through the exams at the end of June, Julek invited me to dinner at the Hotel Metropol. Sitting far away from the band, he filled our shot glasses and toasted my future. He set the empty glass down on the table and said, "I understand you're taking your summer vacation in Poland. I hope you have a good time. You can stay in my apartment in Lodz. I also want you to think about whether you'd like to transfer to the medical school in Lodz or continue to study here. I'll probably be leaving the embassy in the next six months. The government is replacing the Socialist Party members in the diplomatic corps with communists. I don't know what kind of job I'll have or what my financial situation will be in Poland. I'll try to help you with your expenses, but you'll have to come up with some way to live on your own. I'm sure you'll get a Soviet stipend. You can also apply for a Polish stipend from the Polish Ministry of Health. With two stipends, you should be financially secure."

Everything good that had happened to me in Moscow—the relatives and friends I'd met, my entrance into medical school, my luxury food, clothing, and housing—all had been because of Julek. I knew I could get along in the world without him, but his absence would leave a big hole in my life. For a moment I thought about transferring to Lodz to finish my studies, but I couldn't follow Julek everywhere he went. I also wanted to prove to myself that I could live a normal life. "What do you think I should do?" I asked.

Julek thought for a moment. "The Soviets dominate Poland now. A Soviet diploma might be very helpful in your future, especially if you decide to pursue an academic career. In fact, the Party leadership and Polish government consider Polish students studying in the Soviet Union to be part of an elite group that will go back to Poland to lead the new society. You're already in this elite group."

"But I don't want to get entangled in politics," I said.

"If you want a career in Poland, especially an academic one, you have no choice but to become involved in politics. A Soviet diploma will be a great asset. I suggest you stay here and apply for a Polish stipend to continue your studies. You can submit the application for the stipend tomorrow. I'll send it along with the diplomatic mail."

The next day I applied for a stipend from the Polish Ministry of Health. Three days later, as I was getting ready for my trip to Poland, I got a call from the office of Wanda Michalewska, first secretary of the Party in the embassy. She asked me to come to her office the next afternoon. She was curt on the phone and didn't tell me what she wanted.

A phone call from Wanda Michalewska could only mean trouble. She was the Party watchdog in the embassy, and she kept a close eye on everyone. She was a combination of a blindly devoted Stalinist and a devious NKVD operative. People in the embassy, even Party members, were afraid of her, and Julek was extremely careful with her. He told me that several people in the embassy had been recalled to Poland because Michalewska had reported on them. Julek was afraid she was singling me out because I was associated with him. I, of course, was convinced she'd found out about my past and was going to have me expelled from the institute and deported to Poland. I imagined the conversation would be short and gruff, and I would have no defense if she knew the facts about my prison term. Julek and I spent the rest of the evening discussing what I should say to her and how I should behave. He warned me to be extremely careful and to appear to be a deeply devoted Stalinist. We went over my legend, and I practiced answering questions she might ask.

Wanda Michalewska invited me to sit down. "I received your application for a stipend from the Polish Ministry of Health. It's my duty to write up the Party Committee opinion on this matter, and I'd like to ask you a few questions," she said, straightening her skirt beneath her ample hips as she sat down. Her labored breathing filled the room. She stared at me from beneath drooping eyelids. I stared back. She looked away first. In the camps, the *urki* stared at other prisoners to pick out their prey. If the person looked away, it was a sign of weakness and he was likely to be attacked. I learned from the *urki* how to stare forcefully at people, and it worked. Wanda Michalewska was no match.

"Comrade," she said in a commanding voice. "Tell me about your family and education. What did you do during the war? I see you're wearing a Polish officer's uniform. You were probably in the First Polish Army."

Trying to avoid talking about my legend, I told her about my family and recent trip to Wlodzimierz-Wolynski. I talked about my prewar activities in the underground leftist movement. I checked her heavy jowls and thin lips for signs of irritation, and detecting none, I rambled on, telling her how I had become a cell leader and naming my friends who were in the Party. I knew a few of them had survived the war in the Soviet Union, and I hoped she might know one of the names.

Wanda raised her hand to stop me. "Do you *really* know Comrade Genia Rubinstein?"

"I know her very well. She lived across the street from me in Wlodzimierz-Wolynski."

"Her husband's name was Kalinowsky," Wanda broke in. "She's now Rubinstein-Kalinowska. Her husband was killed in the battle at Lenino. He was the first Polish officer awarded the title Hero of the Soviet Union. Comrade Rubinstein-Kalinowska is the most famous Polish widow in Moscow." Wanda gave me a contorted smile.

"Do you have her phone number?" I asked. "I'd like to talk to her." The Rubinstein family owned a small restaurant and an inn for farmers. Genia, four years older than I, was an active communist. We saw each other nearly every day and spent many evenings in our garden, talking about the proletarian Revolution and social justice. Despite our age difference, we were close friends. She was the one who recruited me to join the underground anti-fascist organization, which in essence was organized and led by the underground Communist Party. As my first cell leader, Genia strongly influenced my leftist orientation. "You can't imagine what it means to me that Genia is here. We were close friends. Comrades. She led my cell."

Wanda studied me carefully. Feeling that I was reaching solid ground, I said with authority, "Please, give me her phone number." Not having seen Genia since 1939, I was actually a little worried about calling her. I didn't know how much she'd changed or what she did, or if she'd even be interested in seeing me.

"The question is if she'd like to talk to you. She's a very important person. I can't give you her phone number, but I'll call her myself, if you wish," Wanda said.

Wanda dialed. "Genia, this is Wanda Michalewska. The younger brother of Colonel Bardach is sitting in my office. He says he knows you well." Wanda was silent for some time. Then she abruptly got up and handed me the phone.

"I'd love to see you," Genia said. "My driver can pick you up in half an hour and bring you to my place. We'll have dinner together." I told her I'd be waiting at the entrance.

Puffing up her chest, Wanda said, "You see, Comrade, how wonderful it is that I invited you here tonight. It's always rewarding to bring close friends together." She stood in front of me and put both hands on my shoulders. "I'm sure there won't be any problem with the stipend. When you're in Warsaw, go to the Ministry of Health and talk to Comrade Stysiak. She'll finalize the stipend for you. And by the way, tell Comrade Genia I'll be happy to help you in any way I can. I understand you're one of our best students. I still need your CV in my file, but there's no rush. When you're ready, call me and we'll have a drink together—perhaps with Genia, if she has time. Now you must hurry. The car will be waiting."

It was a short ride to Genia's place. The driver stopped on Gorky Street, next to Pushkin Square, and pointed to the inconspicuous entrance of a huge building, the mysterious Lux Hotel. Julek had said that foreign diplomats lived there, but no one could be sure since there was no directory. I told the officer behind the mammoth desk that I'd come to visit Comrade Rubinstein-Kalinowska. He picked up the phone and dialed a number. "He's here. He'll be escorted to your room right away." Another officer walked me to the elevator in the middle of the lobby and then escorted me to the third floor. As we were riding up, he said, "We prefer that you not look at people who pass you in the hall. Please stop and close your eyes when they pass."

The hallway was long and narrow and had a high ceiling. I wasn't sure if the gray-painted doors were made of wood or metal, but they were definitely soundproof. The officer knocked at the door of the second to last room. The peephole opened and closed, and the chain slid open. The door opened, and Genia appeared, smiling broadly. She thanked the officer, who saluted, turned around, and went back to the elevator.

Genia and I hugged tightly. She stepped back and held me by the shoulders, studying me. "You look so much older than the last time I saw you," she said. "You've really matured."

Surprising myself, I turned her around and said, "You still look like you did when you were eighteen." Genia was thinner now than before the war, but otherwise she hadn't changed. Her wavy, shoulder-length hair was still copper-colored, and her deep-set brown eyes and her smile were just as open and friendly as before. She took me by the hand and led me past a bedroom and a tiny kitchen to a large room with a bed in one corner, desk in another, and a dining room table.

"My five-year-old daughter lives here with me," Genia said. "She's already asleep in her bedroom. I'll be ready with the food in a moment. There's wine on the shelf. You can uncork it."

I poured two glasses of red wine and Genia served barley soup and fresh bread. We talked about our years in Wlodzimierz-Wolynski and our families. Genia, along with her husband and her younger sister, Rosia, survived the war in the Soviet Union. Her parents were murdered at the same time my family was killed. She told me about the years before the war when she studied in Warsaw, met her husband, a devoted communist, and got married. They both worked in Moscow before her husband joined the First Polish Army and was killed.

"So what do you do now?" I asked.

"As much as I'd like, I can't tell you. It isn't because I don't trust you. I just can't talk about my job with anyone. Please, don't ask me about it. Just believe that I'm your very good friend."

Even though both Julek and Genia worked for the Polish government, Genia said they hadn't met yet. In fact, Genia said she rarely went to the embassy, which I found strange.

"Would you like to see Julek?" I asked.

"You know, Julek and I never had much in common. We had different ideas about how to change society. You're very different from him. You've got energy and vision. But I hear Julek's doing a good job in the embassy. He's well respected by his Soviet counterparts."

"I see you know a lot about Julek," I said, thinking that Genia probably knew a great deal about many things and many people. It was clear to me that her job had to do with the Polish or Soviet secret police, or both.

We finished eating and were relaxing with another glass of wine when Genia said, "I heard what happened to you. I'm glad you lived through it. Kolyma breaks people, but those who survive are stronger. You always were and still are strong and resilient. You must forget Kolyma. We must build a new Poland now. It's our great chance."

I wondered how she knew about my past but thought it would be futile to ask. Perhaps she'd heard about it from mutual friends from Wlodzimierz-Wolynski. "I'm studying," I said, "and I want to continue my studies here in Moscow. This was why I visited Wanda Michalewska. I applied for a stipend from the Polish Ministry of Health, and I need her recommendation. I'm studying at the Moscow Medical-Stomatological Institute."

"Don't worry about Wanda," Genia said. "She's hard on everyone. If you have any trouble with her, I'll talk to her."

"She said she'd love to have a drink with us. She respects you very highly."

Genia rolled her eyes. "She respects my position. If you'd like to arrange for us to have a drink, I'll do it for you, but not out of any personal interest in Wanda. Listen, if you need anything or have any problems, call me. I'm your friend." She gave me her home phone number and called downstairs for an escort.

11

POSTWAR POLAND

Julek took me to the Belarussky station to see me off for my summer vacation in Poland. It was already evening and I was relieved when no one else came into the compartment. I pulled down the bunk, stretched out, and fell asleep. Several hours later, I was awakened by loud knocking at the compartment door. I opened it and the Soviet border guard barked, "Give me your passport and prepare your luggage for customs control." He handed me two forms. "Fill them out. Be specific."

The train rolled to a stop. Footsteps pounded across the roof and loud blows rumbled beneath my feet. Border guards walked alongside the train and tapped the sides with long-handled wooden hammers. A unit of guards and German shepherds straining at leashes appeared as if out of a fog. Guards, shotguns, German shepherds—they first appeared in my life in November 1939, when the Soviets deported local capitalists and Jewish refugees from Wlodzimierz-Wolynski. After my arrest their constant presence made me more aware than anything else that I'd lost my freedom. Now I still felt nervous when I saw them. I thought there must be someone on the train they didn't want to leave the country, or that something was being smuggled across the border and the guards were determined to find it. I was relieved that I had refused to carry two letters that an embassy official asked me to smuggle into Poland and post there. The official, Moryc Kornblum, had relatives in the United States, and he didn't want to send them letters from Moscow, since contact with anyone from a capitalist country was considered highly suspicious. In fact it was illegal to carry private letters across the Soviet border. I had felt bad for refusing to take the letters and had even thought that once again my fears were taking control of me, but now I was learning to trust my gut instincts.

Two border guards burst into the corridor. One of them, a lieutenant, asked, "Are you alone in this compartment, or are there others with you?"

"I'm alone," I said. His question made me nervous. He had my passport and he could see I was alone.

"You stay here," he said.

Through the window I saw him sweep a flashlight under the lower bunk and climb on top of the upper one. He tore the sheets off the bed, pinched the pillows, blankets, and mattresses, and left everything lying in a heap on the floor. The other guard unscrewed the light bulb in the ceiling and ran his finger inside the socket. He took the lampshade off the lamp, looked under the table, and tapped on the ceiling, walls, and floor. He opened the door and lumbered out. "Prepare your luggage for customs," he said. When they left I thought maybe they'd planted incriminating material in the compartment for customs to find, so that I would be detained. I began my own search of the compartment, going through the pile of sheets and blankets and feeling the mattress, checking the light socket, searching for gold, diamonds, foreign currency, or papers with secret information. I checked the upper bunk and overhead storage, looked under the lower bunk and under the table. I was struggling with the crank to open the window when two customs agents appeared.

"Do you have anything to declare?" one of them asked, belching garlic. I said no, and he and his buddy rummaged through every item in my suitcase. They dumped everything out of my briefcase and looked at every piece of paper. One agent ripped open the lining in the bottom of my suitcase and groped inside. I was paralyzed with fear, expecting them to pull out papers I'd never seen before and ask me how they happened to be there. They would order me to follow them to the customs compartment for interrogation. Political prisoners in Kolyma told stories of how the NKVD set them up with planted materials, and I didn't doubt they could do it to me.

"Take off your jacket," one of them said. "Empty your pockets. Do you have letters, gold, or foreign currency?" I took off my jacket and answered "no" to all their questions. The guard worked through my clothing, checking the pockets and pinching the hem, collar, and belt of my jacket. He looked in my handkerchief, billfold, and book of matches. He ordered me to hand over my pack of cigarettes, and he examined each one, especially the long, hollow mouthpiece. From the pile of clothes and things from my pockets and briefcase, one agent pulled out a Polish journal. "What language is this in?" he asked.

"Polish. I got it at the embassy, but it isn't a political journal."

"No foreign papers can be taken abroad."

He took the paper and stuffed it under his arm. "Take off your shoes. Put your hands on the bench." I bent over, and both agents frisked me. Then each one took a shoe and tapped the sole and heel, and looked under the lining inside. I hadn't felt more humiliated or frightened since I'd been released from the camps. I didn't believe the search was standard procedure for foreigners. There had to be some reason they singled me out.

They took my customs declaration and left. Two hours later the train arrived at the border station in Brest. The border guards ordered all passengers off the train and separated the foreigners from the Soviet citizens. The guards then formed two columns and told the foreigners to walk down the middle. A white-haired couple carrying heavy suitcases lagged behind the group, stopping every few steps to catch their breath. I turned around to help, but a guard grabbed my arm. "Follow the others. Don't turn around."

"But they need help," I said.

"It's none of your business. We'll take care of them. March ahead."

The border guards stood like wooden statues on both sides of the stairs leading to a special waiting area on the second floor of the train station. The two large rooms there had no phone, not even a loudspeaker, the staple of every Soviet office and private apartment. During the war, every radio in the country had been confiscated and replaced with a loudspeaker, so that the Kremlin could decide what everyone in the country listened to.

Cigarette butts littered the dingy wooden floor and red dashes of mosquito blood stained the gray walls. I went to the bathroom, a small cubicle attached to the larger of the two rooms. One moldy towel lay in the sink, and cut squares of newspaper hung on a long nail next to the toilet. There was no soap and no hot water, just cold water trickling slowly from the faucet.

Three men sat at a long table in the middle of the larger room, sleeping with their heads in the crooks of their arms. Four middle-aged, well-dressed Polish men sat at the end of the table, whispering to each other. Two French-speaking women lay on a green broken-down couch. The elderly couple lay on their coats on the floor. Unlike the passengers in most Soviet train stations, no one ventured outside his own group and everyone spoke in a hushed voice, as if listening for what was going on the other side of the door. The atmosphere was more like that of a prison than a waiting area, with armed guards outside on the landing, making sure that no one would leave and no one would enter. Without my passport I felt extremely vulnerable, subject to the whims of the guards, customs officers, and a web of bureaucracy that I couldn't see but knew was everywhere.

The door banged open and an NKVD officer called out, "Ludwik Ronicki, follow me with your luggage." One of the four Polish men sitting at the end of the table got up. I recognized the name as that of a high official in the Ministry of Foreign Trade. He put on his coat, adjusted his tie, and whispered something to his colleagues.

I looked out at the city. Dark green Soviet passenger trains stretched the length of the railroad yard. Soviet military men and a few civilians strolled across the platforms, carrying huge parcels of goods they'd brought from abroad. I'd visited the city several times before the war. In Polish, Brest was named Brzesc. It was the administrative center of the province of Polesie, in the basin of the river Pripyat, famous for its enormous marshes. Brest dated back to the beginning of the eleventh century. Over the centuries that followed, Brest and the entire Polesie province were alternately under Polish, Lithuanian, and Russian rule. At the end of the sixteenth century, the Uniate Church, which uniated the Roman Catholic Church with the Ukrainian and Belarussian Orthodox Churches, was established in Brest. The Uniates persevered despite harassment from both the Catholic and Orthodox Churches, and some of them still lived in Poland, Ukraine, and Belarus. In January 1918, Germany and the newly created Soviet state signed a peace treaty in Brest, which at the time was called Brest-Litovsk. During the negotiations, Leon Trotsky, who headed the Soviet delegation, came up with the famous formula, "Neither peace nor war." Germany rejected the idea, but Stalin didn't forget it. Ten years later he used this event, among others, to accuse Trotsky of treason and expel him from the country. In 1939, when the Soviet Union annexed the eastern regions of Poland, Brest became part of the Belarussian Soviet republic.

An hour after Ludwik Ronicki had been summoned, the door opened and he reentered the room. He tried to appear confident, but he looked tired and disheveled. His green tie was loosened, and his brown shirt was stained with sweat. He sat down at the table with his colleagues and told them what happened. "They searched everything—all my pockets, the lining of my jacket, and even the soles of my shoes. They asked me over and over if I was bringing anything into Poland from Moscow." Ronicki fumbled through his jacket for his cigarettes and lighter. "My second cousin in Moscow is a professor at the Institute of Technology," he said, his voice quavering. "I visited him while I was there, and the NKVD knows every detail about my visit. They searched me to see if I was carrying anything from him, and they put me through the most insulting interrogation. When they didn't find anything they apologized, saying it was a big mistake." Ronicki put on his jacket and tried to smooth out the wrinkles. "I'm not going to leave it at this," Ronicki said. "I'm reporting this to our prime minister and first secretary of the Party."

"Calm down, Ludwik," one of his colleagues interrupted. "Don't make a scandal out of it. They apologized. They made a mistake. They just wanted to make sure no secret information was passed abroad. This is very legitimate. As a good Party member, you must understand this. Believe me, I know what I'm saying. I work with people from Bezpieka [the Polish NKVD]. I know it was an unpleasant experience, but please, forget about it."

The man's statement robbed Ronicki of his words. I sensed his shame and anger for being suspected of smuggling secret scientific information and noted a radical change in the way his colleagues related to him after he told them how he was treated. He was now a person in trouble, and they didn't need to show him respect anymore, or express sympathy. I figured Ronicki would never report the event to anyone in Poland, but I was sure his colleagues would. They would spread the news that Ronicki had been singled out, searched, and questioned at the border, which could make him a likely target of investigation in Poland. I believed Ronicki had been pegged as unreliable and that his career was coming to an end before he even crossed the border. No high-ranking Polish party or government official in good standing would be searched and interrogated like he had been.

Late in the afternoon we reboarded the train. A Soviet border guard gave us back our passports, and five minutes later a Polish border guard came and took them again. Two Polish customs agents searched the luggage. They politely asked where I was going and for how long. They didn't bother searching my jacket or the light fixture.

The train stopped in Terespol, a small Polish border station, and I got my passport back.

Now that we were in Poland, I wondered why I was subjected to the search without further consequences. Sorting out my paranoid thoughts from the facts of the search, I realized it must have been a routine search and that the scenario I had concocted about planted documents had nothing to do with reality. I was upset with myself for becoming so easily frightened. I had to admit to myself that in some ways I was still unstable, that Kolyma still had its grip on me, and that I couldn't yet trust my perceptions.

Struggling to regain peace of mind, I immersed myself in the view outside the window. The train carved through lush green forests, crossed nameless rivers, circled lakes, and passed through cities and villages. The landscape looked the same on both sides of the border, but other things were strikingly different. From Moscow to Brest, buildings and villages had been abandoned. Gaunt cattle grazed in barren pastures. At the train stations, babushkas peddled lard and bread. But in Poland a mosaic of green and gold fields stretched between towns and villages. Glistening horses pulled plows and wagons. The Polish train stations were newly restored, with well-kept grounds and flowerbeds.

I had mixed feelings going back to Poland. I'd been away for six years, and I wasn't returning to the same Poland where I'd grown up. What I remembered about Poland before the war was the rabid anti-Semitism, fueled by the Catholic Church and supported by the government. But my most painful memories from that time were of the harassment of my father.

I wondered what the war had done to the Polish people. How did they live? How did they survive? How strong were the resistance movements? How many Poles collaborated with the Nazis? Although there were Poles who blackmailed, robbed, and informed on Jews, many others risked their lives to hide and save them. The Polish people also suffered under Nazi occupation. Many were arrested, tortured, forced into slave labor in Germany or sent to concentration camps. I hoped that after the war the Polish people had changed and become more tolerant and compassionate toward Jews. Liberated from the Nazis but now dominated by the Soviets, were the Polish people more humble than before the war, or did they harbor the same prejudice against Jews? I worried that anti-Semitism might be as strong as before, especially since many Jews who survived the war were communists. Now, due to Soviet domination, they were back in Poland and held prominent government and Party positions.

It was not yet midday when the train stopped at the platform at Warszawa-Glowna, the main train station in Warsaw and the one closest to the center of the city. The old building, which I remembered from before the war, had been replaced by a temporary construction. The station was busy with passengers carrying heavy suitcases and yelling for porters, none of whom were in the vicinity. Private cars picked up passengers, but Julek had warned me not to take one because crime was rampant. I waited for a while and then walked to the Hotel Polonia, which was near the station.

Upon their retreat from Warsaw, the Nazis had destroyed most of the city. Every building had collapsed in a different way: staircases hung in the air; bombed-out buildings protruded from the ground like the stumps of amputated limbs; blasted-out windows and doors resembled empty eye sockets. As I walked down Aleje Jerozolimskie Street, strange-looking people appeared from the ruins. I came face to face with a hunched-over man with long, unkempt hair, sunken cheeks, and the look of a scared animal. His eyes darted back and forth, and as I approached he stepped away to keep me at a safe distance. Although I was used to meeting hungry prisoners and hardened criminals, the people living in the ruins frightened me in a way that the unknown and unexpected frightens. I wondered why they were living where they were and how long they intended to stay. Maybe they had returned to their destroyed homes because they had no family and no place else to go, and being in the ruins of their own homes helped them feel close to the memory of their loved ones.

The Warsaw Uprising was known by the code name "Storm" and lasted from August 1 to October 2, 1944. It was planned in London by the Polish nationalistic anti-Soviet government-in-exile. It aimed to use the Home Army, the largest and most popular underground military organization, directed from London, to expel the Germans from Warsaw, regain independence, and establish a nationalistic pro-western government before the Soviet army, along with the First Polish Army, could enter the Polish capital and establish a communist regime. In July 1944, the Soviet army, led by Marshal Rokossowski, and the First Polish Army, created in the Soviet Union and led by General Berling, advanced toward Warsaw. On August 1, the commander-in-chief of the Home Army, General Bor-Komorowski, decided the time was right for the uprising to begin and attacked the Germans in various districts of Warsaw. He staged the uprising to take place when the prime minister of the Polish government in London, Stanislaw Mikolajczyk, was visiting Moscow, making territorial, political, and military demands to Stalin. The Home Army and London government hoped that the uprising would enforce these demands and that all the allies, including the Soviet Union, would hurry to support the insurgents.

However, the foreign governments were not informed of the preparations for or timing of the uprising, nor was Stalin in any hurry to aid the anti-Soviet insurgents. Despite initial success against the larger and better-equipped German forces, without foreign aid the insurgents lost the initiative. The German army and police forces fought the insurgents without mercy, not only killing soldiers and civilians but methodically blowing up building after building. By October 2, nearly eighty percent of the buildings in Warsaw had been destroyed, and sixteen thousand insurgents, over three thousand soldiers of the First Polish Army, and one hundred fifty thousand civilians were killed. Nearly twelve thousand insurgents were captured and sent to concentration camps, and over half a million civilians were sent to slave labor camps in Germany.

Although Warsaw had been nearly demolished only a few years earlier, rebuilding was already in full swing. The city remained the capital of Poland and was very much alive. Heavy traffic and lively crowds of pedestrians wound around the mounds of rubble and gutted buildings. Streetcars and trolley cars rang their bells, parting the crowds, and rickshaws, which I'd only seen in books about China, zig-zagged in and out of traffic. Soviet-made cranes towered over empty lots and workers rushed back and forth unloading bricks and hauling loads of dirt and rubble.

The Hotel Polonia was located in the heart of the city near the intersection of Marszalkowska and Aleje Jerozolimskie Streets, the two main arteries of the city. Before the war the Polonia, along with the Bristol and Europejski Hotels, was the most famous in Warsaw. The two other hotels were in ruins, while the Polonia, miraculously, was undamaged. When I checked in, the attendant asked, "Sir, would you like company for the night? Young or experienced? A boy or a girl? Everything is available, and they're all healthy." I declined the offer and climbed the stairs to my room. The iron military bed was covered with a green military blanket, and the flat pillow smelled of cheap perfume. The unending stream of drunks in the hall kept me awake most of the night with their shouting and door-slamming.

The next morning I went down to the restaurant for a late breakfast. A colorful, noisy medley of people of diverse persuasions filled the room. Polish and Soviet officers in full regalia dominated the crowd. Their table was already cluttered with empty vodka and beer bottles and plates of herring. A group of casually dressed young nouveaux riches talked and laughed loudly, creating their own club. They called the waiters by name, ostentatiously waved bills in the air, and ordered champagne and black caviar. In the far corner was a table of old aristocrats, all formally dressed. The elderly ladies had fresh coiffures, heavy makeup, and long white gloves, and the men wore dark suits and red carnations in their buttonholes.

The adjacent café was much noisier than the restaurant and even more interesting, reminding me of the *tolkuchka* in Moscow. In the back of the room men and women were buying and selling gold coins, jewelry, diamonds, cameos, watches, and cameras. Dealers changed zlotys to rubles, rubles to dollars, German marks to English pounds, and everything back to zlotys. I ate my eggs slowly, unable to take my eyes off the vigorous activity, which in Moscow was punishable by a prison term.

The Ministry of Health was on Miadowa Street, in an old, ornate palace that hadn't been damaged. I climbed the marble staircase to the second floor office of Marysia Stysiak, director of personnel in the Department of Higher Education. The secretary quickly put away her lipstick and mirror as I entered the room. "Do you have an appointment, Mr. . . . ."

"Bardach is my name."

"I don't see your name on the list," she said. She pretended to look seriously at the calendar. "What business would you like to discuss with Comrade Stysiak? She's extremely busy, and looking at her schedule, she won't have time for you for at least two weeks. Maybe someone else can help you."

This petty bureaucratic response irritated me. I said, "Comrade Stysiak is the one who wanted to see me. My name is Janusz Bardach. I arrived yesterday from Moscow, and I'm staying in the Hotel Polonia. Tell her I came to see her. Tomorrow I'll be leaving."

"You're from Moscow? Please, sit down. I'll go and find her." Less than a minute later Mrs. Stysiak opened the door and invited me into her office.

I had expected her to be an older, experienced bureaucrat, but she appeared to be close to my age, with a shapely figure, dark blond hair, and unremarkable but pleasant features. She led me to a coffee table in the corner. Her movements were fast, her speech rapid, as if she were afraid I might run away. "I'd like to be the first to congratulate you as the first recipient of the Ministry of Health stipend to study medicine in the Soviet Union. You must be a very bright man, Comrade Bardach." I thanked her. The secretary came into the room with a tray of coffee and Napoleon pastries. "It must be very exciting to be studying in Moscow. Tell me," Mrs. Stysiak continued, her eyes wide and deferential, "what interests you most in the medical field?"

"I don't know yet. I've only finished my first year."

"Yes, I'm sure it's a difficult decision, especially for a person as talented as you." Mrs. Stysiak flipped her blond hair out from the collar of her jacket and waved the secretary out of the room. "You know, I dream of visiting Moscow one day. What's it like?"

I wanted to tell her about the food shortages and lines at the stores. Instead I said, "It's a vibrant, exciting city."

"I'd like to have you over tonight for dinner with me and my husband. You'll have a lot in common—he's a doctor, an internist. He'd love to hear about studying in Moscow. I hope you don't have any plans for this evening."

"No, I've just arrived."

"Great. Then this afternoon, I'd like to introduce you to some important people here in the ministry, and tomorrow, I'd like you to give a presentation to our department about medical education in Moscow. We have so much to learn from the Soviets."

I was surprised by her request and puzzled by her fawning behavior. "I'm sorry, but I don't think I'm qualified to talk about medical education in the Soviet Union. I've spent only one year at the institute, and I know nothing about clinical work and research. Really, I can't make any presentations."

Mrs. Stysiak waved both hands vigorously to stop me. "You mustn't be so modest, Comrade. The report I received about you from the Party organization in Moscow is highly flattering. But if you don't feel like making a presentation, I won't insist. You'll be here again next summer."

I didn't protest anymore. I realized that Wanda Michalewska must have called Mrs. Stysiak about my stipend, and, seeing me as an ambassador from Moscow, she was trying to make a good impression. Julek was right—studying in Moscow would elevate me in the eyes of Polish bureaucrats in the Ministry of Health. I was surprised by how quickly it had happened.

Mrs. Stysiak disappeared for a moment and returned with two envelopes, gifts from the Polish government. One envelope contained a stipend for a two-month vacation; the other contained a voucher for a month of free lodging in a villa belonging to the Ministry of Health in Zakopane, the most fashionable resort in the Tatra Mountains. Mrs. Stysiak also scheduled me to meet with several prospective medical students and two doctors who had been recently selected to study in Moscow.

On the tour of the ministry I met and shook hands with at least a dozen different directors, associate directors, and officials, as Mrs. Stysiak showed off her connection with "the stipendiary from Moscow." Of all the short, meaningless visits, I remember the one with Professor Rowinski the best. He was a famous prewar radiologist and director of the Department of Higher Education, as well as chairman of the Department of Radiology at the medical school in Warsaw. Tall, white-haired, and impeccably dressed, with an inquisitive gaze and aristocratic manner, he was a distinguished-looking gentleman who, as Mrs. Stysiak warned me, didn't like to be called "comrade." Mrs. Stysiak curtsied when Professor Rowinski ceremoniously kissed her hand. "It's nice of you, Professor, to see us on such short notice. We have a special guest from Moscow. He's the first student to receive a stipend from the ministry to study medicine in the Soviet Union. He's going to meet some new young men who will follow in his footsteps."

While Professor Rowinski listened attentively to Mrs. Stysiak, I realized that she must be a trusted and devoted Party member and was probably closely connected to the Polish secret police. Professor Rowinski was not a Party member but a distinguished professional employed by the regime because of his name, expertise, and international connections. Professor Rowinski sized me up and knew right away how ignorant I was. He wasn't about to discuss anything with me. "It was very thoughtful of you to introduce this young man to me," Professor Rowinski said. "I'm pleased to meet our first stipendiary from Moscow." He turned toward me. "You have a long road ahead of you. I'm sure we'll meet again next year or the year after. If I can be of any help to you, please don't hesitate to contact me through Mrs. Stysiak. I can see that you're already her protégé." He didn't shake my hand on the way out, and I felt that he despised me, considering me a communist and arrogant Jew.

Trying to cover up her embarrassment, Mrs. Stysiak said, "Now you've seen for yourself how the old bourgeoisie and Polish nationalists hate us. Did you see how he treated us? We need him right now, but I can't wait until we get rid of all the people like him. His behavior was offensive, and I apologize. But now let me introduce you to his first associate and my good friend, Comrade Jerzy Pomianowski. He's a different person. I'm sure you'll like him. He'll be at the dinner tonight." Without knocking, Mrs. Stysiak entered his office. "Jerzy, I want you to meet Janusz Bardach. He's right from Moscow."

Pomianowski invited me to sit down. He asked me about my studies, and he told me he too had spent the war years in the Soviet Union. The longer we talked the more I felt a close connection developing with him. I thought that despite his typical Polish name and bushy mustache, he must be Jewish. There was something in the way he looked at me and smiled with kindness that made me feel that both of us could read deeper into each other than was revealed in our superficial conversation. On my way out he told me to call him if I ever needed anything.

The evening at Mrs. Stysiak's home was an unending inquiry about Moscow, Stalin, and Soviet lifestyle and culture. No one discussed politics, and no one asked about the Soviet economy. Luckily, the evening ended early because everyone was in a hurry to get home. Walking in the streets in Warsaw after dark was dangerous.

Early the next morning I took the train to Lodz.

12

FAMILY OF FRIENDS

The warehouses lined up along the tracks were scorched and pitted, but none of them had been bombed or burned to the ground. The station name, Lodz-Fabryczna, was painted in faded black letters on the sides of the warehouses. Before the war Lodz had been the second largest city in Poland and had had the largest textile industry in the country, and the Jewish population had been the second largest in Poland, next to Warsaw's.

Julek's apartment at 74 Gdanska Street was in a modern, four-story building that had belonged to a German manufacturer during the war. The man left town when the Soviets came, and now it belonged to the Polish army. The luxurious apartments had been assigned to high-ranking officers, and Julek received an apartment on the second floor. Halina was there with her cousin Antoni. He'd just returned from England, where he'd been in the Anders army. He was my age or a little older, with wiry dark hair and baleful brown eyes. We sat around a large ebony table. The German manufacturer must have left in a hurry, because the credenza was loaded with crystal, marble sculptures, and fine porcelain figurines. A crystal chandelier hung above the table. Halina tried to cajole Antoni into conversation, but he was depressed.

When Halina went into the kitchen Antoni remained quiet. He looked out the window, lost in thought, as if there weren't anyone else in the room. His aloofness reminded me of my own behavior when I had a lot on my mind. "Why did you leave England?" I asked.

"I don't know. I don't know. I should've listened to my friends and stayed. The communist emissaries promised us a welcome return home to our families and homeland, and I believed them. But now,

I'm trapped. Bezpieka is after me. Everyone who comes back from England is suspected of being an English spy. I've already been interrogated several times."

"But you were just serving in the army."

"They don't trust anyone from the west. They're afraid we'll spread news of a better life, or worse, turn out to be spies. I don't know what will happen to me." Antoni's bitterness and fear reverberated with my own.

General Wladislaw Anders had been imprisoned in the Soviet Union from October 1939 until August 1941. Upon his release he was appointed commander-in-chief of the Polish army, which was formed in the Soviet Union after the prime minister of the Polish government in London, General Wladislaw Sikorski, signed a Soviet-Polish treaty in July 1941. The Soviet government supported the formation of the Polish army, but the cooperation between the Soviet government and Polish government-in-exile broke down after Stalin refused to promise to restore Poland to its 1939 borders. In mid-1942, General Anders, following orders from London, evacuated the Polish army through Iran, Syria, and Palestine to Egypt, where they joined the English army fighting the Nazis on the African front. In 1944 the Polish and English armies liberated Italy. The most famous successful battle of the Anders army was the takeover of Monte Cassino, an important strategic sector of German defense. Over four thousand Polish soldiers were killed and wounded in the battle. After the war, General Anders and his army settled in England.

"I can't even write to my friends in England anymore," Antoni said, looking away from me. "Every letter I receive from England has been opened, and I'm afraid to write back."

"I wouldn't write to anyone," I said. "It's dangerous to send and receive mail from the west." Antoni was right, he was trapped. He'd never be able to go to a university, get a good job, or even get good housing.

That evening we ate outdoors at the restaurant Tivoli. Dim lights hung from tree branches above the tables. It was quiet, with only a faint sound of music coming from inside the restaurant. I was surprised to find myself relaxing and enjoying being with Halina and Antoni.

. . .

The first person I wanted to find was our close friend and neighbor from the house on the hill, Nuchem Spielberg. He was about fifteen years younger than my parents and fifteen years older than me, and therefore he was somewhat of an uncle figure to me. In fact, as a child I believed Nuchem was a close relative because he was always in our home. Before he got married, he ate dinner with us every evening and listened to the radio with my parents. I wondered why he never worked and how he made his living, and how he could afford to have a large house and garden right next to ours. He was a generous person, always bringing liquor and presents for my parents and me. He was present at all family celebrations, and he came to dinner every Saturday, which my father provided for his friends after morning services at the synagogue.

I got to know Nuchem better and liked him even more when he invited me to spend a week at his estate. I was fifteen and was surprised to find out that he and his two older brothers, Pinia and Lowa, owned the forests surrounding the village Turia. They also owned two sawmills, herds of cattle, a dairy, and stables with half-Arabian horses. Nearly every family in Turia worked for the Spielbergs, and the relationship between the villagers and the Spielbergs seemed to be quite friendly.

Nuchem liked me, and he loved the outdoors. He taught me a great deal about horses, wildlife, and the forest. He taught me to climb trees, walk in the woods, and distinguish good mushrooms from poisonous ones. He encouraged me to raise pigeons, and he stood with me in the yard watching them fly high in the sky. I learned to identify the sounds of owls, pheasants, wild geese, black grouse, and black cocks. He taught me to distinguish the smells of moss and mold and swamps and rotten leaves. I learned to recognize edible wild berries and wild nuts. On horseback we sometimes got disoriented, and I was afraid we'd get lost, but Nuchem always found our way back to the village. I considered him a dear, close friend, and the prospect of meeting him after seven years made me happy and sad at the same time. He was closer to me than anyone else I hoped to meet in Lodz. He also reminded me more than anyone else of my family.

I was afraid I wouldn't find anyone in a city that after the war had swelled to over a million people. I went to the Jewish center to track down my old friends from Wlodzimierz-Wolynski. Piotkowska Street, the main and longest street in Lodz, was pulsating with life. The Jewish center was located in a prewar building that had once belonged to the Jewish congregation. In the large quadrangular inner yard, men and women, young and old, wealthy and poor, searched for friends and loved ones. Everyone in the yard was a stranger to Lodz, even those who had been born and raised there, because the war had changed the city so drastically. Several men and women stopped me and asked where I was from and where I had survived the war, and I did the same, hoping to find someone from my hometown or someone who knew about survivors from there.

I was overwhelmed with feelings I had hardly been aware of before I came here. For the first time in eight years I was surrounded by a crowd of truly Jewish Jews. To me only the Polish Jews, the Jews I grew up with, had the Jewish heart, Jewish soul, and Jewish intellect. The Soviet Jews were too Soviet to remain sensitive and devoted. During eight years of living in the Soviet Union, I'd lost a great deal of my Jewishness. It had become a fading memory, not a part of daily life like before the war. But in the yard of the Jewish center, in a city I'd never been to before, the talking, yelling, laughing, crying Jews made me feel like I was back on Farna Street.

In the office I checked the lists of names on the information board and heard people talking about affidavits and visas in Russian, Polish, and Yiddish. The name Kielce kept cropping up. Kielce, a well-known, middle-sized Polish city, had a large Jewish population before the war. After the war many survivors returned to Kielce and tried to repossess their property. One day in 1946 a crowd of Poles attacked them, killing forty-two of them. The remaining Jews fled the city.

The clerk gave me a list of people from my hometown and asked me to add my and Julek's names and addresses to the list. Many names were familiar to me. Nuchem's name was listed, along with his home and work addresses.

I ran practically without stopping to Nuchem's office. On the door of the second-floor landing a signboard read "Tie Factory and Shop." Under this, in smaller letters, were the names Moniek Gorny and Nuchem Spielberg. I was getting ready to knock when the door opened and a man said to someone inside the room, "I'll be there at six o'clock. Don't you be late. Shalom."

Nuchem was sitting at his desk, cigarette in hand and an open newspaper in front of him. I stood in the doorway waiting for him to look up. Hundreds of memories flashed through my mind: Nuchem with my parents in our living room; Nuchem and I riding horses; Nuchem and I walking in the forest on his estate. Sensing someone in the room, Nuchem looked over the top of his reading glasses toward the door. The paper dropped to the floor, and next thing I knew Nuchem was hugging me closely.

"You don't know how I've been waiting for this day," Nuchem said. "Julek told me you were alive, but you were still in the camps." Nuchem had always had deep creases in his cheeks and forehead, and now they were deeper. His sunken cheeks were wrinkled, and his thin hair was white. He looked as if he'd shrunk, and I couldn't figure out if he really had been bigger and stronger or if he had just looked that way to me when I was young. I hugged him again and kissed both of his hands. "Let's surprise Moniek," Nuchem said. "He'll be happy to see you."

He led me to a back room where five men were playing poker. Poker chips and paper bills lay in the middle of the table. "Fifty and another one hundred fifty," one man said.

"One hundred fifty and three hundred," Moniek said and displayed his cards. "Full house."

A husky man wearing a cap and suspenders hissed in Moniek's face and fanned out his cards. "Not good enough. My full house is higher than yours."

"Now there's an old friend," Moniek said when he saw me. He hugged me and introduced me to his friends. He looked like I remembered him the last time I saw him on Farna Street in the summer of 1940: tall and slim with angular features, his lower jaw protruding slightly, which made his lower teeth jut out farther than the upper ones. His nose was sharply contoured, and his neck was long and thin, like that of an ostrich. "Wonderful to see you," he said. "We'll go for dinner. Nuchem, bring Janusz to our restaurant. I'll be there at three o'clock. Then we can talk."

"Moniek gambles quite a bit," Nuchem said on the way to his apartment. "He and Jacek Grembecki are real gamblers." I'd known Jacek as Grisha Greenberg. Like many other Jews, he'd changed his name during the war.

Nuchem's apartment was furnished with Biedermeier furniture, and oil paintings hung on the walls. The parquet floor was gleaming. Sunlight and a bouquet of freshly cut flowers warmed the room. "Jacek invited me to share the apartment. He has everything now— women, money, power. He's drunk with it. He's the chief prosecutor of the city." The apartment had probably been confiscated by the state, and the owner was now in prison or had fled the country. "But he doesn't have an easy life. It all comes with a price. Sometimes he tells me what the Party or secret police tell him to do. He's been or- dered to prosecute Poles returning from abroad, where they lived during the war. He prosecutes land and factory owners as enemies of the people. When his conscience bothers him he gets drunk or calls a girlfriend to come over. Then he goes back to work the next day. I don't know how long he can do this. I worry about him."

Nuchem treated me to a ham sandwich, strong coffee, and a glass of cognac. "Nuchem, what can you tell me about my family? Were you in touch with them? Did you see them during the occupation?"

"Don't torture yourself," Nuchem said. "We don't need to talk about the war. It's gone. We must forget and keep living." He took off his shoes and socks. "Since the war, my feet swell a lot. I have to rest them a couple of times a day. The doctor told me to keep them up." He lay down on the couch and rested his feet on the armrest.

"I know what you're saying, but I want to know everything. It's not to torture myself or to think about it again and again, it's just to know and remember and live my life as a normal person. It will help me. Believe me, I know myself."

"L'Chaim," he said, clinking his glass of cognac with mine. He loosened his tie and began talking in Yiddish but switched to Rus- sian, the language he used with my parents and me. "During the first six months that the Germans occupied our town, there was no ghetto, but Jews were ordered to wear white armbands and yellow stars. After that no one could live a normal life. We could be harassed, beaten, and robbed. It was hard on everyone. Friends and neighbors changed overnight. Some of them stopped associating with us, some openly harassed us. I visited your family every day. Your father was a main source of information because many army and Gestapo offi- cers were his patients. Villagers brought him food from their farms, and many people came to your home to get a good meal. Your mother was ill, but she cared for everyone who came through your door. I admired her more than ever. There were also some decent people from our estate in Turia who gave my brothers and me food. They offered us shelter if we decided to leave our homes."

With his glasses off, Nuchem looked not only old but helpless. His upper eyelids drooped, nearly covering his pupils. I wanted to tell him how much it meant to me to hear about my parents, but I was afraid to interrupt him.

"Your mother and I spent hours talking. With others she tried to hide her feelings. She was pessimistic about the future. She worried a great deal about you and Julek. No one knew what had happened to either of you. Taubcia, Rachel, and Fruma took good care of her and your grandmother. They cooked and cleaned. Taubcia was the strongest of the three. You would've been proud of her. She changed quickly from a frightened teenager to a strong, responsible woman. She was the one who went with Chaim to the market, and she dealt with your father's patients from the nearby villages. Your father relied on Taubcia. She was the only one who could make him rest from work. Both she and Rachel took special care of your parents.

"Then the news came that you were being held prisoner in a POW camp. Two of your Polish classmates told your father that they could bribe the guards to get you released if he gave them enough money. They came back again and again until Chaim Ochs found out they were using a similar story to extort money from other families, and he told your father to stop paying.

"Life was terrifying from the first day of the occupation onward, but it got even worse when the Ukrainian police began fencing off the area of the ghetto. It was early spring 1942. There wasn't much time left to go into hiding. We all knew that." Nuchem got up from the couch and walked to the window. I stood next to him.

"Why didn't my family go into hiding? There was so much time at the beginning of the occupation. They could have survived in hiding with the help of their friends."

"I talked to your parents again and again about hiding with us. I decided to take my family to Turia to hide in the house of my close Polish friends, Stefan and Krystyna Jurewicz. They prepared a hiding place next to their cellar, and there was enough space for both our families. Turia was far enough away from the train station that the Germans never went there, although Polish partisans had headquarters in the nearby forests. I told your parents about the place. But your mother was afraid that she and your grandmother would be a burden to everyone because of their frail conditions, and she refused to consider hiding in a shelter. Under no circumstances would she leave the house. Your father became angry whenever I talked about Turia.

"In the spring, just before we left for Turia, your mother and I had one of our last talks. I begged her to come with my family and me, but she refused. She took my hand and said, 'Nuchem, you're my dear, close friend. I don't want you to feel that I don't trust you, I trust you with my life. But I just can't go to Turia. You understand.' She wasn't crying, and she didn't sound as despairing as she had in the past. She told me your father had gotten them cyanide capsules. I went to your father's office and told him I was leaving. That's when he told me that a patient of his, the chief of the local Gestapo, had promised to protect your family if there was a pogrom. I couldn't figure out if he really believed this or was just repeating the promise to ease his mind and convey a sense of security to the family. He felt that he couldn't subject your mother and his mother to the misery of living in a cellar, and he held on to the promise as their only hope. Later on I suspected that maybe he invented the story to make the family feel safe.

"Your parents told Fruma, Taubcia, and Rachel that they could leave with us to hide in Turia. Your father had money and gold coins prepared for them. Your mother tried to persuade them to go, but they didn't want to leave your parents. Taubcia said simply that whatever happened to your parents would happen to all of them, and at least they would be together. The next day I left with my family. We couldn't wait any longer. Your family decided together what they wanted to do, and they were together until the end."

Nuchem sighed deeply and closed his eyes, and I waited nervously for him to continue. When he didn't, I said, "Nuchem, how did you—"

Nuchem put his hand out to stop me. He was quiet for a moment longer. He sighed again and said, "I don't need to tell you how it feels to live in hiding, to be trapped and hunted. My wife was losing her mind. She began praying all the time. Every day she sprinkled her and Rachel's heads with dirt and prayed for forgiveness. She spoke only Yiddish. You remember how beautiful and gracious she was? In two years her face wrinkled and her hair turned gray. She became emaciated and could hardly move because she fasted so often. The only news we heard was from the Jurewiczs, who traveled to the market in Wlodzimierz-Wolynski once a week. In September 1942 they told us that thousands of Jews from the ghetto had been killed in the Piatydnie forest.

"During the second year in hiding the partisans started coming to the village for food and moonshine. One night Stefan told me that someone had reported them, and that we had to leave immediately. He gave us a horse-drawn wagon furnished with straw and sheepskins and the directions to two of his relatives living nearby. It was late March, and the dirt road was muddy and bumpy. We drove into the forest, taking a road I knew by heart. Before dawn, I heard shouting in Ukrainian, and the next moment shots were fired. I struck the horses and they galloped wildly, throwing the wagon up and down, and when we were hidden safely in the forest I stopped." Nuchem buried his face in his hands and sobbed loudly. "They'd both been killed. There was nothing I could do. I drove off as far as I could and buried them in a thicket, and when I went back after the war, I couldn't find the place." He broke off and cried quietly. I looked out the window so Nuchem wouldn't see me crying.

The Jewish restaurant was a world I thought no longer existed. There was no sign on the building indicating a restaurant inside, and not until we climbed three flights of stairs did I smell the homemade soup and heavy tobacco smoke and hear the crowd of people. I'd never been in a Jewish restaurant. There were none in either Wlodzimierz-Wolynski or Moscow, and I had wondered what they were like. But much more important was meeting people I'd known since childhood. Nuchem told me that Moniek had invited many of my family's friends from Wlodzimierz-Wolynski.

The large dining room was dim, with clouds of smoke blocking out the daylight. The four windows were open and strips of flypaper hung over the tables. Waiters glided between tables, balancing bowls of steaming soup. Greetings and toasts erupted in Yiddish, Polish, and Russian. The sound of Yiddish touched me in a different way than it had in the morning at the Jewish center. The special atmosphere of the restaurant and Nuchem's presence made Yiddish sound to me like a rhapsody of joy and nostalgia, a happiness of being and a longing for what was lost. I was enveloped again in my Jewishness with the people I'd been forced to desert years before.

Nuchem led me to a small room in the back. A note that read "Private Party" was pinned on the door. I was stirred by the anticipation of seeing so many people I used to know, but I was also unsettled. Being with a group of survivors, enjoying life, I couldn't stop thinking about my family and couldn't stop blaming myself for being far away from them.

Moniek and three other men sat at a long table set for twelve. Moniek, at the head of the table, pulled out a chair for me to sit next to him. Zelman Wasser, whom everyone in Wlodzimierz-Wolynski referred to as the "gentle giant," came over and hugged me. An old bachelor, he'd owned the largest printing shop in Wlodzimierz-Wolynski, located right below our apartment on Farna Street. I had seen him every day back then, but we had hardly spoken to each other. He was much older than me, and I never knew what to talk to him about. My father and uncle considered him wise and were always talking to him. He survived the war hiding with a Polish family for more than two years and then hiding with several other Jews on the farm of a Ukrainian family.

Jacek Grembecki came around the table to embrace me. In Wlodzimierz-Wolynski Jacek had been a very active and somewhat arrogant young man. He had been very popular on the river and in the club of Jewish intelligentsia. He was an excellent orator, great bridge player, and highly sought-after lady's man. He studied law in Warsaw, receiving his degree before the war started. He survived the war with his brother, Isaac, a doctor, in various locations. Isaac emigrated to the United States immediately after the war.

I saw my close friend and classmate Izia Geller. His father, a pharmacist, had built a large two-story house next to ours on Farna Street. I laughed to myself when remembering how my father forbade me to play with Izia, believing he had a bad influence on me because he stole pigeons and cheated in class. My father didn't realize I didn't need Izia's tutoring. I'd developed my own techniques for luring someone else's pigeons away and capturing them, as well as for cheating in class. Izia survived with a family of circus performers, and after the war he married their daughter.

Basia Hammerman, one of the most attractive and fashionable

women in Wlodzimierz-Wolynski, arrived with her two younger sisters, Milka and Bronka. Basia and her husband, Max, lived next to us when we lived in the house on the hill. She owned a fashionable women's clothing and cosmetics store, while her husband owned a men's clothing store. Max was killed during the first wave of terror, when the Nazis rounded up eight hundred Jewish men in the big synagogue and executed them. Basia had later been blackmailed by my classmate from the Polish gymnasium, Antoni Shimanski. He recognized her on a street in Warsaw and threatened to report her as a Jew unless she paid him off. She offered him the jewelry she still had in her apartment and the little money she'd saved. Basia and her sisters, all natural blonds with no signs of Jewishness in their facial features, survived the war in Warsaw, living and working on the Aryan side. They left Warsaw at the time of the uprising, and now they lived in Lodz.

More and more people came to greet me and join us at the dinner table. Zygmunt Podlipski, my parents' close friend, was the one who had diagnosed my mother's colon cancer and took care of her after surgery. He and his wife survived along with another thirteen Jews on a farm owned by a Mrs. Pruchniewicz in the village of Wodzinek, not far from Wlodzimierz-Wolynski. In January 1944 a group of Polish partisans from the Home Army recruited Zygmunt to join them. Although they didn't accept Jews in their ranks, they needed a surgeon, and he remained with the unit until the Soviet army took over the area. At the end of the war, the Soviets arrested him when they were arresting others from the Home Army. They were considered enemies because the Home Army had been led by the anti-Soviet Polish government-in-exile in London. In early 1946, Julek noticed Zygmunt's name on a list of Polish prisoners in the labor camps and arranged for his release.

The last person who came was Zygmunt Pawlowski, a dentist who found shelter in our home during the initial Nazi occupation of Warsaw in 1939. For over a year he worked with my father, and then he and his wife left and settled in Lwow. Now he was associate professor of maxillofacial surgery at the medical school in Lodz.

The waiter, whom everyone called Abramek, spread out chopped liver and herring, carp in aspic, cold meats with pickles and beets, and horseradish. A large carafe of vodka stood at each end of the table. Moniek announced that the dinner in honor of my arrival was on him, and he made a toast in Yiddish: "Thank God for saving another Jew and bringing him back to his family. Now each of us is a member of this family, because each of us lost someone we loved." At the end he said a kaddish, a prayer for the dead. Everyone sat quietly, heads bowed, holding handkerchiefs to their eyes. I wanted to cry loudly, feeling very sad and very happy.

13

SUMMER 1947

In Lodz I met more Jews from Wlodzimierz-Wolynski than I expected, but only two were friends from the Jewish gymnasium: Izia Geller and Silek Shternfeld. Silek had completed his studies at the Moscow Theatrical Institute and was now acting in the Jewish theater in Lodz. The other Jews I met were my parents' friends. Although they quickly became my friends, their presence disturbed me because it reminded me of my parents' absence, the untimeliness of their deaths, and their refusal to go into hiding. I could picture them getting ready for guests to come over, greeting them at the door, eating leisurely meals, not aware of the dark days ahead. Sometimes Nuchem caught me in this state of despairing nostalgia, and he tried to pull me out of it by offering to go for a walk or talking to me about his life in Lodz. I felt comforted by his presence and I needed it frequently.

Nuchem was pleased with his new business. He'd come out of the war penniless, and before that had never had a profession or education to support himself. He was fortunate that Moniek Gorny had brought him to Lodz and made him a partner in a business he didn't know anything about. He was honest, although sometimes to a fault, and everyone liked and trusted him. He was put in charge of keeping the books, a skill he'd become adept at when running his own estate.

For the first time ever I was drawn into Jewish life, which made me feel more Jewish than I felt before coming to Lodz. I continued to go to the Jewish center and Jewish theater. I went to the synagogue once, despite my atheism. There was something special about sitting on the bench with other Jews, wrapped in tallis and tefillin and wearing yarmulkes. I listened to the prayers and familiar music. I stood with everyone else and I listened as if for the first time to the kaddish being recited. I felt that simply being there and participating in the rituals was the right thing to do. My grandparents, parents, Taubcia's parents, and Taubcia and Rachel would have liked to know that I prayed for them in the temple and listened to the words of the Torah. But at the same time I resisted being drawn too deeply into the Jewish life around me. Silek and Nuchem wanted me to see the site of the ghetto and attend prayers at the Jewish cemetery, but I was too afraid. I was just learning to navigate through daily life without being reminded every minute of the suffering and death of my family and friends.

It took several weeks of living in Lodz to understand the political climate and economy of postwar Poland. On July 22, 1944, the first provisional Polish communist government was established in Lublin. Even though war was still raging, with only one-third of the Polish territories liberated, Stalin was already scheming to take control of Poland and make sure that it would be ruled by a communist government when the war was over. Boleslaw Bierut, a devoted Polish communist, was designated the first Polish postwar president, and Edvard Osobka-Morawski, a representative of the Polish Socialist Party, was named prime minister. Choosing a socialist as prime minister was a slick maneuver because it camouflaged the Communist Party and communist-led government. The new government promptly declared itself the only legitimate Polish government, and it was recognized immediately by the Soviet Union and later by the allies. The opposition, supported by the Polish government-in-exile in London, still existed in 1947, but any efforts it might make toward establishing a democratic government were doomed once Poland was in the clutches of the Soviet Union. The new regime was solidly established and included two groups of hard-core communists: those who survived the war in the Soviet Union, and those who were active in Nazi-occupied Poland. But the real strength of the new regime rested on Soviet bayonets. Armies of special Soviet advisers infiltrated all levels of the Polish Communist Party, government, army, and secret police.

The Potsdam conference, held in the suburbs of Berlin from July 17 to August 2, 1945, clinched Stalin's takeover of eastern Europe. At that meeting Harry Truman, Winston Churchill and subsequently

Clement Attlee, and Joseph Stalin discussed the proceedings of the postwar peace settlement in Europe. They agreed to divide Germany, Berlin, Austria, and Vienna into four zones governed separately by the Americans, British, French, and Soviets. Poland received German lands reaching the Oder and Neisse rivers to the west, as well as East Prussia. The prewar eastern Polish lands of the so-called Western Ukraine and Western Belarus were incorporated into the Ukraine and Belarus Soviet republics. Less than one year later, Winston Churchill coined the term "iron curtain." On March 5, 1946, during a speech at Westminster College in Fulton, Missouri, he talked about the Soviet zeal to seal off the Soviet Union and its European satellites from any contact with the west, in order to prevent the dissemination of democratic ideals. Churchill's phrase made history: "From Stettin in the Baltic to Trieste in the Adriatic, an iron curtain has descended across the continent."

The effects in Poland of the iron curtain were swift. After Poland was liberated, a major land reform was enacted in which large estates were broken up and parceled out to peasants, paving the way for collectivization, which never took place. However, around the country, transportation, coal mines, factories, and electric stations had been nationalized, and high taxation forced the few large private businesses still in existence out of business. Only in the numerous small factories and privately owned establishments did prewar capitalism prevail. Polish and Soviet military men roamed the streets as if they owned them, and in defiance, the Polish people filled the churches on Sundays, ignoring the call for an atheistic state.

Reality was changing rapidly, and interpretations of that reality were constantly in conflict. People who should have been angry with the regime praised it; people who should have been praised by the regime were persecuted by it. A man I thought would have been sympathetic to the plight of Polish prisoners in the gulag was Stanislaw Okencki, a general in the Polish army. I first met him at the embassy in Moscow, and he was in Lodz at the same time I was. In 1938, when the Polish Communist Party leadership was accused of Trotskyism, Okencki was arrested. He'd been summoned to Moscow along with other Party leaders for consultations with Soviets, but instead of having consultations, the Poles were arrested, and most were shot in Lubyanka Prison. Okencki, a minor functionary, was given ten years in the labor camps. He was released in 1941 under the Stalin-Sikorski

Pact. I thought he would have become disillusioned with communism, especially with Stalinism, but to my surprise he supported it more than ever before.

One day Okencki and I were talking about the labor camps when I mentioned a mutual friend, Witold Hirschbaum, who had just gotten out of the camps and come to Lodz. He had been a doctor in the same hospital in Kolyma where I worked. I told Okencki that Witold had such bad memories of the labor camps and so much hatred toward the Stalinist regime that he was going to leave Poland as soon as possible. Okencki wrinkled his face and spit out the words, "We need to forget about people like him. You and I went through the same hardships as he, but we don't dwell on it. Don't forget that most of those arrested and executed were true enemies. Stalin was right in cleaning up the Party. So what if you and I were swept up in the tide. You can't make an omelet without breaking eggs. I never think about the past, and you must forget it as well and help to build a new society here. Poland's future is only with the great family of socialist republics led by the Soviet Union." He sounded like a *politruk*, a political leader, reading from the Party booklet *Sputnik of the Agitator*, prepared by the Department of Agitation and Propaganda of the Central Party Committee. "Everyone in the world is afraid of the Soviet might," he continued, "and we're its closest ally. That's why the imperialists want to lock us up behind the iron curtain."

I'd met many zealots like Okencki in the camps and in the embassy. No matter what abuse and injustice they'd suffered, they supported Stalin blindly, making excuses for him such as that he was "cleaning up the Party." I learned to be extremely careful when talking to them.

Antoni, on the other hand, had fought against the Nazis and was now being routinely interrogated by the secret police. He couldn't find a good job and had been asked to inform on his friends. He was threatened that if he didn't, he wouldn't be allowed to live in Lodz or get an education. Antoni no longer wore his crisp green British military uniform. He worked in construction now and wore drab workers' garb. His hands were callused. He was depressed. Whenever we got together he mulled over the same topic. "Look at what the Soviets are doing in this country. They have military bases on the German borders and around large cities. Soviet military men and their families have special privileges. The Polish government builds special housing for them and special clubs and restaurants. They shop at special stores which are stocked with foods and goods you can't get anywhere else. Soviet civilians run our industry Soviet-style, which means they steal everything they can get their hands on and ship it to their country. The whole nation hates the Soviets and the communist regime. I don't think it can last."

After two or three shots of vodka Antoni either got more depressed and fell silent or became more agitated and talkative. I frequently had to tell him to shut up and stop his anti-Soviet tirades. If he shared these thoughts with me I was sure he was sharing them with others, some of whom would denounce him to Bezpieka. To complicate matters further, the attitude of Poles toward communism and communists was entwined with their attitude toward Jews, who now held many high positions in Poland.

Before the war, there were more Jews in the Polish Communist Party than there were Poles, because the ideals of social justice and equality appealed to many poor and intellectual Jews, myself included. When the war ended, many Jewish communists became high-profile members of the Politburo and Central Committee of the Communist Party and rose to high positions in the Polish government, military, Bezpieka, commerce, and foreign service. Poles often used this fact to dismiss accusations of anti-Semitism both before and after the war. The goal of many Jewish communists was to stay in Poland and, with the help of the Soviet Union, actively build a new socialist society in Poland. For them, Poland was the final destination. Poland was home. Many Jews who were not communists also considered Poland their homeland because they had been raised there. They considered themselves to be Poles of Jewish origin. They had always wanted to assimilate, and they hoped that under the new communist regime, assimilation would be easier because there would no longer be an ethnic or religious barrier. Many Poles, however, continued to resent Jews.

When talking to me, some Poles carefully hid their true sentiments toward Jews, while others emphasized their friendship with them. Henryk, an engineer I met through Moniek, was typical of many Poles in this regard. I used to see him on the weekends, when I went with Moniek and Nuchem to visit him at his summer cottage. Henryk would be sitting on the veranda talking to his friends about the political changes and their implications for the Polish economy and the Catholic Church. He seemed to be politically more seasoned than his friends and neighbors, and we had many good discussions, but basically, Henryk was an opportunist. As such he was proud of his daughter's marriage to a Party functionary, who happened to be Jewish, but if the Nazis had won the war, Henryk would have been equally proud to have his daughter marry a Nazi officer. And if she had met her Jewish husband before the war, Henryk would have thrown her out of the house. But now, with a Jew as his son-in-law, he watched himself carefully around me and tried to show his most compassionate side, expressing anguish over the fate of the Jews in the Lodz ghetto. However, Henryk's friends didn't bother to take such care in expressing their sentiments toward the new regime or the Jews.

Franek, a prewar major in the Polish army, was now a housing inspector, a position he considered far beneath him and one that caused him great bitterness. He pressed the tobacco down in his pipe with a stained, callused thumb and lit it. "Before the war, the communists were in prison and there wasn't a single Jew in the government or even in the local administration in Lodz. Now Jews and communists are running the country, with no experience in how to govern. They don't know how to deal with people or how to run the economy and industry. They certainly don't know how to train the military. All they know is how to follow Soviet orders." Franek rocked forward and leaned toward me. "Can you explain to me how the communists, with Soviet advisers and Jews, will govern thirty-five million Polish Catholics who hate them? I hear all the time that over three million Polish Jews were murdered by the Nazis, but look around and you'll see that enough of them survived to run a country. They're in the highest positions in the Party, government, and military, not to mention the secret police and industry. They're a very small fraction of our nation, and it's not right that they rule over us.

"And I'll tell you another thing," Franek said, puffing on his pipe. "Poles won't put up with it." He sat up straight and looked me in the eye. "I feel free to talk about this. Many other people would be afraid to talk to you so openly, but I'm not. Some of my best friends before the war were Jewish. I'm very sorry for what happened to them during the war, but this doesn't give them the right to run the country as if it's their fiefdom. You know what's going to happen? Having so many Jews in power will incite such rampant anti-Semitism that it may end badly. Don't forget how Jews were treated before the war. People won't forget what can be done to them. Poles can be provoked, like those in Kielce. And one last thing. The communists cannot start closing down the churches and arresting our priests. I've heard that the Soviets closed all of their churches and arrested and even shot their own clergy, and that they'll try to do the same here. But we Poles will never give up our religion. Our Madonna took care of us throughout the centuries, and she will never abandon us."

I listened with interest to the new twists in Franek's anti-Semitic tirades. I thought about debating him on some of his points, but when he commented that he "had many friends who were Jews," I felt no urge to reply. This comment was almost always used to justify anti-Semitic remarks and often indicated that the person was speaking from ignorance rather than reason and observation.

That summer Basia's apartment, dubbed the Ludmir Club (Ludmir being the Yiddish name for Wlodzimierz-Wolynski), was the headquarters where my friends—Nuchem, Zelman, Moniek, Jacek, Edek, Izia, Silek, Basia's sisters, and Zygmunt Podlipski—met to talk about our lives, the future, and politics. We shared whatever news we could get from abroad—it was as tightly censored in Poland as it was in the Soviet Union. Everyone came and went as they pleased, and everyone helped themselves to the food and liquor, playing host and guest at the same time. By the end of the evening everyone was sprawled across the floor or draped across the orange sofa. I sat in the corner and listened to the conversations but was reluctant to join in. Since I didn't live in Poland I didn't feel I had a good enough grasp of life there to comment on it. But when the conversation turned to the new regime and the influence of the Soviet Union on Poland, everyone turned to me.

I felt an obligation to tell my friends about my experiences in the Soviet Union because they had such high hopes for the Soviet-controlled regime in Poland. They didn't see the danger inherent in the kind of open discussions we were having. They didn't know they'd be watched and informed on or the extent to which they'd have to change their behavior. I told them about my arrest, experiences in the prisons and camps, and about life in Moscow. I was aware of what the consequences might be if anyone reported me to

Bezpieka, but I wanted them to know about me and felt that this might be the last time I ever felt safe enough to reveal my true thoughts. It was difficult for them to hear about the conditions in Kolyma, but it was even more difficult for them to hear me break their illusions of the great socialist nation.

"What do you mean when you say that everyone in Moscow is afraid of talking openly to their friends?" Jacek said.

"I mean that no one talks openly, not even to their best friends. Soviet citizens are raised to watch the behavior of others and inform on them if they say anything critical about the country or the regime. Friends are not devoted to friends over there, they're devoted to the state and Party first," I said.

Jacek leaned against the doorframe and crossed his arms. "I don't believe it's that bad," he said. "Maybe your experiences in the prisons and camps have skewed your perceptions and made you feel that it's worse than it really is."

"No, Jacek, as a matter of fact, it's worse than what I just told you. I don't want to frighten you, but I want you to know what's like. I would never talk like this with my friends in Moscow. Despite all the propaganda they feed you about the wonderful lives of the proletariat, the Soviet people are poor and exhausted. They spend hours standing in lines waiting for food and other goods. They live in cramped apartments, three to five people in a room without basic amenities. This is the truth about life in the Soviet Union. Money is spent on boosting the armed forces and supporting communist regimes abroad, not on the people." I was surprised by the force of my emotions and tried to detach myself, not knowing how deeply my anger ran.

"Look, you want to talk about hardship? I can tell you about hardship," Jacek said. "Everyone in this room has gone through unimaginable hardship. I don't doubt that you're telling the truth about life in the Soviet Union, but I do know that I would prefer hardship to being treated the way I was by Poles before the new regime came. I feel safer now than I've ever felt in Poland."

The long silence in the room and the concentrated looks on the faces made me pause and think over what I said. No one was sure whom to believe—Jacek or me. They had wandered far, they had been hungry and filthy, they had lived with the relentless threat of being shot like stray dogs or locked in the gas chambers. "I have to admit that the Soviet prisons and camps, as horrifying as they were, offered more hope for survival than the Nazi gas chambers," I said. "You're right, Jews weren't singled out to be slaughtered in the Soviet Union. But life in Soviet society isn't what you think it is. Everyone is afraid of the secret police, and no one feels free to express themselves. It's a different kind of fear."

Jacek walked over to the window and looked out at the clay-shingled roof on the building next door. His face reddened and the veins in his neck bulged. "Things in Poland are much more complicated than you think. I need to tell you something, and I trust that none of this information will leave this room. What I'm about to tell you could cost me my job, maybe worse. One month ago I got a directive from the Minister of Justice to mitigate the prosecution of Poles who collaborated with the Nazis if the only crimes they committed were against Jews, with the exception of murder. The new regime is taking great pains to avoid antagonizing the Poles. They want to quell any public outcry that the Jewish communists now in power are taking revenge on Poles."

"What do you mean?" Zelman asked. "Are you saying that Poles who blackmailed, raped, or robbed Jews won't be arrested and tried for their crimes? You're in the Party. Explain to me how Jews in the Politburo, Central Committee, and Bezpieka can allow this."

Jacek sighed heavily. "You don't understand the fragile balance of power in this country. Yes, Jews do have power, but the majority of Poles hate both us and the Soviets. Every trial of a Pole accused of war crimes against Jews is perceived as revenge and incites more anti-Semitism. Therefore, we must try to win over the Poles, not antagonize them further. The Party must be particularly careful right now to lessen the impression of there being too many Jews in powerful positions. We must be on guard to avoid being accused of conducting an anti-Polish witchhunt. Haven't you noticed that Party members are changing their names so they don't sound Jewish? I think Jacek Grembecki sounds better to the public than Grisha Greenberg, don't you?"

"Jacek," Basia said, shaking her head, "what about sticking together like we always have? That's how we've survived all this, not by trying to assimilate or deny our Jewishness. We shouldn't have to hide."

"You mean the Party orders you and people like yourself to denounce your Jewishness?" Zelman asked.

"Listen, all I'm saying is that we need to make a choice. We can't sit on the fence anymore. None of us can support both the communist regime and Zionism at the same time. I was a communist before the war, and I believe that only by being internationalists can the Jewish people be led out of oppression. Either we forget about our Jewishness and accept the brotherhood of communism or we become nationalists and try to create an independent Jewish state. Most of you here are not Party members, so you can go to the Jewish center and the synagogue. You can contact Jewish international centers to help you emigrate, but I can't nor do I want to do this. Before the war I never dreamed that the communists would rule Poland and that a poor, ordinary Jew from Wlodzimierz-Wolynski would be chief prosecutor in Poland's most populated city. But it's a new world now."

Zygmunt Podlipski walked around and filled everyone's glass with vodka. He raised his glass and spoke softly. "L'Chaim."

"L'Chaim." We raised our glasses and drank.

Zygmunt cocked his head and looked at Jacek with interest. "How do you really feel inside yourself? Are you still a Jew? Are you still our friend?"

Jacek stopped him with an outstretched hand. "Zygmunt, I'm a Jew and I'll always be a Jew. But I'm a different kind of Jew than you are. I'm your friend and I'll always be your friend. But to me Poland is my homeland. I want to assimilate, develop feelings for the Polish people, understand them, help them, and win them over to our side. To tell you the truth, I strongly believe that Polish Jews can help to build a new society, but only under the leadership of the Communist Party and in close partnership with the Soviets."

Jacek's rapid switch from a friendly tone to a firm, authoritative statement made me realize the difficult position he was in.

"So what do you intend to do?" Nuchem addressed Moniek and Zelman. "We have a good life here—our business, the Jewish center, the theater and synagogue. I want to stay here because you're all here."

Moniek tossed down another shot of vodka and stuffed a piece of herring in his mouth. "Nuchem and Jacek, let's face the truth: how much longer do you think we'll be allowed to run our business? I don't want to go bankrupt."

"I'm with Moniek," Zelman said. "Who knows how much longer the communists will tolerate private enterprise. I think we should leave. But Nuchem, you'll come with us. We came here together, and we'll leave together. We'll always have each other. What about the rest of you? Basia, you're planning to leave too, aren't you?"

Basia sat on the arm of the couch listening to the conversation. "I'm thinking very seriously about leaving. But first I want to sell my business. I need to find out what my sisters want to do. I know that Bronka and her fiancé want to go to Palestine. Milka and I have been talking about going to Germany."

I sat speechless while this conversation whirled around me. The issue of emigrating was a new predicament for me. I definitely didn't understand the complexity of my friends' lives. When I arrived in Lodz I was so happy to be with them that I thought that every one of them was happy in the new Polish reality.

"Nuchem, I understand you so well," Basia said. "I don't know what I want to do either. When I'm alone and am tormented by my memories of the war, I want to run away the next day. But there are days when I'm happy here, and just being with all of you and having my sisters with me makes me feel I can spend the rest of my life here."

"I have thoughts like you do, Basia," Zygmunt Podlipski said. "I'm not sure where I want to live the rest of my life. Busia wants to stay here. I want to leave. When I was with the Polish partisans, they shot Jews when they found them hiding in the forests and refused to feed them when they were hungry. But this was during the war. Many of those partisans have been arrested and are in prison. I don't feel safe here, but I still think I have time to decide. I don't want to make a rapid decision."

The only person who hadn't spoken was Edek. He sat stretched out on the floor, his back leaning against a wall. He had survived the war in Lodz, living with a working-class couple who knew he was Jewish. Their two adult sons lived in Pabienice, a nearby industrial town, and they too knew about Edek.

After liberation Edek became a successful businessman and lived with his Polish girlfriend, a student at Lodz University. His curly blond hair and delicate facial features allowed him to live on the Aryan side, working initially as a bookkeeper and then as a floor manager in a German textile factory in Lodz. In the Jewish gymnasium Edek had been a bright, creative student, a high achiever without arrogance or the need to impress. No doubt these traits had helped him blend in as a Pole on the Aryan side.

"What do you think, Edek?" Basia said. "You've lived here for the past six years, do you want to stay or leave?"

"You really want to know?" Edek looked around the room. "I'm getting out of here as soon as I can. I've listened too many times to Poles talk about 'eradicating Jews like rats.' When I worked with them, I had to laugh at their jokes. I've been called a Christ-killer, bloodsucker, and parasite too many times. Can you imagine some of these people believe we kidnap Christian children and kill them to use their blood for making matzo at Passover? They still hand out anti-Semitic publications at the entrance to the Catholic Church. Priests still have strong anti-Semitic messages in their sermons. I'm in the process of selling my business, and I'm going to leave for Germany, where I have close connections in the textile business. You'd be surprised, but when I visit West Berlin I feel safer than I do in Lodz. There is no future for us in this country. I think Moniek and Zelman are right: the regime won't tolerate private business much longer. They'll raise taxes higher and higher until they force us out of business. To them we're capitalists, and one day they might deal with us like they did with capitalists after the October Revolution. The Poles will never love Jews. Anti-Semitism is in their blood. They only tolerate us because so many Jews are in powerful positions. But should anything change in the future, you'll witness the same or worse than what happened during the war. I dearly love many Poles. A Polish family saved me. My fiancée is Polish. But I don't want to live here."

Edek's decision to emigrate to Germany threw me into turmoil. Now I no longer knew what I wanted for my future. Despite my hopes that Poland had changed over the years, it clearly hadn't. I would be leaving with my heart heavier than when I arrived, and I was very sad to realize that when I returned next summer there would only be a few friends left. Nuchem, Izia, and Silek assured me that they were going to stay in Poland and would be looking forward to my next visit, but Basia and her sisters, Edek, Zelman, and Moniek would probably be gone.

14

FINDING MY WAY

As the train cut across swollen rivers and furrowed through the golden grasses of eastern Poland, I had an untidy sense that I'd failed to find what I was looking for. I wanted Poland to be my homeland and the Poles to be my compatriots because after completing my studies, I'd be going back to Poland and would have to adjust to the new conditions there. I wanted to have the same attitude toward Poles as Julek, Jacek, Genia, and Silek did, but I believed that no matter how hard Jews might try to be assimilated, they weren't going to be integrated into Polish society. If Poland wasn't my homeland, where did I belong? The only other country I knew was the Soviet Union, and although I would never consider becoming a Soviet citizen, I liked the Russian people and understood them and their soul.

To me the Russian soul seemed vast and enigmatic, rich and full of suffering, difficult to grasp and not always easy to live with. It was vulnerable and volatile, humble and revolting, sensitive to a fault, and yearned permanently for love and friendship. The Russians easily got depressed, drunk, and weepy, but just as easily they danced, drank, and sang despite the poverty and oppression they lived under. They would share their only shirt and last piece of bread. There was a time early in my prison term when I didn't want to live. A group of *urki* had stolen my possessions, which meant more to me than gold: a pair of gloves, a towel I used as a scarf, an old cap with earflaps, and my wooden spoon. I was homesick and worried about my family, and I still hadn't come to terms with what had happened to me. After a grueling day of work in the mine, I fell on the bedboard and closed my eyes, not sure how long I would last. Then I heard the rhythmic sounds of a guitar playing a gypsy melody. A low voice joined the guitar, and the music carried me into nostalgia and longing for someone far away. I cried as I listened to the strings being plucked gently by a redheaded young man. I knew the song and mumbled the words. It was a song about a gypsy girl, Tamara, who fell in love with a boy from town but decided to die rather than leave her tribe.

Without a pause, the redheaded singer altered the melody and played another gypsy song from my youth. I had seen a gypsy girl dancing to it in the Piatydnie forest. The men sat in a circle and played guitars and beat rhythmically on drums, and everyone clapped and sang "Ochi Chornya." The melody soon picked up, making me want to join the girl in the circle and whirl with her in a dizzying crescendo of joy. The music got faster, the clapping got louder, and the girl's colorful skirts twirled faster and faster above the grass. She clapped the castanets between her fingers and shook the tambourine. Then in a climax of twirling ecstasy, she shook her arms and small breasts, moving faster and faster in synchrony, which made me feel the music inside myself. I lay on the bedboard feeling the song inside me. I felt stronger, and I knew I wouldn't give up. This was how I met Jora, my closest criminal friend, and how I rediscovered my own Russian soul, the soul of my youth, which had been immersed in gypsy music. There were no songs about the Polish soul. There were songs about honor, courage, and even lawlessness—Poles would sacrifice their lives fighting for an honorable cause, even if the fight was hopeless. They revolted against powerful enemies not so much to succeed as to express their bravery and honor. But they hid their feelings behind a façade of formalities and pleasantries which, oftentimes, were insincere.

I reentered the Soviet Union at the border station in Brest and went through the same routine with the border guards and customs agents. The foreigners were crammed into the same two rooms, and every time the door opened I waited to hear the guard call my name. In the evening I boarded the train for Moscow and I arrived at the Belarussky train station the next morning.

That evening Julek and I went for a walk so we could talk freely without worrying about having each word analyzed by NKVD experts. It was nearly 11:00 p.m., but the downtown area was as alive as in daytime. The food stores were open twenty-four hours, and the windows in the government buildings were lit. Every government and Party office functioned fully as long as Comrade Stalin, an insomniac, was awake and working. Even Politburo members and those in the highest government ranks remained vigilant, ready to be summoned, until the lights in Stalin's study went out.

It was good to be back with Julek, even though our conversation lapsed here and there, like a slow-moving train stopping at the tiniest stations. I loved walking among the swarming crowds of pedestrians on Gorky Street, the city pulsating with life. We found an empty bench on Tverskoy Boulevard and sat silently for a while. Julek sat slumped over, his head pulled between his shoulders and eyes facing the ground. He shuffled a large piece of gravel between his feet. "I've got problems in the embassy with the new ambassador, Marian Naszkowski," he said. "He wants to get rid of me to prove he's cleaning the embassy of anyone who's not a communist. Polish Socialist Party members are no longer welcome here. It'll only be a matter of months before I'm forced to leave. As I told you before you left, you need to decide if you want to stay here and be on your own or transfer to the medical school in Lodz or Warsaw. I have no idea what I'll do. I'd like to get out of the military and return to the university."

"I think I'll stay here," I said. "I want to stay with you, but I should get my diploma in the institute. I'll adapt to life in the dormitory. I think you should go back to your academic career. University classes are a safer place to be than diplomatic receptions." I wanted to tell him I had met more diplomats than professors in the camps, but he wasn't in the mood for joking, and on second thought, both professions had been well represented. "You could continue the teaching and research that you began so successfully as a student in Vilnius," I said.

"You should think about this route for yourself," Julek said.

His comment surprised me. I'd never thought of an academic career for myself. I was still struggling with my doubts about my ability to study in depth, and I thought I'd be lucky if I made it through medical school and became an ordinary doctor. I wanted to believe that Julek saw something in me that I didn't see in myself, but I didn't take his suggestion seriously.

We returned to the Grand Hotel well after midnight. I worried about Julek; his life was in upheaval only because he belonged to the wrong party. I also worried about what I would do after he left. I thought about living with Katia and Sioma, who would probably like the idea of having me live with them, filling the empty space left after their son was killed on the front, but I would have to get official permission from OVIR, and this task was less than appealing. Everyone in the Soviet Union faced housing restrictions.

I got together with Viktor and Mark. They'd both spent two months at a resort in Gagra on the Black Sea. They looked lean and sporty in white shirts that showed off their tans. It wasn't customary for students in either the Soviet Union or Poland to work during the school year or summer vacation. As a matter of fact, high school and university students never worked, because to do so was considered shameful evidence of their parents' poverty, something everyone tried to hide in both Polish and Soviet societies. During summer and winter vacations students traveled around the country visiting relatives and friends, went to resorts, or lived in the suburbs. Those who had no means to travel stayed at home to rest, but working to earn money was not an option. The fact that working at a young age was considered shameful in the Soviet Union, just as it had been in pre-war Poland, greatly surprised me. I'd become used to the Soviet slogan "Work is an act of honor and heroism," and I thought that everyone worked from an early age.

Sitting in a downtown café, I realized how much I had missed these two friends, who had such joyful spirits, intellect, humor, and ambitious plans for the future. Their friendships were different from most of those I'd experienced in life. Before the war my friendships were tried by harsh circumstances and adversity. I trusted my friends from the Jewish gymnasium with my life. My friendships in the labor camps were the strongest I'd ever known. In a place where everyone was degraded and diminished, they gave me the things that were most difficult to give—a good word, a lighter workload, an extra piece of bread. The friends I left behind in Lodz were dear to me because we shared the past and personal loss. I hadn't gone through difficult times with them, we didn't sacrifice anything for each other, but I felt a special kinship with them. However, as much as I liked Mark and Viktor, I wasn't confident that they would risk anything for me. They'd been taught since childhood not to trust anyone, and I had no idea how much they trusted me. But we liked to be with each other, and I was satisfied with this.

On September 1, 1947, I attended the inauguration of the new academic year. In the same grand hall of the institute, I listened to the same speeches by the same people in the same sequence as the year before. The same people sat at the presiding table. The audience clapped and cheered the same chants whenever Stalin's name was mentioned.

The adulation of Stalin had escalated to new heights. In every medical publication the author paid tribute to Stalin for the progress of medical care and research. Professors began every lecture with the same homage, and students developed their own accolades and invocations to Stalin's genius before speaking. I developed my own brief formula of introduction praising Stalin: "Comrade Stalin's genius has fostered the progress of all medical sciences, particularly in (insert course name), and this has helped me to understand (insert subject)."

There was another twist in the lectures and professional journals: the names of foreign scientists disappeared and were replaced by the names of Russian scientists. It was no longer Edison who developed the lightbulb; no longer Marconi who developed the telegraph; no longer the Wright brothers who constructed the first airplane; no longer Pasteur who established the field of microbiology. These inventions and scientific breakthroughs, along with many others, were now attributed to Russian inventors whose names became popularized, forcing the Soviet people to acknowledge the might of the Russian mind instead of bowing to western pseudo-science. When I discussed this phenomenon with Julek, it became clear to me that this trend fostered Soviet nationalism and disdain for anything foreign, especially western.

I did my own kowtowing to Russian greatness. When students asked me about my vacation in Poland, I was restrained in my answers. If I had told the truth, that in Poland food and other goods were readily available and the country was in much better condition than the Soviet Union, my Russian classmates would have become envious and thought I was spreading propaganda. So I told them how impoverished Poland had become during Nazi occupation, and that highly sought-after items were harder to find in Warsaw than in Moscow. I also emphasized the close friendship between our countries and the brotherly help Poland received from the Soviet Union. I rehearsed the account of my trip, keeping in mind that there might be one or more informers in the audience.

It was good to be occupied with my studies and Soviet friends. I felt more settled with them than with my friends in Lodz, who were so uncertain about the future. The time would come when I would face going back to Poland for good, but I didn't need to think about it now, in contrast to Julek, who expected to be recalled to Warsaw any time.

Rising Soviet nationalism strained relations between Poland and the Soviet Union. The first secretary of the Polish Communist Party, Wladyslaw Gomulka, was not as subservient to the Soviets as other party chiefs in eastern Europe. He wasn't highly enthusiastic about the creation of the Cominform, which was under Soviet domination, to replace the now dissolved Comintern, nor was he committed to collectivizing agriculture. Gomulka understood too well the fierce Polish nationalism and deep-seated anti-Russian and anti-Soviet feelings of the population. Instead of copying the Soviet model, he opted for the "Polish way to socialism," which was anathema to the Stalinist regime. The news that the Polish Communist Party first secretary was showing signs of independence surprised both me and my friend Ziemovit Fedecki, the press attaché in the Polish embassy. We agreed that the Soviets would need to use much more pressure to bring Gomulka and his supporters in line, or else they would have to eliminate them completely and replace them with a more obedient team of devoted Stalinists.

Gomulka's resistance to copying the Soviet model in all spheres of Polish life wasn't shared by all Poles. In Moscow hundreds of Polish students were now attending Soviet institutions of higher education. At the meeting of the newly formed Association of Polish Students, held in the Polish embassy, there were over one hundred new students and postgraduate fellows; the previous academic year there had been only nine. Sitting at the presiding table were Naszkowski, the Polish ambassador, Mazur, a member of the Politburo, and Jan Chylinski, the son of President Bierut. In his keynote address, Mazur summed up the feelings of the Polish Stalinists about Polish students being educated in the Soviet Union, a prejudice I was soon to discover for myself. "You are the most precious treasure of Polish society," Mazur thundered. "The Politburo, Central Committee, and Polish government count on every one of you to be leaders in the new socialist society. You are the elite guard. You are in the front line of the most progressive scientific ideas, and you will be the first to bring the ideas of Marxism-Leninism to the Polish people. Every one of you will be cared for and supported by our government. I came here specially to meet with you and to convey to you personal greetings and best wishes from our president, Boleslaw Bierut, and the first secretary of the Communist Party, Wladyslaw Gomulka. You are the future of our homeland. Long live Comrade Stalin! Long live Comrade Bierut! Long live Soviet-Polish friendship!"

Listening to Mazur's speech and watching the reaction of the audience, I didn't feel like I belonged to this group. I wasn't selected by a Party organization to become a stipendiary of the Ministry of Health, and I wasn't a Party member.

Two months later I was invited to the embassy to meet with the executive committee of the association. I was terrified. They hadn't given me any idea why I was being invited.

Three young zealots wearing green Polish military uniforms sat at a conference table. Jan Chylinski led the meeting. "Comrade," he said, "the executive committee is preparing materials for the Central Committee of the Party and we cannot locate your file. Could you please explain this to us?"

"I don't understand your question. You want my file—the Ministry of Health has my file. They awarded me a stipend to study here. If you need my file then contact Comrade Stysiak at the Ministry personnel department. I was there this summer, and Comrade Stysiak has my information."

"I'm not talking about your file in the personnel office. I'm talking about your file in the Party committee," Chylinski said.

"I don't have one. I'm not a Party member."

"Then how did you get here?"

"I was studying in the Soviet Union before the association was created. I've lived in the Soviet Union since 1939, and I served in the Soviet army. A year ago I was accepted to the institute, and I was awarded a stipend by the Ministry of Health on the recommendation of the Party committee. Just ask Comrade Michalewska."

Chylinski ignored my reference to Wanda Michalewska. "I'd still like to have your file completed and your personal questionnaire filled out. I'm sure that our Party committee would support your nomination as a Party member."

"I would consider this a great honor, but I've never thought about participating in any political activities. I was always interested in sports, and now my only interest is to study hard and become a Soviet-trained specialist so that I can help people in our homeland with my skills."

"What were your grades for the first year? Did you perform adequately?"

"I received A's and B's," I said. "I worked very hard, and I intend to work even harder this year. I'm not interested in doing anything but following the direction set by the Party to become a highly skilled specialist and to transfer the knowledge I gain here to the Polish medical community."

"It sounds like you're doing well in school," Chylinski said, sitting back in his chair. "Make sure you attend the association's monthly meetings to study Marxism-Leninism and the *Short Course*. This is obligatory for all members of the organization."

"I'll be grateful to attend the meetings."

Chylinski gave me the questionnaire to fill out, and we all shook hands.

Back at the hotel I worried about being one of the only students in the association who wasn't a Party member. The young communists were very zealous, and applying for Party membership would expose me to a scrupulous review. I decided to fill out the questionnaire following the original formula I had concocted with Julek but not to join the Party. From then on I adopted the persona of an apolitical but highly studious person, hoping this might protect me and allow me to complete my studies.

15

ENEMIES EVERYWHERE

Pathology was the most boring class I had during my second year. Professor Soloveyev, a tall, gaunt, somber man, lectured as if he were giving a sermon at a funeral. Accustomed to dealing with corpses, he didn't notice that no one listened to his lectures. I felt as if I were suffocating in class with each passing minute and tried to rouse myself by looking out the window at the squirrels jumping around in the elm trees. When the bell rang no one waited for Professor Soloveyev to finish the lecture. Our books were packed, and we were out the door.

One autumn day after the leaves had dropped, I was staring out at the spindling branches when Yasha Frumkin, a second-year medical student and Party leader, burst into the classroom at the end of the hour. He jumped up on a table and shouted, "The independent state of Israel has been created, and the Soviet Union is the first country in the world to recognize it. Long live Comrade Stalin! Long live the Soviet-Israeli friendship!" Everyone cheered and hugged each other and fell into mindless chanting. "There will be an open meeting tomorrow at the big synagogue downtown. Everyone is invited."

I was surprised that so many students, Jews and non-Jews, were sympathetic to the Zionist cause of establishing an independent Jewish state in the land of Palestine, which had been a British mandate since 1920. But then again the announcement had been instigated by the Party committee, and so the reaction had less to do with supporting Israel than with following Comrade Stalin's cue: If another state had been established, the students would have reacted the same. But among my Jewish friends I sensed a deeper enthusiasm; the handshakes were stronger, and the cheering was louder. Misha Hitterer shouted, "We aren't stateless anymore. We have a homeland!"

The next day the newspapers affirmed the resolution passed by the

United Nations on November 29, 1947, establishing the state of Israel. The Soviet Union was indeed the first country to acknowledge and establish diplomatic relations with the new state.

I'd never been a Zionist and didn't know much about the Zionist movement or the fight of the underground Jewish organizations against the British for independence. In my late teens, I believed that the Soviet Union provided the best solution for the Jews by including them in the international family of nations. But I was as happy as my friends that the state of Israel had been established.

When I arrived at the synagogue the next day, hordes of people were spilling out into the side streets. Bursts of cheering from inside the building led to chaotic chanting and whistling outside. I stayed toward the back of the crowd. Down a narrow side street, several dozen civilians disembarked from a chartered bus. The driver wore an NKVD uniform, and the passengers, although they wore civilian clothing, didn't look like they were there to praise the new state of Israel. They neither clapped nor shouted but spread out and waded slowly into the crowd. Another bus arrived and parked behind the first one. Dozens more suspicious-looking civilians got out and dispersed. Afraid of being "taken on the pencil"—registered by the NKVD—I went to the nearby metro station and left.

Refreshed after summer vacation, I studied hard. The coursework came to me more easily than the year before. I'd caught up with my peers, learned to study diligently, and had few outside interests to distract me from my tasks. I was truly interested in learning how the normal human body functioned and what happened when it was affected by various diseases. Biochemistry, physiology, pathology, and microbiology all made sense now that I could apply them to physiological and pathological processes. I felt more secure in the classroom and more independent in my classwork, and I no longer minded studying alone. I'd even begun studying at the medical library, which was only two blocks away from the embassy and across the street from the mansion of Lavrenty Beria, who was in charge of the secret police and internal security.

During my first year the medical library had intimidated me; every book was an indictment of how much I didn't know. I felt entombed in the concentrated silence, as bored and impatient as I now felt in Soloveyev's classroom. But this semester, as my only refuge from the suspicious atmosphere of the institute and embassy, the library felt like home. I was tired of being on guard around the Polish students, who struck me as more zealous and blindly indoctrinated than the Soviet students.

Two librarians sat behind a large information desk, answering questions and retrieving books for the borrowers. One of them registered everyone who entered, noting the times of their arrival and departure. The library provided a lamp, ashtray, and two pencils at the tables, but not a sheet of paper, and I had to bring my own eraser. I carried my books, papers, sandwiches, and flask of water in a brown leather briefcase Julek had given to me. On a given evening there were usually no more than ten to twenty people in the library. Several of the patrons were regulars. A biology professor with a shock of white hair and a white goatee always had a stack of books on his table. A young woman and her aunt sat next to each other and whispered frequently. The younger woman was writing her dissertation on lung cancer, and her aunt, a professor in pulmonology, was tutoring her. Then there were the lone medical students grinding out formulas and the researchers flipping endlessly through the card catalogue. Although we rarely talked to each other, I felt a kinship with these people. In moments of boredom or fatigue, I could look around and know that everyone else was struggling too and it made me feel less alone. We were in tune with each other's rhythms: when someone unwrapped a sandwich, everyone else in the room did the same, and when someone stopped working for the evening, several other people packed up their books, too.

Before long I felt the impetus to learn more than was mandated by the courses, and this ambition surprised me. Perhaps I was still trying to make up for the years I'd lost as a prisoner. I pushed myself harder and harder, trying to learn more than other students. I was both amazed and dismayed by the discrepancy between what I learned in class and what I found in the medical textbooks and journals. With every foray into the card catalogue and bibliographical references, the chasm between student and scientist, the university and the real world, closed a little more. I often recalled what Dr. Piasetsky used to tell me when I worked on the TB ward in the camp hospital. He said studying was like listening to music: the more you listen, the more you want to hear and the better you understand and enjoy the melody.

I developed a routine to quiet my mind after a hectic day. I studied at the same table every night, with the same view of the bright yellow walls of the pediatric hospital across the street. Like most of the
regulars, I was territorial about my table. If I found someone there
when I arrived, I considered it an infringement and felt the urge to tell
the person to leave. I'd take a nearby table and try to study there, but
I'd catch myself staring at the intruder. If I worked efficiently and finished my assignments, I allowed myself to browse through old
books. Many of them hadn't been opened in years. At first I was interested in the books as objects. I loved smelling and touching them.
The older the book, the closer I examined the worn, gold letters
pressed into the leather cover. I noted the large print and high quality of paper, which was still shiny. I became interested in medical history. It appeared that progress was a slow enterprise; sometimes it
seemed to be completely absent. One day I came upon drawings in
our physiology book that I'd seen in one of the old manuals. The au-
thors had plagiarized the paragraphs and presented the drawings as
their own. This finding disturbed me. Ever since my first days at the
institute, I had believed that every professor was the ultimate authority in his or her field, and that the manuals we used in the classroom were the most up-to-date on the subject.

I still spent some evenings studying with Viktor, and at the end of
the semester we got together with Mark. I didn't prepare any more
crib sheets but relied on the knowledge I'd accumulated and my
memory, which was restored. I felt solid in my role as a medical student. The feeling that I'd found my path in life and was doing what I
was meant to do offset much of the anxiety and sense of loss and
homelessness I'd felt the year before. But now Julek had problems.

He still worked long hours repatriating Polish citizens, and he
complained about how difficult and time-consuming it was to deal
with the ridiculous Soviet bureaucracy. He had trouble locating
people scattered across the immense territory of the Soviet Union,
and when he did find them, he had trouble contacting them because
of red tape. The problem was that no Soviet bureaucrat was willing
to make a decision without getting approval from the higher-ups. The
modus operandi was to send everything up the line so that responsibility was spread among several people, especially if the last level of
approval was from a person so high up that he couldn't be touched.
Simple, straightforward issues were moved across desks, through of-

fices, and between floors until they reached the top officials, prefer-ably members of the Politburo.

Ambassador Naszkowski gave Julek no support. When Julek re-quested more people in his office, Naszkowski told him not to make excessive demands. Julek sought support in Warsaw with the party leadership, but times had changed, and the Polish Socialist Party was no longer an equal partner with the Communist Party. The Commu-nist Party had pushed hard to eliminate the socialists from the polit-ical scene by uniting both parties and creating a Polish United Work-ers' Party, which in essence was a communist party. No one wanted to spoil the unity because of a minor quarrel between a communist ambassador and the socialist military attaché.

When Julek came back from spending the winter holidays in Poland, he told me he would be leaving Moscow at the end of Febru-ary or the beginning of March. "I don't know my new assignment," he said, "but I'll get it when I return to Warsaw. I won't be living in Lodz. Halina and I are separating. She's going to stay in Lodz with Krystyna. I've met someone else. Her name is Zofia Szyszko. She's the widow of a high government official." Julek's face flushed as he talked about Zofia. I was happy that he'd found a more suitable com-panion, but I felt sorry that Krystyna would grow up without a father. "You must decide if you want to move with me back to Poland or stay here. If you decide to finish your studies here, you'll have to move into a dormitory."

"I'll stay here," I said.

"It's your choice. But if you change your mind, you can join me. My home will always be open to you." I sensed a new tone in Julek's voice. I could tell that his upcoming departure and our separation worried him. He wanted me to move with him to Warsaw, but he also seemed to admire my readiness to stand on my own. I sensed he would miss playing such an important role in my life, but as I con-sidered the changes taking place in Poland, I was convinced that stay-ing in the lion's den would be safer for me and better for my future than going back to Poland without a Soviet diploma.

On March 9, 1948, Julek left Moscow for Warsaw. I stayed in the Grand Hotel until the end of the month, then moved to the institute's dormitory, a desolate, two-story building with broken entry doors. Twenty-eight women were crammed into six rooms on the first floor. Ten men were crammed into two rooms on the second.

The handrail shook and stairs creaked as I climbed up to the second-floor landing. I explored the narrow hall to the left of the landing and found one restroom with a sink that ran cold water only. The hallway reeked of stale cigarette smoke and cooking grease. There were two more doors down the hall, each with a heavy lock dangling from it. I opened the door to my dorm room and walked into a haze of smoke. Someone was frying potatoes, and everyone was smoking. The room was small, with five beds, five nightstands, a clay wood-burning stove, and a small table with three chairs. There was no wardrobe. There weren't even hangers or pegs to hang my coat on. I took the one unoccupied bed in a corner, pushed my suitcase under it, and lay my coat at the foot like everyone else had done.

A brawny man with dark hair on his arms extended his hand and said, "Welcome to your new home." Viktor Kulikov was a fourth-year medical student, and as the most senior student in the room, he was in charge. He introduced me to the three other men who shared the room. "I should tell you the rules around here. Every morning someone is responsible for bringing firewood from the shed and starting a fire to warm up the room before everyone else gets up. The same person is responsible for boiling a full kettle of water for the breakfast tea, clearing the table after everyone has eaten, emptying the ashtrays, washing the dishes, and sweeping the floor. Everyone is responsible for making his bed neatly, just like in the army. And everyone is allowed ten minutes in the restroom. You'll need to get your own knife, fork, and spoon and mark them with your initials. Keep them in your nightstand. We all share the plates and tea glasses." He nodded toward the array of chipped, mismatched plates and glasses sitting on the stove. Two burned frying pans also sat on the stove. Old tin cans filled with ashes and cigarette butts lay everywhere, and a dirty lightbulb hung above the table, the only place one could even attempt to read or write.

I spent the first several days exploring the neighborhood, finding the nearest food stores, cheap cafeterias, dry cleaning shops, and public baths. I kept a small supply of bread, sugar, and cheese in my nightstand. I took cheese sandwiches with me to the institute every day. My dorm room wasn't any worse than those of other Polish students; the dormitories they lived in were swarming with hundreds of students on each floor who watched and informed on each other. I enjoyed being close to the main building of the institute, especially in winter, when I could cross the yard in a minute without a coat. I didn't complain about my new living conditions. I'd lived through worse, and I was committed to staying until I became a doctor.

The war had been over for three years and it seemed that the eastern bloc countries had solidified their ties with the Soviet Union. The goal of spreading communism all over the world had established a good footing in eastern Europe and was even starting to spill over onto other continents. In this atmosphere of adulation of Stalin, the Supreme Leader of the proletariat and savior from fascist oppression, Yugoslavian leader Josip Bros-Tito's refusal to submit to Soviet dominance threatened to shatter the unity of the eastern bloc. No one could believe that Tito had the audacity to take a stand against Stalin, and everyone was terrified of the repercussions.

Since coming to Moscow I had followed closely the political events in the Soviet Union, the eastern bloc countries, and the west. Like all Soviet citizens, I was cut off from important political news since the Soviet press, radio, and TV fed the public propaganda. When Julek was in Moscow he shared what he knew with me, but after he left my only source of information was my press attaché friend Ziemovit Fedecki. He was the one who told me about the feud between Stalin and Tito. Tito had broken ties with the Soviet Union and expelled all Soviet advisers from Yugoslavia. Stalin's response to Tito's defiance was swift and harsh: On May 28, 1948, he expelled Yugoslavia from the Cominform and condemned Tito as a lackey of imperialism and traitor of the working class. The next day's newspapers called Tito a "bloody butcher of the communists," a "traitor of the proletarian unity," and the "worst enemy of the working class." Political cartoons portrayed him as another Hitler. The Yugoslavian affair frightened everyone in the eastern bloc countries because Tito had been considered Stalin's closest and most devoted ally, and overnight he had become the greatest enemy of communism.

At the end of June, I passed my finals with straight A's and celebrated the results with Viktor, Mark, and other friends. Lova Feinberg, who lived with his parents in a large downtown apartment, threw a party. We sang popular Soviet songs, all of them sentimental. Group singing was the most common form of entertainment in Soviet society, popular in all circles, in all places, at all times. I enjoyed singing with my friends because it created an atmosphere of closeness and warmth.

On July 1, I was again crossing the border on my way to Warsaw, but this time I checked and rechecked my documents, especially my passport and student identification, and made sure I had no books or journals that might raise suspicion. Julek met me at the train station and the first thing he did was introduce me to his new girlfriend, Zofia. In the evening we went to her luxury apartment in a building reserved for high officials of the Polish government. She had many high-powered admirers, and Julek seemed to be very proud to be chosen as her partner. He'd become director of the Military Department of the Central Planning Committee and was responsible for planning the structure of the military forces and the industrial site of the defense system. He wasn't happy with his new job. He dealt with highly sensitive material, which put him at serious risk of arrest. All of his projects were under special scrutiny by top military leaders, some of whom were Soviet generals. Also, a rumor was going around that there might be drastic changes in the leadership of the Polish Communist Party because of first secretary Gomulka's resistance to the Soviet leadership. Julek believed the fight between Stalin and Tito would stir up dissent among the eastern European countries. We both thought Tito's action would lead to increased terror in the eastern bloc countries and increased suspicion of anyone from the west. Even though he was overwhelmed with work, Julek took on an additional job lecturing on the history of law at the Academy of the General Staff. He hoped this would be the first step to leaving the military and becoming a university professor.

Mrs. Stysiak and her associates treated me well at the Ministry of Health, and Professor Rowinski complimented me on my achievements, saying that if I continued to study hard, I might be selected to perform my residency training in Moscow. The Ministry of Health again sent me on a month-long paid vacation to the mountain resort Zakopane. I visited my friends in Lodz, but only Nuchem, Jacek, and a few others remained. Basia and her sisters, Zelman, and several others had already left Poland for other parts of the world.

Soon after the 1948 academic year began, new political events uprooted the peaceful life I'd gotten used to living. As I'd feared, the break-up with Yugoslavia spurred a new wave of terror in the Soviet Union, spilling over into all of the satellite countries. Tito became "Enemy Number One," and Titoism replaced Trotskyism as the number-one evil. Tito's stubborn defiance infuriated Stalin and triggered an avalanche of purges and show trials modeled after the Soviet show trials of 1937 and 1938. Beria got his orders and was back at work fabricating group conspiracies and extracting confessions from tortured Party officials in the process of "purifying Party lines" and teaching by example that no one was safe in Stalin's empire. Even communist leaders in many eastern bloc countries were treated as enemies of the people and brought down.

In September 1948, Gomulka was dismissed from his post in the Polish Communist Party, and many members of the Politburo and Central Committee were purged from their positions. In 1949 and 1950, the elite guard of the Polish Communist Party was arrested and tried. Gomulka was finally arrested in 1951. Poland was the only country that didn't have a show trial of its first secretary, although thousands of old communists lost their positions, and many of them, their lives.

In September 1949, Laszlo Rajk, an old communist, devoted Stalinist, member of the Hungarian Politburo, and minister of the interior, along with a large group of his supporters, was arrested and accused of Titoism and spying for the imperialists. Rajk and his associates were sentenced to death and hanged. The general secretary of the Communist Party of Czechoslovakia, Rudolf Slansky, who was Jewish, and fourteen co-defendants were arrested in 1951 and accused of Titoism, Trotskyism, and Zionism. They were tried in Prague five years later in what was called the "Trial of the Leadership of the Anti-State Conspiratorial Center." The trial had strong anti-Semitic overtones. Slansky and his co-defendants were executed after Stalin's death. The leadership of the Czechoslovak Communist Party was unique in continuing the purges and executions even after Beria was executed in 1954.

Terror spread like wildfire to Bulgaria, Romania, and the German Democratic Republic, following the same pattern of extorted confessions, show trials, and executions. At the same time, a new wave of internal terror unfolded according to the directives of the Kremlin. News on the radio and in the newspapers boasted about the uncovering of enemies of the people, Titoists, Zionists, Trotskyists, and spies among top Party dignitaries in the eastern bloc countries. But the events in Moscow touched a raw nerve by their transparent anti-Semitism.

In November 1948, Stalin dissolved the Jewish Anti-Fascist Committee, a harbinger of the anti-Semitism to come. The committee had been created in April 1942 on Stalin's order, to solicit political support and financial help primarily from Jews in the United States and Great Britain. The committee seemed to be of great importance at the time, since the deputy minister of foreign affairs, Solomon Lozovsky, was appointed its chairman, and the director of the Jewish theater in Moscow, the most renowned Jewish actor in the Soviet Union, Solomon Mikhoels, ran the committee. Members of the committee included famous Jewish writers, poets, academicians, doctors, musicians, artists, aviators, engineers, journalists, and other renowned intellectuals. In January 1948, Mikhoels was killed in a car accident in Minsk, and the government arranged a grandiose funeral. A Jewish theater was named after him. But rumors circulated that Mikhoels had actually been murdered because he was too outspoken, both abroad and in Moscow, on Jewish nationalistic issues.

Soon afterward the Central Committee passed a resolution against "rootless cosmopolites." The media was encouraged to uncover these cosmopolites by putting the Jewish name of the person involved in parentheses. This euphemism was widely used to indicate that people who had no roots in the Soviet Union—primarily Jews—couldn't be trusted or considered to be true Soviet patriots. The epithet was a masterful way to single out Jews and harass, discriminate against, and persecute them.

I first noticed a change in public behavior toward Jews in the buses and metro stations and in the lines in food stores. Before the war, anti-Semitic slurs had been a crime, but by 1948–1949, Jews were being openly insulted. The few people who expressed indignation and condemned the vulgar remarks were called "Jew-lovers" and were ridiculed, even physically attacked. One day I was standing in line at a bakery waiting for fresh bread to be unloaded from a truck. The manager of the store, a middle-aged Jewish woman, came out from the back of the store and announced that the sale would start in five or ten minutes. As she returned to the back room, two Russian women rushed to the counter and shouted, "You Jewish whore! Open the door so we can see how much you steal!" An elderly man in an army uniform joined in, shouting, "Don't let those bloodsuckers steal and cheat. It's time to be done with them." Finally a young army officer stepped in and told everyone to shut up. "I don't know her or you," he said, addressing the trio at the counter. "But I don't like what I see or hear. We're not Nazis."

In the following months newspapers became more virulently anti-Semitic, accusing Jews of nationalism and connections with western imperialism. More famous writers and intellectuals were arrested, and the name of Mikhoels became a symbol of Zionism and connection to American intelligence. Mark told me that a close friend of his, a young professor of quantum physics at Moscow University who worked in a lab with a Nobel laureate, was suddenly dismissed from his position and transferred to Novosibirsk. At the beginning of 1948, Molotov's wife, Paulina Zhemchuzina, was arrested. At the time, Molotov was the number-two man in the Party and government. The wife of Kalinin, the president of the Soviet Union, and the wife of Poskrebyshev, Stalin's longtime trusted private secretary, were also arrested. All three women were Jewish, and all were accused of Zionism, connections with Mikhoels or Israeli ambassador Golda Meir, and dealings with foreign intelligence. The repercussions of this organized, top-down campaign against "rootless cosmopolites" and "sell-out Zionists" had a ripple effect across the country and in the satellite eastern European countries.

The institute was no safe haven for Jewish professors. The Party committee and the leadership of the institute began weeding out the Jewish professors one by one. Three of them resigned after being called to meet with the director of the institute and the Party committee. My friends and I were sorry to see Professor Shabadash, a famous histologist and department chair, removed from his position. This highly educated man, with the appearance and manners of an old aristocrat, was one of the top researchers in his field and the author of several books. He vanished suddenly, and no one heard anything more about him. He'd probably been arrested. Professors Ginsberg and Omlinsky were also removed, as well as some young professors from the department of surgery. Someone was missing from nearly every clinic and seminar I attended. It was just the beginning of the thinning of the herd.

In May, as I began preparing for finals in June, I met Viktor at the institute. "I suppose it's time to get ready for final exams," I said. "In three weeks we'll be done with our third year. I'm ready to be done. I need a vacation."

Viktor turned away from me. "I've been meaning to talk to you about something," he said. His face was flushed and jaw set. "It's hard for me to say this, but I have to ask you not to come to my place anymore."

"Viktor, what happened? What did I do wrong?"

"You didn't do anything wrong," he said gruffly. "I just have to insist that you not visit me anymore or talk to me at the institute. I can't explain why."

"But what happened?"

Viktor backed away and said, "I can't tell you anything else. Please, just don't talk to me anymore." He continued walking.

I stood in the same place for a long time, watching him weave among the pedestrians, hoping he would turn to look back at me or come back and explain what had happened.

16

COMING INTO MY OWN

It takes a long time for memories to fade and to learn how to concentrate on things not connected to the past. Going into the third year in the institute I obsessed less and could immerse myself for longer periods of time in my studies. I got better at weeding out the bad memories and retaining the good ones. Like training my muscles with daily exercise, I trained my mind to memorize information quickly, and I worked hard not only to survive but to succeed. I was ready to begin classes, but my summer visit to Poland, Julek's departure, and the loss of Viktor's friendship threw me again into turmoil. When I parted from my few friends remaining in Lodz, I felt as anguished as the summer before, and when classes started I fought hard not to fall into the same malignant apathy I'd felt when I returned from the camps.

I began my third year in the Department of Internal Medicine in the hospital on Sokolinaya Gora, a complex of fifteen red- and yellow-brick buildings sprawled across a spacious wooded area. With their clipped grass and flowerbeds, the grounds resembled a park more than a hospital. At first the system of separate pavilions, each housing separate departments, was impressive, but in reality it was impractical and excessively wasteful. Each building required its own emergency room, laboratory, X-ray section, kitchen, administration, and janitorial services. Consultants who had to travel between departments lacked transportation, which was especially hard during the long winters. In addition, there was a shortage of hospital beds. There were one hundred sixty beds in the internal medicine department, and there were usually thirty to fifty extra patients lying on beds in the corridors and conference rooms. Staff members were squeezed into two rooms and residents were squeezed into one.

Since the department had only one secretary and one typewriter, the doctors' reports were written by hand, and many of them were indecipherable.

There were more doctors than nurses on the wards, and ward attendants were in the shortest supply. Higher education was free, and young people, mostly women, preferred to become doctors rather than nurses because doctors' salaries and prestige were higher. Therefore the level of patient care and hygiene was far below the quite low standard I had been used to in the Kolyma hospital. In Kolyma, perhaps because there was so little else we could do to help the patients, we bathed the very sick patients at their bedside, brushed their teeth, changed their linens and gowns daily, and quickly removed bedpans. But in Moscow bathing patients and changing linens weren't done until midday, and the stench of urine and feces fouled every room and corridor.

The internal medicine rotation lasted four months. We spent the first six weeks listening to lectures and following our instructor around the ward like chicks behind a mother hen. Natalya Fyodorovna, a shapely, middle-aged woman with curly brown hair, was considered to be one of the most experienced internists in the department. She was charming toward the doctors, authoritarian with students, and abrasive toward nurses, patients, and their families. For her, medicine was a purely scientific endeavor: she procured information, made diagnoses, and ordered treatments. The patient as a person did not exist. "When you interview the patient, you must lead the conversation," she told us. "Interrupt the patient anytime he goes off on a tangent. Most patients like to talk not only about their sickness but also about their personal problems. You must prevent this. You're not psychiatrists or psychologists. You're here to cure disease as best you can."

Natalya Fyodorovna enjoyed demonstrating her interviewing and diagnostic skills. She liked to teach through experience, especially through our experience when we made mistakes. My classmates wore expressions of mute concentration as Natalya Fyodorovna explained different techniques. She'd choose one student to perform a procedure—to palpate the liver and spleen, for example—and correct the student along the way. She'd ask another student to repeat the procedure. I was in a precarious position during these rounds, because although I could display what I had learned in the Kolyma hospital when asked to perform a procedure, I had to be careful not to show off too much. Certain procedures could only be learned with a great deal of practice, and my proficiency would attract attention. As I watched my classmates struggle to train their senses in the art of medicine, I remembered my own arduous journey.

Two and half years after I'd begun working in the gold mines, I was declining rapidly, and I conned my way into a job in the labor camp hospital by claiming I'd been a second-year medical student when the war began. Nikolai Rafaelovich Piasetsky, the chief of the TB ward, took me in, but it wasn't long before he caught on to my ignorance. He confronted me about it, and I told him the truth. That's when my real medical education began. Instead of firing me, he kept me on and became my mentor. For the next two years Dr. Piasetsky and I held one-on-one seminars. He gave me reading assignments from his textbooks, and he taught me how to perform physical examinations and some procedures. Dr. Piasetsky was my idol. He'd been a professor of endocrinology and a distinguished researcher in Moscow before his arrest. He'd published numerous articles and books and delivered presentations at national and international congresses, all before being arrested when he was in his late thirties.

I held the doctors in the Kolyma hospital in high esteem, especially because I thought they'd achieved something in life I would never come close to achieving. In the institute I continued to idolize the professors, convinced that each one of them possessed deep knowledge and extraordinary talent. I believed there was an abysmal distance between them and the students—me in particular—and that I would never be able to cross that divide. It was a long time before I had the audacity to ask a professor a question. I didn't do it in front of the class but one on one, in the hall or in the professor's office. I was terrified of revealing my ignorant, provincial nature. I derived my identity from my twenty years of boyhood in my hometown, one year as a soldier, four years as a prisoner, and now two years as a medical student. I'd had no time to learn about the fine arts, the things I had admired in my mother and that set her apart from others.

Entering the world of clinical medicine, I felt that I'd reached the doorstep of my destination. I was confident among the patients, nurses, and doctors, but Natalya Fyodorovna wasn't as enthusiastic about my progress. One day toward the end of our rotation I performed a physical examination on a new patient. He was an older man and had been brought to the emergency room by ambulance. He'd fainted on the bus on his way to work. He lay on his back on the table in the examining room, his gaunt, pale face grimacing with pain. I kneeled down next to him and asked, "What are your complaints?"

Through clenched teeth he whispered, "I'm in pain."

"When did it start?" I asked.

"Please follow the order of the interview as I taught you," Natalya Fyodorovna interrupted. "Establish personal data first."

"I know the routine, Natalya Fyodorovna," I said respectfully, "but since the patient is in so much pain I thought I'd start with the complaints first. I think we should get to the source of his pain and do something to relieve it."

"Don't start your own order of the interview." The shrillness in her voice surprised me. She breathed deeply and said in a softer voice, "I realize you're probably nervous. You'll get used to seeing patients in pain. Please continue the interview."

The patient rolled onto his side and pulled his legs into a fetal position. He whimpered quietly. "When did you start to feel sick?" I asked.

The patient held his abdomen with both hands as if trying to keep me from touching it. "I was in the bus," he whispered. "It came on suddenly, as if someone had stuck a knife in me. Then I woke up here. Please, help me. It's getting worse."

"Did you ever feel sick like this before?" I asked.

"Never like this," he said. "Maybe a year ago I had abdominal pains. I just needed to eat something, and then the pain went away. The doctor in the ambulatory clinic told me not to get too hungry."

"I need to examine you," I said. "Please, lie on your back."

He turned on his back but couldn't extend his legs. When he tried, the pain worsened and he drew up his knees again. He clutched his abdomen with both hands when I tried to raise his hospital shirt. "Please, don't touch. Don't push."

I put my hand gently on his abdomen but he cried out loudly and I stopped. Any place I touched was painful. "There is diffuse pain all over the abdomen," I reported to Natalya Fyodorovna. "I think we need to relieve his pain now and run tests to confirm a diagnosis."

"I can see that the patient has severe abdominal pain," Natalya Fyodorovna said. She stood back, clutching her clipboard to her chest.

"Before treating the pain, I want you to complete the interview as I taught you. Then we'll work on a differential diagnosis. We'll transport the patient to the ward, and there we'll begin treatment."

I could feel the man's pain as he lay cringing on the examining table. "I'm sorry, Natalya Fyodorovna," I said, "but I think he needs an injection of morphine now. Then we can continue the examination and discussion."

My classmates were dead silent. I could feel their fear and resentment toward me growing the longer this went on. Natalya Fyodorovna stepped between me and the patient. "It seems that you know everything already. You didn't need to volunteer to interview the patient, and I don't think you need to attend my seminars anymore. I'd like to discuss your status in Professor Badylkis's office after class. You're dismissed." I walked out of the room.

Professor Badylkis was the chair of the Department of Internal Medicine. His office was spacious, with dark oak furniture, a few paintings on one wall, and a large portrait of Stalin behind his chair. He was an engaging lecturer, and, I had heard, a very good cardiologist.

Natalya Fyodorovna sat comfortably in an armchair at the side of his desk. I wasn't invited to sit down. "I don't like what I hear about you," Badylkis said. "You're here to learn and follow your instructors, not to be argumentative. I don't tolerate arrogance and disobedience in my department. Apologize right now to Natalya Fyodorovna, and from now on, follow her orders."

"But I don't think I acted out of line by asking Natalya Fyodorovna to relieve the patient's pain," I said.

"I'm not interested in your side of the story," Badylkis said. "I warn you, if there is conflict between you and any of my staff, I'll find ways to discipline you. Now apologize."

His gruff tone infuriated me, and I stared at him and said loudly, "I'm sorry, but I don't apologize for things I strongly believe I did right. I'd like to know how you personally would deal with a patient in severe pain. Would you let him lie there and suffer? I'm here to learn medicine, not be ordered around like a recruit in boot camp. I don't like to be treated this way." At that moment, I didn't care what would happen to me; the way Professor Badylkis was treating me reminded me of the days when army officers and camp guards ordered me to do things that served no purpose. "I have high respect for my teachers, but I also want to be treated with respect, not to be kept standing like an imbecilic child in front of the class and ordered to do things without an explanation."

Professor Badylkis swivelled around and reached for the phone. I caught Natalya Fyodorovna looking questioningly at him as he mumbled into the phone and shuffled papers on his desk. "I'm running late," he said to the person on the line. He put his papers in a folder and stood up. "You two make peace and go back to work." When he was out the door I faced Natalya Fyodorovna, who tried to regain her composure.

"I've got to go too," she said.

I tried to brush off the incident with Natalya Fyodorovna, but I felt as if I'd been personally deceived or deprived of something I'd been promised. I thought I was right, which was why I had argued with her, but now I felt sorry the incident had taken place. I lost respect for her and Professor Badylkis as my teachers, but I also blamed myself for my temper and excessive compassion.

Despite the unpleasant incident with Natalya Fyodorovna, I made good progress in internal medicine. The students from my group recognized my knowledge and abilities in dealing with patients, and they were surprised that I could perform some of the procedures and discuss diagnoses. I never spilled a word about my past experiences but instead attributed everything I knew to our teachers. I was truly pleased and avenged when, at the end of the rotation, Natalya Fyodorovna and Professor Badylkis mentioned me as an outstanding student in class. Although the friction between us was forgotten, my respect for them was never restored.

Working in the hospital in Kolyma, I'd gotten acquainted with the clinical disciplines, and so I didn't go through the phase of fascination with every specialty that most students go through. I already had an idea of what kind of doctor I wanted to be. Working all day in internal medicine, diagnosing patients through lab tests and treating them with medication, bored me. Obstetrics and gynecology was somewhat more interesting, but the excitement of delivering a baby was counteracted by the numerous routine prenatal exams. I thought perhaps general surgery would appeal to me. In the introductory seminars we learned about antiseptics, sterilization, wound healing, and wound infection, and after each seminar we went on rounds or assisted in the operating room. I loved to wash up in the special sterilization chamber and to don the surgeon's gown. I loved the instruments laid out on a tray and the attentive audience of nurses and other residents. But before long general surgery, in which we had to follow to the letter the techniques we learned in our lectures and textbooks, became too routine. I liked the immediacy of surgical treatment, but I needed more variety and contact with people.

One evening I stayed late at the library, preparing notes for the next day's seminar on wound infection. It was the first week in April, and I was looking forward to warmer, sunnier days. As I was leafing through my general surgery textbook, I came across a name and address I'd written at the top of a page: Lena, Sretensky Tupik, 1, apartment 13. I'd written down the note in the dead of winter and forgotten about it.

I had been standing in the aisle of the train in the metro station Arbat, holding onto a strap, pushed and squeezed by people moving in and out, when I found myself facing a blond woman with gentle features and gray-green eyes. "Lena," I said, surprised. We'd been in the same biology class first semester, but after that I saw her only in the large auditorium during lectures or in the corridor during breaks. She sat in the back row with two other attractive blonds who giggled and whispered to each other. She seemed very young. Her eyes stood out, framed by the dark gray scarf she clutched around her face. I was charmed by the way she cocked her head and raised her upper lip slightly in a childish half-smile when talking to me. Standing next to me and holding onto the strap, she asked, "Is it Jan or Janusz?"

"Janusz," I said.

"What rotation are you on now?"

"General surgery." I had to change trains at the next station and added, "Give me your phone number."

"I don't have a phone, and besides, I have no free time." The train slowed down. The white marble walls of the station rushed by and the car stopped in front of a multicolored map of the metro lines. Passengers pushed us against each other as they scrambled for a place to sit or a strap to hold onto.

Afraid the door would close any second, I said, "Give me your address."

She came close to my ear and whispered, "Sretensky Tupik, 1, apartment 13." I jumped out of the car and stood on the platform, furiously writing down her address in my textbook.

For several days after that I thought I'd like to visit her, but I stopped myself every time, thinking that since she was just out of high school we wouldn't have much in common. But months later, when I found the note, I was feeling lonelier than ever. I dreaded going back to the dorm, to the rank odors of fried lard, stale cigarette smoke, and unwashed men. I dreaded hearing the same crude jokes, and I had no interest in drinking warm, poorly distilled vodka. I was determined to study for another hour or two, but I couldn't stop thinking about Lena. I imagined her eyes, full lips, and curly blond hair. I analyzed the way she had whispered her address. Since it was shortly after eight o'clock, early by Moscow standards, I packed up my books and headed for the bus stop to go to Sretensky Tupik.

The first street to the left of Kolkhoznaya Plaza was Srtenka Street. The street was essentially a high-class *tolkuchka*. I'd been on it many times before, visiting second-hand stores. I felt at home here among the hustlers and pickpockets, whom I could identify by their signs and gestures. It didn't matter that they were well dressed and well mannered, when it came to searching for a "deer" or "fryer"—a target for their unsophisticated schemes—they spoke the same language as the *urki* on the shady side of town.

I found Sretensky Tupik without any trouble. It was a dead-end street and the shortest one I'd ever seen, no more than two hundred feet long. Two five-story tenement houses were on each side, and at the end of the street were a tall brick wall and a huge garbage bin. A group of youngsters who reminded me of young *urki* lurked beneath the overhang of Lena's building. Rain pelted the tin overhang and slid off in a continuous sheet, splattering on the pavement. I stopped in front of the group, which had pulled in tightly to block the entrance. My stylish Polish overcoat aroused their curiosity. The leader, who had red bushy hair and a long wool scarf, reminded me of Jora from the camps, and I wasn't intimidated when he asked gruffly, "What are you doing here?"

I said firmly, "Where is apartment thirteen? Lena is waiting for me."

He held my gaze for several seconds, and when I didn't look away, he said, "Follow me." I followed him into the vestibule, which reeked of cat urine. To the left was a staircase. The door on the right was marked number thirteen. The redheaded ringleader knocked on the door and said, "There's a guy here. Lena's expecting him." He waited for the door to open, and I waited nervously, hoping Lena was home. I no longer felt safe standing in the vestibule, surrounded by a bunch of hoodlums who looked ready to strip me naked and beat me if they caught me lying. The latch clicked open, and Lena appeared at the door. She grabbed my hand and pulled me into another vestibule inside the apartment.

"Thank you, Vovka," she said. "He's a good friend." Lena was barefoot and dressed in a light blue robe, and I worried that I'd embarrassed or annoyed her with my unannounced visit. As we stood talking, an older woman cracked her door and looked at us. Another door opened and an attractive woman and tall young man came out. "Lala," the woman said, "who's your friend?"

"Lidia is my cousin. This is her husband, Lova." Lidia and Lova were dressed up like they were ready to go out.

"It's our anniversary," Lova said. "Come in. Help us celebrate."

Another door cracked open. "Lala, what are you doing out there?"

"I have a friend here, Mother. He's from the institute."

"Do I know him?" the woman asked.

"No, you've never met him. He's Polish," Lena said. A middle-aged woman dressed in a white blouse and a long black skirt came out. She extended her hand, and in elegant Polish style I raised it to my lips and kissed it. Lidia was next in line with her extended hand, and before I knew it the older woman had come out and I greeted her, too. Her name was Alexandra Ivanovna, and she was the head nurse at the emergency hospital. Someone took my coat, and Lena's mother led me into Lidia and Lova's room, where a large, round table was stacked with food. Before sitting down, Lova filled our glasses with vodka and made a toast. "It's a happy occasion, and you came at a happy hour, bringing good luck to all of us."

"Wait for me," Lena said. She'd gone and changed into a flowery dress. "I want a glass, too." Lena and I sat together eating, drinking, and talking. From time to time we looked closely at each other, she with interest and I with adoration. When the party ended at midnight, Lena walked me to the door. "The guys are probably still outside. I'll introduce you to them. They don't like strangers, but once they know you're my friend, they won't bother you."

"Would you like to go to a movie or restaurant sometime?" I asked.

"I'm sorry, but I'm very busy in the evenings. And I have a friend who doesn't like it when I go out with other men."

When we reached the bus stop I asked her again to go out with me.

"Really, I enjoyed the evening, but I'm afraid I can't go out. Goodnight." She squeezed my hand and was gone.

The next Sunday I was back at her apartment. Lena's mother, Sophia Konstantinovna, opened the door and invited me in to wait for Lena. She was running errands, and her mother expected her home soon.

Living space in Moscow was extremely tight, with a limited amount of square footage assigned to each person by law. Apartments were divided into rooms, and a family of three, four, or five people often lived in a single room. Lena and her mother lived in one of three rooms in a large apartment. Another room belonged to her cousin and her family, and the third room, the size of a large closet, belonged to Alexandra Ivanovna. There was a common kitchen with one stove and a small sink that ran only cold water. The bathroom had a sink and toilet but no shower or bathtub.

Sophia Konstantinovna led me into a large room artfully partitioned into three areas by curtains and a large wardrobe. She parted a heavy red velvet curtain and invited me into the living area, which served as a dining room, living room, study, and guest bedroom. I sat down on the sofa, which was covered with an old Persian rug. A newer Persian rug hung on the wall behind the sofa, and in the corner was an old dresser with elaborate wood carvings around the mirror. A bay window faced the asphalt inner yard. Next to the bay window was a piano and next to it, a bookshelf.

Lena was surprised when she came home and found me sitting on the sofa petting her gray cat, Murka. She sat in the chair next to me, and he jumped up and landed on her lap. "Do you have any plans for the evening?" I asked. "I wanted to see you again, but if you have plans, I'll leave."

"No, I don't have plans. I'm just tired. It's nice of you to think about me, but I prefer to stay home. We'll have tea with cherry jam."

She unlaced her shoes, took them off, and rubbed her feet. She told me that three times a week she taught ballroom dancing and etiquette to young Soviet diplomats in the Ministry of Foreign Affairs. She also worked as a seamstress to support her mother's modest income. Her mother was a technician in a pharmacy. Lena had attended ballet school and taken piano lessons since she was seven. She loved music, books, and theater. When I asked her to play the piano, she sat down and played several of Brahms's "Hungarian Dances" and the "Sabre Dance" by Khachaturian, transporting me to a world of dreams and fantasy far beyond the cramped room in the multi-family apartment at the end of a dimly lit dead-end street.

Walking home, I tried to sort out what attracted me most in Lena. She didn't fit her surroundings or her friendship with the local *urki*. I could feel the richness of her intellect and softness of her soul, which she kept hidden from the public. I knew I would be seeing much more of her.

Our rotation in reconstructive plastic surgery was in the veterans hospital on Shablovka Street. The instructor, Dr. Vladimir Zausayev, had spent the war years in field hospitals treating victims of trauma. His main interest was in reconstructive surgery of the face, an area he considered to be the most challenging and badly in need of surgeons. Although he was tall and gangly, Dr. Zausayev was surprisingly co-ordinated, with a cat-like gait and quick, precise movements of his hands and fingers. I liked his self-assurance and delicate manners. His seminars were informative and to the point, and he was the only professor who didn't punctuate his lectures with politically correct slogans and praise of Stalin. Despite his distinguished military career, he wasn't authoritarian in the operating room, as many surgeons were, and he had a special way of showing his patients how much he cared for them and how much he respected them.

The patients with facial disfigurements were different from other surgical patients. For the most part they were young or middle-aged men with strong, healthy bodies. They played cards, walked the cor-ridors, exercised in the gym. Someone on the ward was usually play-ing a guitar. But all of them had suffered facial injuries during the war. With some patients it was difficult to recognize that they'd once had a human face. I was used to seeing prisoners with disfigured faces, and so the men on the fourth floor of the veterans hospital didn't frighten me. To the contrary, I felt the same way toward them as I felt toward the patients on the TB and psychiatric wards in the camp hospital. Unlike war invalids, they avoided going out in public because the outside world wouldn't tolerate them. They were shunned and insulted, and I wanted to make them feel that I saw the person inside them, not just their deformity. Perhaps I sensed some similarity between the disfigured patients and myself. We'd all been injured during the war, they externally and I internally, and reconstruction and convalescence took a long time.

Every morning Dr. Zausayev and his assistants presented patients in different stages of reconstructive procedures and discussed plans for upcoming surgeries or told us what had already been done. Vitali, a twenty-seven-year-old war veteran, was the first patient we met. He sat in an examining chair, and Dr. Zausayev pulled a chair up next to him. "When Vitali arrived two years ago, he had one large hole in the middle of his face," Dr. Zausayev said, opening Vitali's chart and showing us the initial photos. In them, Vitali's nose, upper jaw, upper lip, and most of one cheek were completely gone. Miraculously, both eyes had been spared. His forehead was intact, as were his lower jaw and lip, although they were pulled strangely upward almost to the orbits. "You can see how the tissue around the defect contracted and scarred at the margins. I had to remove it, so we couldn't use any local soft tissue for reconstruction. I decided to close the defect first and re-create the upper lip, cheeks, and nose in stages. Now come close. Examine him carefully." Dr. Zausayev waved us over. "I showed you Vitali so you could see what can be done using the new techniques. They allow us to bring tissue from other areas of the body and model it into missing parts of the face. You can ask me and Vitali any questions you'd like." I liked it that he referred to Vitali by his first name. This kind of familiarity seemed to put both patients and students at ease.

I couldn't believe that the person I saw in the initial photographs was the same person sitting in front of me. Vitali now had an upper lip, both cheeks, and a nose. The new features differed in color and texture from the surrounding skin, and the lip and reconstructed part of the cheek didn't move normally, but the hole was gone. Dr. Zausayev explained how skin and underlying fat from Vitali's abdomen had been "tubed" into a cylinder, covered with skin, and transferred to the face, where it was used to fill the defect and build the missing parts. He showed us photos and schematic drawings of each stage of the procedure, pointing out the difficulties and complications. Vitali enjoyed our praise and attention. He said that when he arrived he could hardly speak or swallow because he had no mouth cavity, and that he communicated mostly through writing and was fed through a gastric tube. Now he had none of these problems.

Another day we watched Dr. Zausayev operate on a young man who'd been severely injured on one side of the face. Looking at him from both sides, I had the impression that I was looking at two different people with two different personalities. Dr. Zausayev showed us how the unattended wounds had healed with severe scarring. "If the patient doesn't have enough skin left around the wound to cover the defect, we have to harvest skin from other places on the body and bring it to the facial wound to close it." He taught us how unforgiving scars can be, especially in patients who'd been burned. Scars from burns contracted forcefully, pulling parts of the face in various directions and fixing them in unnatural, distorted positions. Sometimes the eyes or mouth were permanently open. Sometimes patients lost their lips, nose, and eyelids. Patients who couldn't open their mouths had to be fed through a straw.

Dr. Zausayev stressed the importance of treating each facial deformity with an individual treatment plan, because each patient was unique and differed in the way he dealt with the dramatic change in his appearance. These patients looked at Dr. Zausayev the same way that the patients on the TB ward had looked at me and Dr. Piasetsky—their eyes asked the questions they were afraid to utter. Their eyes also asked for hope. They wanted to believe the surgeons had the skills to make them look the way they looked before, or at least in a way that would allow them to live comfortably outside the hospital. But Dr. Zausayev, like Dr. Piasetsky, was short on promises. He told us straightforwardly that most of the patients would never look good because there were no surgical techniques to reconstruct perfectly such severely damaged facial features. Another similarity between the patients with facial injuries and the TB patients was that many of them were severely depressed. Some became resigned, lost hope, stayed in bed, and covered their heads with blankets. Others were openly hostile. They cursed in the worst possible ways, got drunk or drugged, and fought for no reason. They didn't care, because they knew they'd never have a life outside the hospital. Their sexual drive caused permanent problems. No one took care of their damaged self-images. For that they needed special psychiatric treatment, which was never available.

In addition to the many disfigured patients I met, one person in particular raised my interest in reconstructive surgery. While I was getting to know Lena, she introduced me to a neighbor nicknamed Lipless Boris. In contrast to the other young men in the building, who were fresh out of prison or heading in that direction, Boris was studying physical education at a sports institute. He was an outstanding skier and member of the national long-distance ski team. He was lean and muscular, with sandy blond hair, but his face startled me the first time I met him. It was disturbing and somewhat frightening. His upper jaw, flat, wide nose, and upper lip were severely retruded, and his lower jaw and lip jutted forward, making him look angry. His speech was unintelligible to me at first, but Lena was used to him and understood him well. She told me he was born with bilateral cleft lip and palate. As an infant he had lip surgery, and at nine years of age he had palate surgery. After the second operation his parents were told nothing else could be done to improve his appearance or speech. When I met him he was twenty-four years old. Despite his severe handicap, he had gained the respect of his peers and even had a girlfriend from the sports institute. He was a kind, gentle person, and I wanted to help him. I talked to Dr. Zauseyev about him, but he said that cleft lip and palate surgery hadn't progressed very far and nothing more could be done for Boris.

Several weeks into the reconstructive surgery rotation, Dr. Zausayev surprised everyone by asking who wanted to scrub and assist him in the operating room. I volunteered. A forty-two-year-old war veteran diagnosed with cancer of the lip was scheduled for surgery. "Be prepared for screaming and bleeding," Dr. Zausayev said as the patient was rolled into the operating room. "We don't have enough anesthesiologists in the hospital to give everyone general anesthesia, so we'll have to operate under a local. Also, the equipment is outdated, so we'll have to make do with what we have. Let's go scrub."

I couldn't believe Dr. Zausayev's critical remarks about the surgical conditions—they could have landed him in the camps for ten years. I wondered if it was inexperience, bravado, or simple honesty that caused him to speak so openly. My classmates and I changed into white pants and shirts, all of which were stamped in black letters with the name of the hospital. I grabbed a cotton mask and cap. The first mask I picked up smelled of powder and perfume, so I threw it back and grabbed another. With some effort I found a cap that didn't smell oily.

Dr. Zausayev led me into a small corridor just outside the operating room. He let the cigarette burning between his lips drop into the sink and ran water over it. He rinsed his hands and forearms. "Watch me and do the same," he said. We each took a bar of lye soap and scrubbed for five minutes. Then we plunged our hands into a metal basin of pure alcohol for two minutes. We dried our hands and scrubbed beneath our nails with cotton balls saturated with iodine. Dr. Zausayev stuck out his arms and a nurse slipped a sterile gown over them and tied it around the back. She did the same for me. I waited for a pair of gloves, but they never appeared. We'd be operating with our bare hands.

Dr. Zausayev began the surgery by injecting an anesthetic into the patient's lower lip and the area under the jaw. He dipped a small wooden stick in methyline blue ink and drew a small vertical line on each side of the ulceration, down toward the chin. In the crease of the chin, he drew a third horizontal line linking the two vertical lines. "Would you like to make the cuts?" he asked. I said yes. He showed me how to hold the scalpel and said, "Grab the lip on your side and cut slowly through the skin, muscle, and mucosa. Cut through and through. Expect bleeding when you hit the muscle." I felt a surge of adrenaline as I squeezed the lower lip hard on one side. Still pinching it, I cut downward in one decisive move. As Dr. Zausayev clamped the bleeding arteries his eyes widened with surprise. "Good. Continue," he said. Again I cut swiftly through the tissue without hesitation. Dr. Zausayev let me make the horizontal incision and remove the cancerous growth. He handed the tissue to the nurse and told her to send it to pathology. With the middle section of the lip gone, the sides of the lower lip contracted, making the defect look twice as large and exposing the lower teeth and gum in a hideous grin.

"Any idea how to close the defect?" he asked.

I didn't know, and none of the other students offered advice.

Dr. Zausayev drew more blue lines around the stumps of the lower lip and on both cheeks. He cut swiftly and then moved the segments of tissue around, re-creating the missing lower lip. It was magical to see how every incision and every move not only closed the gaping defect but truly rebuilt the lip. I held my breath as I watched him extend the incisions a little bit and pull the tissue in one direction and then in another. When he was done pulling and adjusting, he handed me the scissors and sutured the segments of the reconstructed lip together. I cut the thread after he tied each suture. He thoroughly removed the lymph nodes, sent them to pathology, and finished the operation.

Dr. Zausayev's performance imprinted itself in my memory and left me fascinated with reconstructive facial surgery for the rest of my life. I wasn't interested in the reconstruction of other body parts; it was the face, with its complex structures and various functions, that attracted me. I wanted to learn how to repair facial deformities so that patients could look in the mirror and see a face, go out in the world without wearing a veil. Throughout the rest of my studies I wouldn't find another field of medicine where I could have such a strong physical and psychological impact on patients' lives. It was exactly what I was looking for.

17

ASPIRANTURA

As I lay on my bed listening to my snoring, hacking, farting room-mates, the camp saying "No animal would survive the conditions in the labor camps, but a human being can adjust to anything" ran through my mind. But I never compared my present quarters to the embassy or Grand Hotel. I compared them only to the overcrowded barracks where I slept on raw bedboards fully dressed and full of lice. Before long the cramped, stinky dorm room became my refuge. My iron-spring bed was the only space I claimed as home, and my suit-case, shoved under the bed and secured with two locks, contained all my possessions. I loved the feeling of freedom that came with being a poor, anonymous student. I embraced my new life, making friends with my roommates and with the female students from the ground floor. It was good to be out of the embassy, no longer pretending to be somebody I wasn't.

Into my fourth year, clinical rotations went well, especially since I knew I would specialize in reconstructive surgery. I admired Dr. Zausayev's imagination, the way he could see three, four, or five sur-geries ahead, and the courage it took to undertake these lengthy sur-gical journeys. I wanted to learn his skills and I dreamed of adding my own personal touch of counseling and encouraging every patient. I didn't know if I could achieve my goal because I wasn't sure I would be capable of becoming a sculptor of human flesh. It required a spe-cial gift of imagination and foresight, and special talent for dealing with material so different from wood, clay, stone, or metal.

I continued to see Lena. We went to concerts and museums, and she taught me about the fine arts. I couldn't figure out where she'd gotten her refined taste and scholarly talents. I was sure it wasn't from her mother, who struck me as a very ordinary, pompous person. She certainly didn't get it from the friends and neighbors in her building. One evening, after attending a concert at the Moscow Philharmonic, I asked her how she knew music so well, and about her past.

"I don't like anyone digging into my life," she said sharply. She never talked about her childhood, but she liked to listen to my stories and asked me many questions about my early years, family, and friends. I found her behavior strange. It became clear to me she was hiding something, but I was the last person to fault her. I hoped that with time we would both open up to each other.

We were cautious about jumping into a close relationship. She'd recently broken up with someone, and I wasn't ready to risk dating a Soviet citizen. The more interested I became in Lena, the more I worried about the law forbidding relationships with foreigners. When I got the courage to bring it up, Lena responded without a moment's hesitation. "If we both like being together, we should be together for as long as possible. If we can catch a happy day in our lives, let's do it. We owe it to ourselves. There isn't much happiness around." I was elated by her determination to take the risk but taken aback by her despairing tone of voice. It sounded as if there was much more to her response than determination.

We continued to see each other, taking long walks in Gorky Park on the bank of the Moscow River, but only as friends. I wanted to start a relationship, but she was so closed and sometimes so remote that I decided to wait and let time do its work. We usually ate in a local café after standing in line for half an hour or longer, and then we stood in line again at a kiosk to get ice cream. Standing in line was usually boring and tiring for me, but with Lena it became romantic. We laughed, told each other stories, and joked that we even enjoyed standing in line and would look for another one to stand in after eating our ice cream.

In 1949 and 1950 terror was again on the rise. Andrei Zhdanov, the Party's ideological leader and one of Stalin's closest allies and his likely successor, had launched attacks on prominent poets, writers, and composers, accusing them of deviating from socialist realism and slipping into an opportunistic bourgeois style where art was for art's

sake and not for the masses. Among those listed by name were the famous writer Mikhail Zoshchenko and the renowned poet Anna
Akhmatova. They were expelled from the Association of Soviet Writers and banned from publishing. Meanwhile, the Party- and state-
orchestrated campaign against "rootless cosmopolites" spread in
ever-widening circles across the country. This initial effort to harass
and humiliate Jewish intellectuals soon transmuted into an openly
anti-Semitic campaign under the new phraseology of "anti-Zion-
ism." The Ministry of Foreign Affairs, Ministry of Defense, Ministry
of Internal Affairs, and the Party Central Committee cleaned their
ranks of Jews, who were now called "foreign elements." Jews were
transferred to jobs in other provinces or forced into early retirement.

In the midst of the hunting season on Jews, the NKVD discovered—or rather fabricated—another hostile plot. It was called the
Leningrad Case and implicated the Leningrad Party and city leadership in a plot to kill Stalin. Rumors circulated that the investigation
of the plot had been carried out on the direct orders of Stalin, starting
a new wave of terror. The announcement that the conspiracy against
Stalin was led by the most revered Soviet economist and member of
the Politburo, Nikolai Voznesensky, and the secretary of the Central
Committee of the Party, Alexei Kuznetsov, reminded me of the
Moscow trials of other members of the Politburo and Central Committee in 1937 and 1938. Like those officials, the accused in the
Leningrad case were executed.

Many of my Jewish friends were already "sitting on packed suitcases." Even Katia and Sioma panicked and asked me not to visit
them for a while. Rumors spread that political prisoners from the
1936–1939 purges who'd been released were being rearrested. Fear
poisoned the air we breathed, and it was capable of touching everyone, not only Jews. There was no telling where it would end.

In the spring I had an unexpected meeting with an old friend. I was
at the metro station Ochotnoy Riad when I saw Nikolai Rafaelovich
Piasetsky, my dear friend from the camp hospital in Kolyma, running
to catch a train. Out of breath, I caught up with him on the platform.
He held a briefcase in one hand and an *avoska* full of food in the other.
He no longer stood straight, with his chin held high. His dark wavy
hair had thinned and grayed. His dark jacket and pants were crumpled, as if he'd slept in them. I remembered our years together and
everything he'd done for me, saving me from a return to the gold

mines, where I would surely have died, caring for me and treating me when I was sick with contagious TB. "Nikolai Rafaelovich!" I called out.

He turned around and when he saw me he looked startled.

"How wonderful to see you!" I said. He hugged me tightly. But when we stood back to look at each other, I could see how tired and visibly worried he was. His chubby, rosy cheeks sagged and his face had deep wrinkles.

"Are you here for good?" I asked. "I want to know everything about you. What have you been doing since I left Magadan?" It had been over four years since I'd seen him, and I had many more questions to ask.

But Nikolai Rafaelovich, in a gesture I knew so well, raised his hand to stop me. "It's really good to see you," he said, turning to look for the arriving train. "I have to hurry, but if you have time, come with me." I felt he wanted to be with me, and I stepped on the train with him.

We got out at the Sokol metro station. "I live close by, very close, but I can't invite you to my place. It's in disarray. I have a wife and two daughters. One is three and the other nine months. Let's sit down on the square."

There was so much bitterness in his voice that I didn't want to risk opening wounds by asking more questions. We found a bench under an oak tree, and I sat quietly.

"What are you doing in Moscow?" he asked with awakened interest. "I thought you'd be living in Poland."

I told him briefly what had happened since leaving Kolyma, and again we both fell silent. We used to be the closest friends, but here we were sitting next to each other tense and uneasy, afraid to open our hearts as we used to do in the camp hospital. Trying to breach the barrier between us, I said, "Tell me what's happening with you. You know I'm your friend."

He lowered his head and crossed his arms. "It would be better for both of us if we hadn't met. We would live with good memories about each other, even though it was in Kolyma. Now I don't know what you're going to think about me. Next week I'm leaving for Yakutsk, going back to Siberia, if you can believe that. I'm scared of being arrested again. I've got a wife and children who depend on me. I've been working at the Institute of Endocrinology for the last three years, but now, as a past political prisoner and Jew, I'm a prime target for being rearrested. I hope we'll be safe in Yakutsk. Thank God my wife isn't Jewish. Who knows what will happen. They might even find me there." His last words were barely audible.

I walked Nikolai Rafaelovich to the door of his building. We hugged briefly, and he didn't ask for my address. I wished him good luck.

As a Polish citizen I felt safe, but not safe enough to quell my fear of being rearrested and sent back to Kolyma. Although it was against my nature to live in the shadows, life in the Soviet Union taught me to stay out of the public eye, not to draw attention to myself, not to expose myself to any danger, and not to discuss politics. The assumed role of nobody fit me well, lessening my fears and obsessions. My instincts told me it was good to be forgotten, to keep a low profile, to keep my contacts to a minimum, to be a very ordinary student. During this scary time I stayed away from the Polish embassy, cut down on socializing with Polish students, and built up an image of a loner, a one-track medical fanatic with no other interests.

Final exams were scheduled for the last week in June. My classmates were nervous because they didn't know where they'd be working after graduation. In the Soviet Union, graduates from every trade school and institution of higher education were subject to the process of central distribution in order to fill positions in the provinces. It was the price graduates paid for their free education. In theory, the distribution was based on need and planned by the appropriate ministry governing that profession. In practice, central distribution was a corrupt and chaotic endeavor meant to control individuals and break up families. My classmates from Moscow might be sent to remote regions in the vast territories, while graduates from institutions thousands of miles away could end up in Moscow.

The power of the state over the life of every working person extended far beyond the post-graduation period. Since everyone in the Soviet Union worked for the state, the state was empowered to transfer people from one city to another, one position to another, and one institution to another. It was easy to order the transfer of undesirable people from Moscow to the farthest corners of the country and keep them there forever. Disobeying an order to appear at a specific destination on a specific date was interpreted as an act of sabotage and punished by a prison sentence. Everyone lived permanently under the threat that one day they might be dislodged. No one, including top Party and state officials, was untouchable.

I was relieved that as a foreigner I didn't need to worry about being sent to work in some remote region. Instead I looked forward to devoting all my time to studying for the final exams, which again included Marxism-Leninism—the advanced course—and four major clinical subjects: internal medicine, surgery, pediatrics, and gynecology and obstetrics.

During the last several months before graduation I decided to specialize in reconstructive plastic surgery of the face, and Dr. Zausayev had already offered to train me. He suggested I apply for a postgraduate studies program called *aspirantura*. It was the most highly sought, most prestigious graduate position in Soviet academia. It consisted of three or four years of specialty training, research, a dissertation, and a defense in front of the Council of Professors with three outside professors evaluating the study. There were only one or two positions open every year in each department. The successful completion of the program resulted in a scientific degree equal to a Ph.D. and the title of specialist in the student's field. Many top students competed fiercely for the positions. I was certain I was well qualified, but I studied extra hard on my last final exams so that I'd get straight A's and graduate with the highest academic award: the Red Diploma. It would guarantee my admission into *aspirantura*. Julek's suggestion several years earlier that I go into academia had never left me. I didn't want to end my studies with an M.D. and work in the public health service. I wanted an academic career, following the tradition of scholars in my mother's and father's families. My mother especially would have been proud that I'd continued in the medical field like her uncle and brother. I also wanted to spend three or four more years with Lena.

I got straight A's on my exams, but graduation was anticlimactic. In the Soviet Union there was no cap and gown ceremony, no celebration with the professorial staff and families. When I went to get my diploma in the dean's office, the secretary told me that the Red Diplomas weren't ready yet and that I had to come back the following week. When I went back she barely looked up from her work to find my diploma and hand it to me. No one shook my hand or congratulated me, even though less than ten percent of the class received the award. Along with the diploma the secretary handed me two letters. One was from Professor Yevdokimov, accepting me into *aspi-rantura* in his program; the other was from Professor Zausayev concerning my training in reconstructive plastic surgery. I put the diploma and letters in my pocket and went to show Katia and Sioma. Then I went to the embassy. With great satisfaction I showed my diploma and the letters to Wanda Michalewska and to the officials at the Association of Polish Students. I was the first among the Polish students to receive the Red Diploma. Now the fate of my *aspirantura* lay in the hands of the Ministry of Health in Warsaw, depending to a great degree on the opinion of the director of personnel, Mrs. Stysiak.

The week before I left for summer vacation in Poland, Mark and his friends arranged a big farewell party. This was the first party Lena and I attended together. Before leaving her apartment for Mark's party, I told her that I honestly didn't know if I'd be back in Moscow in the fall as we both had hoped. I hadn't yet gotten approval from the Polish Ministry of Health to start my *aspirantura*. "I'll do everything I can to come back," I told her. "I want to be with you as long as possible. Maybe the law will change and we'll be able to be together forever." I tried to sound optimistic.

But Lena looked sad and said, "I like being with you, but I don't want to get involved with you until you come back from Poland. The time apart will give us a chance to see how we really feel about each other."

It was great to be with Lena at the party. A current ran between our fingers when we touched each other, and I felt warmth and excitement and a desire to grab her in my arms and hold her close for a long time. Despite the crowd of classmates and friends, I felt that we were alone on the whole planet. We hadn't yet kissed, but the gentle touches we exchanged were more than kisses. I smelled the fragrance of her perfume and the scent of her hair whenever I whispered an invitation to dance or share a drink. I discovered that whispering brought us closer. Although no words of love were exchanged, it hung thick in the air. I tried not to think that I might not be back in Moscow and that a moment like this might never happen again in my life. When we danced I held her firmly, leading confidently, seeing and thinking about her only. Lena in my arms was light and fiery, and so close that I felt dizzy. I wished we could dance all night.

After midnight, as people began to leave, the mood of the party became somber. Many of our classmates were saying goodbye not only for the evening but for good. They were leaving Moscow to go God knew where, and we all wondered if we would ever see each other again. The mood of uncertainty and angst rubbed off on Lena and me, and we stopped dancing. We sat quietly holding hands, looking at each other with warmth and despair. Mark, who was still waiting for his appointment, was joyful as usual and tried to keep the party alive, but Lena and I left, and when I dropped her off at home she asked me not to see her again before my departure.

The next week passed slowly, and since Julek was gone there was no one to see me off for my trip to Poland. The thought of not having him in Moscow when I came back, coupled with the thought of not having Lena in my life—she could easily meet someone else over the summer—made me deeply lonely. I even thought it might not be so bad if I stayed in Poland and began working as a general practitioner. But as I waited for the train I couldn't stop thinking about Lena, and while I was lost in fantasy she suddenly appeared on the platform. The surprise took my breath away. She gave me a tiny bouquet of lily of the valley and a small passport photo with the inscription "To Janusz. Fondly, Lena." We walked back and forth on the platform, hoping the train wouldn't leave on time, but after the conductor blew the whistle for the third time, we rushed over to the car. The moment I turned to embrace her, we kissed, and I carried the taste and warmth of her lips with me on the two-day journey to Poland. "I know you'll be back," she whispered. "I'll be waiting for you." The door closed and Lena ran after the train and waved until the platform ended.

When I arrived in Warsaw in July 1950, I found the political situation in Poland to be as frightening as it was in the Soviet Union. Julek was very nervous. He told me his deputy in the embassy in Moscow, Major Zurawski, had been arrested, as had one of Julek's previous bosses, Colonel Komar, the chief of military intelligence. If the secret police were fabricating a group conspiracy in the military, Julek could easily be pulled in. Marian Naszkowski, who had been ambassador in Moscow and was Julek's nemesis, had been promoted to the rank of general and was the new vice minister of defense. He hadn't approved the military discharge for which Julek had applied, and Julek was afraid he'd be sent to the "green garrisons" deep in some province and left to stagnate. He was more secretive than ever, afraid his apartment was bugged and that he was being watched by the secret police. I was afraid he might be arrested, and that scared me to the point that I decided to spend the whole summer with him in Warsaw and give up my voucher from the Ministry of Health for one month's vacation.

Julek and Zofia had married and moved into a spacious apartment on Nemtzevicha Street, number 12. He had an efficiency apartment in the other wing of the same building and he put me up there. He said he would keep it for me in case I decided to live in Warsaw after completing my studies. The apartment awaited me newly furnished, with fresh flowers on the table and food and liquor in the pantry. I was deeply touched by Julek's thoughtfulness and generosity at such a troubled time in his life.

Every two or three days I wrote at least a four-page letter to Lena, just as I had promised when we parted at the Belarussky train station, and two or three times a week I received a letter from her. There was something romantic and exciting in exchanging letters, running each day to the mailbox, recognizing the envelope, and looking for solitude in which to read it. Never before had I had the chance to express my feelings in writing, and I found it difficult because ordinary words seemed too pedestrian to touch the heart and convey deep emotions. It was torturous to tear up page after page because I couldn't find enough refined and meaningful words to convey my longings. However, just sitting at the desk and staring at the empty page with only a salutation, "Dear Lena," made me imagine her close and sweet and beautiful, the way I had left her at the train station. Before long the "Dear" changed to "Dearest" and then to "Beloved." At the end of two months I was overwhelmed with feelings for her. I read and reread each letter she sent to absorb every thought and feeling she conveyed in her dashing handwriting.

Once I was settled in Warsaw, the first visit I paid was to Mrs. Stysiak, who'd been elevated to the position of deputy director in the Department of Higher Education. Her influence and power in the ministry had grown immensely since she had become the first secretary of the Party committee there. She had a big office and two secretaries, and although she had gotten busier every year, she always found time for me. At our first meeting four years earlier, I had sensed in her the devotion and enthusiasm of a neophyte. But over the years her expressions of devotion became more fervent. It was Party talk, the need to prove to everyone how devoted she was to the Party. I showed her the Red Diploma, and she hugged me and shook my hand vigorously. "I'm so proud and happy that our first stipendiary has excelled in Moscow. You'll serve as an example for all of our medical students and residents who want to follow in your footsteps. I still remember when you were the only Polish representative, and I remember our first meeting. It took me great effort to convince Professor Rowinski to grant you a stipend," she said, as if I were a prize puppy and she my handler.

"I have much to be thankful for," I said. "You were always supportive and encouraging over the years. I'm grateful for your personal interest in me and for inviting me to your home. I'd like to celebrate my Red Diploma along with you and maybe also your husband and Director Pomianowski. Lunch or dinner, your choice. But it's my invitation. Now I'm a doctor." By showing off I was hoping to lay the groundwork for asking to be sent back to Moscow for *aspirantura*.

"Janusz, it's a good idea, but Pomianowski isn't with us anymore. He's in the Central Committee. I miss him, but we're still good friends. He was always fond of you. Perhaps I'll call him and ask him to join us." She reached him on the phone and extended the invitation, but he declined. She handed me the receiver. "Comrade Pomianowski would like to talk to you." We chatted briefly, and he apologized for not being able to come but invited me for lunch at the end of the week.

When I hung up, Mrs. Stysiak said, "So, Janusz, have you applied to join the Party—or are you already a Party member?"

Caught off guard, I said, "No, not yet. I've been working very hard in my studies. In fact, I'd like to continue my postgraduate studies. I brought two letters of recommendation to show you." I reached into my pocket and handed her the letter from Professor Yevdokimov, who accepted me as an *aspirant* in the department of Maxillofacial and Reconstructive Facial Surgery. When she finished reading it I gave her the letter from Professor Zausayev, who praised me as a gifted student with a special talent for reconstructive surgery. He offered to provide me with special training in the field.

"Why didn't you show me these letters before?" Mrs. Stysiak asked. "First you show me your Red Diploma, and then your acceptance in *aspirantura*. Again, you're the first one to graduate from a Soviet medical school and to be offered the prestigious position of *aspirant*. Congratulations. I'm very proud of you. But we're following the Soviet system of central distribution now. The ministry has decided that every medical graduate must serve in the country for at least two years as a general practitioner before specializing in any particular field—you do understand that this is how you'll pay back the state and improve the health of the masses?"

"But Comrade Stysiak, the place in *aspirantura* won't wait for me. It's offered now, and if I don't accept it, it'll be filled immediately. There are too many excellent candidates for this position. And who knows what will be in two or three years. It's the only opportunity I have."

"I'm sorry, but as the first medical graduate from Moscow, you must follow the law and set an example. Don't be so discouraged. If you tell me where you'd like to go, I'll arrange a placement for you. Would you like to be in the mountains, next to a lake, or near the sea? We can talk about it. After two years working in the country, you'll be a prime candidate to continue your studies in Moscow, but right now I can't support your application. I can't go against the decision of the Party committee and leadership of the ministry."

"I don't think the law applies to me. I'm not a graduate of a Polish medical school, I'm a foreign graduate, and on this basis I don't think I should be treated like graduates from Polish institutions."

"No, no, no. Don't try to sway me from my decision. This is the law created for us by our ministry. As first secretary of the Party committee in the ministry, I must follow the rules without exception. You'll be a prime example of the socialist approach to health care."

Too shocked and defeated to come up with another angle, I didn't argue with her any further.

That night I lay in bed feeling cheated and angry. I didn't need a Red Diploma to work in some faraway region where I might be the only Jew. I didn't need to meet Lena only months before graduation. I didn't need to get excited about becoming a reconstructive plastic surgeon when my destiny was to be a general practitioner in a Polish province. I knew Mrs. Stysiak would follow the Party line and wouldn't change her mind. If I'd been a Party member and activist, it might have been easier for her to speak on my behalf. Now I was paying the price for not having joined.

I went to see Pomianowski on Friday. He looked tired and depressed. "So I hear anti-Semitism is raging in Moscow," he said. "I'm afraid the wave is coming here. We still have Jews in the Politburo and Central Committee, but I wonder when the Polish nationalists will start kicking us out. I can see it coming, and I'm not sure what I'll do when it gets here." Pomianowski sighed. He smoothed a trembling hand over his hair. "But how are you? What can I do for you?"

"I've got problems, but I don't know if I should trouble you now," I said.

"Go ahead. Maybe I can be of some help. As long as I have my position in the Central Committee, people will listen to me. What's the matter?"

I told him about the Red Diploma, my acceptance into *aspirantura*, and Mrs. Stysiak's decision to send me to work for two years in the provinces. I gave him the letters and watched his face closely as he read them.

"Did Comrade Stysiak see these?"

"Yes."

"With these credentials it would be a waste of your time and talent to send you into the country. What was she thinking?" Pomianowski shook his head. "Marysia Stysiak isn't a bad person, just rigid when it comes to deviating from the Party line. I'll talk to her." He picked up the phone. "Marysia, glad I caught you. Sorry it's so late, but Janusz is sitting here with me. He has a unique offer to get a postgraduate education. You aren't breaking any laws if you send him back to Moscow. He isn't a graduate from a Polish school. I think you need to rethink your decision." In another minute he handed me the receiver.

"Janusz," Mrs. Stysiak said, "Jerzy gave me some good advice. I think it's better if you go ahead with *aspirantura*. You're an ideal representative of Polish students in the Soviet Union. I was going to present this at the next committee meeting, but with Jerzy's approval, I don't think I need to."

When I got off the phone, Pomianowski poured two shots of vodka. "L'Chaim," he toasted. "I know how hard you worked. You deserve it. You know, there aren't many people I can talk to openly around here, but I can trust you. This isn't the Poland it used to be.

The communist zealots are changing everything to fit the Soviet model. You seem to understand the system and have a sense of the undercurrents. I think you'll do well here. But I'm too filled with the past to change my ways." His voice trailed off. We talked for several hours about Poland and my future, and I enjoyed his praise and the interest he took in me. It seemed like the kind of talk I might have had with my father.

The next day I sat in Professor Rowinski's office in the same place I had sat four years earlier, when my only distinction was that I was a medical student in Moscow. Over the years I'd seen him several times, but I always had the impression he hadn't changed his initial opinion of me—that I was a fake and lightweight. I handed him the Red Diploma and the two letters. He looked surprised when he read the letters. He congratulated me, and for the first time he shook my hand.

Julek was extremely proud and immediately began making plans for me to pursue an academic career. We talked about what university I might go to—Warsaw or Lodz. We talked about my interest in plastic and reconstructive surgery. We also celebrated his good news: he'd finally been discharged from the military and had been offered a professorial position to teach history of law at Warsaw University.

I hadn't written to Lena during the week in which I feared we wouldn't see each other again, and I didn't write to her now even though the stipend was granted. I was superstitious, and I didn't want to spoil my good luck. I would wait to surprise her at her doorstep.

18

LOWER THAN GRASS,
QUIETER THAN STILL WATER

Back in Moscow I dropped off my suitcase at the dormitory and hurried to Sretensky Tupik to see Lena. I carried the last letter I had received from her, which I'd read so many times on the train it had torn along the creases. Holding a small bouquet of flowers in one hand and a bottle of wine in the other, I knocked on the door. Now I regretted not having written to her about the stipend, worrying that perhaps she was gone or worse, that she'd started seeing someone else. But when the door clicked open and Lena threw her arms around my neck, I knew everything I needed to know.

Lena held my hand firmly and said to her mother, "Janusz is going to sleep here tonight on the sofa. I don't want him going back to that filthy dormitory." Lena's decisiveness surprised me and was a quality I'd see much more frequently.

There are moments in life and love when things turn upside down, like the way the current of a stream suddenly changes direction during an earthquake. It seems totally impossible but happens all the time. Lying on Lena's sofa that night, rubbing my cheek against her pillow, feeling her sheets around my body, smelling her scent, I knew I'd finally found home. From that night on I spent every weekend at Lena's, not minding the cramped conditions and presence of other people. During the week I saw Lena every day, no matter how tired I was. We were both working and we both had a lot of homework to do. She was doing her residency in prosthodontics, while I followed my detailed program in *aspirantura*.

The greatest obstacle in our relationship was finding privacy. In the park we searched for secluded benches, but everyone else had the same thing in mind. Often we sat on a bench on the main promenade because in the current of pedestrians, there seemed to be less of a chance of someone listening to every word we said. In the camps there was an expression, "Thoughts may torment you, but words can kill," and this saying was just as true in Moscow. Lena and I felt especially vulnerable to eavesdropping by informers because I had the look of a foreigner. Lena said there was something in the way I walked and dressed that marked me as one. I would've preferred being with Lena in a jungle with lurking leopards and venomous snakes than in Moscow. As a result, the only time we could talk freely was when we were alone in her apartment, and this opportunity arose much too infrequently. So we followed another camp saying, to be "lower than grass and quieter than still water." We put on blinders in order to forget about the outside world. I had learned to put on blinders in the camps, to focus on one thing at a time. It could be dangerous for me to take my eyes off the outside world, but sometimes it was more dangerous to see the horror and cruelty around me. Living in Moscow was the same way, with the difference that focusing on Lena was much easier than focusing on work in the camps.

One evening in late December we were alone in her apartment and took the opportunity to celebrate the coming new year ahead of time. We'd both made good progress in our work and studies, and our relationship was growing deeper. Lena prepared some simple appetizers, and I bought vodka and more food from a store across the street. I made a toast to our love and our future, but the moment I pronounced the toast I regretted mentioning the future, which hung over our heads like Damocles' sword.

Lena emptied her glass and snuggled close to me on the sofa. "I know there might not be a future for us after you're finished with *aspirantura*," she said. "But right now I'm happier than I've ever been."

"Maybe the law will change," I said. "Lots of Polish students and officers are in relationships with Soviet citizens. They wrote a petition to Bierut to get permission to marry. Something has to change."

Lena pulled back and looked at me. "How can you believe our leaders would do something just because the people ask them to? They'll do anything for political benefit, but they don't care about us. You haven't lived here long enough to understand the system."

When Lena got upset she talked loudly, and I got up to make sure no one was in the hallway.

"You know why I never belonged to the Komsomol or Party? Because this country terrorizes everyone. Everyone spies on everyone. My mother and I eat meat only once a week or less, even though we can afford it more often, because we don't want our neighbors to envy us and start digging into where our money comes from." Lena opened the window and let Murka into the room. She held the cat in her arms and petted him gently. We listened to him purr. "Murka is the only animal I can trust," she said bitterly. "I trust him because I don't trust anyone around me. People in this country are worse than animals. They'll denounce, destroy, do anything just to save their skin."

"I don't think it's that bad," I said. "I've lived long enough in this country. I've met scoundrels and crooks, but I've met good, honest people, too."

"Well, you've had better luck than I." Lena put the cat down and walked over to the piano. She played a few notes and stopped. "This piano is the only thing I have from my past life. We didn't always live in this dump. Look at the people in this building. Most of them are born in poverty and stay in poverty. They rob, steal, go to prison, get out, and do it all over again. I want out of here. Boris is getting out of here. But only a few of us have any chance to escape." Lena filled our glasses with more vodka. "To those we love, and to those who aren't with us anymore."

Lena came back to the couch. The tension eased in her voice. "My father was a communist and Red Army officer. He met my mother in a field hospital during the Revolution. He was wounded in both legs. My mother was a volunteer nurse. She hadn't trained as a nurse, but she volunteered for the Red Army and was sent to help in the hospital. They fell in love and married after the war. My father worked in the city government. When the New Economic Policy was introduced, encouraging private enterprise and allowing private ownership, he opened a fur and leather business, following in his father's footsteps. He was successful, and we lived in a nice apartment with beautiful furniture. I had a nanny, and we had a live-in maid. We were very happy. But when I was ten years old, it ended. One night NKVD officers stormed into our apartment and took all our valuables. They beat my father in front of us and took him away. We never saw him again."

As the story poured out of Lena I understood her anger and despair. I'd known thousands of men like her father in Kolyma, tormented not only by their fate but by the fate of the family they'd left behind. I'd heard their side of the story, how they were arrested in front of their family, interrogated, and sentenced to hard labor without ever seeing their family again. I always wondered what became of the families left behind, and as Lena talked I saw the other side of the story take shape.

"His business was confiscated, and my mother had no money and no profession. Soon we were ordered to leave the apartment. We were forced to leave behind the furniture, Persian rugs, crystal, silver—everything. The piano was at the repair shop. That's how it got here. I changed schools and grew up here, but I've never forgotten my father and the life we lived with him. I still don't know what happened to him, if he's dead or alive in some prison or labor camp. My mother's inquiries were never answered."

As Lena talked she squeezed my hand and cuddled closer to me. I could feel her body shivering. I'd learned how to lift the spirits of the dying, but I'd never learned how to console those who were left behind. I kissed her eyes, the way I kissed my mother's whenever she cried.

As Lena was telling her story, my own secret swelled inside me. "Lena," I said. "I might have met your father. We might have worked together in a gold mine or slept in the same barracks."

Lena pressed her face against my chest, and I kept talking. It was strange to hear the words come out, but I didn't want any secrets between us, and I told her my tale, every bit of it.

When I finished, Lena said, "I always knew there was something strange about you, some deep, sad secret that you hid from the world. Even since the first day you came here I've wondered how you could relate so well to the guys in the building. I wondered how you knew their lingo, why they liked you. Now I know."

We stayed up all night talking, but after that night we rarely talked about our pasts. We'd built our lives around our secrets. We'd learned to guard them well and no longer felt their burden. Instead, we made the present as happy and interesting as possible. There were no clouds in our sky as long as we could be together.

When I started *aspirantura*, I had grandiose plans for research despite my meager experience. My youthful dreams and ambitions resurfaced. I didn't want to be an ordinary reconstructive surgeon; I wanted to be famous. During my years as a student, I worked in the Department of Biochemistry on a team investigating the metabolism of the bones of the skull as compared to the long bones. Although my role on the team was limited to injecting various isotopes into the femoral arteries of rats and using a Geiger counter, I spent a great deal of time thinking about how medical problems could be solved and what questions needed to be asked and answered. I hoped to come up with a fresh angle that no one on the team had thought of, which never happened. Professor Bronovecky, who lectured on pathophysiology, invited me to assist him in experiments in the Institute of Experimental Medicine. The institute was created and led by Professor Speransky, author of the monotheistic theory of medicine that asserted the primacy of the central nervous system in the pathogenesis of various diseases. According to this theory, the cure of these maladies could be achieved through the central nervous system. Professor Bronovecky's research was aimed at inducing pathological processes by stimulating certain segments of the central nervous system. Under his guidance, I learned how to design experimental studies and ask pertinent questions.

When designing my research proposals, I thought I might find a way to apply Speransky's theory to the treatment of cancer in the head and neck area, accessing the central nervous system from the peripheral nerves. I wrote a proposal to isolate the peripheral nerves that supplied the cancerous tumor and inject them with a substance that would cut off the nervous impulses to the tumor, which in turn would make it shrink and disappear. Another idea I had for research was to transplant the ears and noses of accident victims to people who'd lost their ears and noses. I also wanted to perfect cleft lip and palate surgery, imagining I could reshape Boris's face and make him look and speak normally. Ideas whirled through my mind, each one aimed at discovering a new method in the surgical treatment of facial deformities or diseases in the head and neck area. Filled with these ideas, I went to get Dr. Zausayev's advice on which research topic I should work on for the next three or four years.

Dr. Zausayev had just returned from vacationing in the country, and he looked tan and rested. I cleared a little place on his desk and laid down my proposals. His desk and shelves were loaded with books, papers, photographs, and plaster models of patients' faces, but

I was under the impression that he was quite familiar with the topography of the office and could find whatever he needed.

"I've brought you three proposals for my research," I said, pointing to the neatly typed manuscripts with transparent covers. "I'm ready to begin. I just need to know which one you think will work best. The ideas will probably have to be refined, of course, but I think the proposals will give you a picture of what I'd like to do." I didn't intend to get into a discussion right away, I just wanted to know he was as enthusiastic about my ideas as I was.

"First of all, please call me Volodia. You're no longer a student, you're a colleague, and we'll be working closely together for the next several years. Second, let's talk about the program. Here's what I expect from you during the years of your *aspirantura*. This is a highly privileged position, but it's also a highly demanding one. In three to four years you must learn how to treat all kinds of facial disfigurements, congenital and acquired. You need to learn to analyze each defect, design a surgical plan, discuss other surgical options, and finally, be able to perform a variety of surgical procedures. This is what I and a few other staff surgeons will teach you. Most of your time will be spent in the hospital with me. You'll also have to take classes and spend time in the emergency room, surgical intensive care, general surgery, and internal medicine. You must pass the exams in all of these disciplines before defending your dissertation. Every year you'll spend three months in one of the areas, while the remaining nine months you'll work here with me or with Professor Chitrov at the institute. He's a true master in reconstructive surgery. You'll be on twenty-four-hour duty twice a week. This schedule should give you a lot of experience."

More than a little taken aback, I was getting ready to say that the clinical program didn't seem to leave me much time for research, not to mention my private life, when Dr. Zausayev cleared his throat and continued.

"Your week will be full of clinical work, but don't worry, you'll be finished at 3:00 or 4:00 in the afternoon. You'll work from 7:00 a.m. until 3:00 p.m. If there isn't any more work, you can leave earlier. That leaves you the afternoon and evening to work on your research—and of course you'll have nights and Sundays."

He picked up the proposals and looked at the titles. "So, what do you have here?" He didn't wait for an answer but shuffled through the pages and grunted several times. He put the proposals back on his desk. "Let me give you some advice. Since you'll be very busy with your surgical training, classes, and studying for exams, I advise you to select a clinical research topic that can be completed on time. Don't venture into unknown territories. Don't try to select something over your head. Don't fantasize that your dissertation will bring you fame. Leave those dreams for later. In *aspirantura* your prime goal is to get good surgical training and get your scientific degree. This will open the door for your academic career."

"So you don't think any of my ideas will work?" I tried to hide it, but I was crushed.

"I don't even want to discuss them. It's a waste of time. I only want to talk about research that can be completed, that will result in a written dissertation. You've got good potential as a reconstructive plastic surgeon. You've got a good imagination and analytical ability. I'm anxious to see how you do in the operating room."

With his last comment, a new image of myself replaced the stinging disappointment I'd felt at having my research plans scrapped. I pictured myself at the operating table, working on a difficult case, surrounded by admiring doctors and residents as I made cuts, moved tissue around, and transformed faces.

Dr. Zausayev hesitated as if he wanted to say something else, but instead picked up his briefcase and loaded it up with papers. "Let's get out of here. We'll have plenty of time to talk later."

Dr. Zausayev assigned me to ten patients on the ward, all of whom were veterans. In the beginning my duties were to perform daily rounds, change dressings, fill out charts, present proposed treatments to Dr. Zausayev, and assist him in the operating room. I also wrote up the operating room protocols. When new patients arrived, I performed physical exams and noted in detail the existing deformity and my plan for the reconstructive procedure. One day, while sitting in the lounge after surgery, Dr. Zausayev's mentor, Professor Vasilyev, asked me if I was still looking for a research topic. He was studying the use of contrasting agents for diagnostic purposes, focusing primarily on the detection of cancer in the sinuses. The use of these agents was a novelty at the time, and he invited me to join him in the research, promising it was a topic certain to complete an easy dissertation. I accepted.

The other *aspirants* and I attended weekly staff meetings in Professor Yevdokimov's office. Viktor was there. It was strange meeting him, because we hadn't talked for the last two years. I was still hurt and puzzled by the abrupt ending of our friendship, but I still liked him. We were civil to each other, but we worked in different hospitals and were interested in different aspects of specialization. Our friendship was never resuscitated.

At faculty meetings I learned about the façade of academic life. Everyone was polite and friendly. Everyone used the same wooden, Party-approved jargon praising each other's achievements, and everyone constantly paid lip service to the Great Teacher. Faculty members presented progress of their current research and discussed problems concerning teaching. From time to time there was a slapdash critique of manuscripts prepared for publication or doctoral theses. Rarely did they discuss complex clinical cases, and I never heard anyone mention the psychological status of patients who were depressed because of their severe facial deformities. Not even the problem of postoperative infection, which was rampant, was raised for discussion. Faculty members would never admit that sterility and hygiene were worse than primitive, and with one bathtub and two toilets for forty-five patients, there was no way to prevent infection.

I slipped into a routine divided between my professional and personal lives. In my professional life I lived in the dormitory, rushed to the hospital in the morning, took care of patients, and found myself more immersed in reconstructive surgery than I ever expected. But I was torn apart by how much I didn't know, and I couldn't wait to become more independent in the operating room.

Months passed. The calendar pages rolled into another year. Through my relationship with Lena I had regained an inner peace I hadn't felt in years. Following her philosophy to live each day to the fullest, the knots in my stomach rose less often to my throat, and the anxiety that had knitted together my fears and obsessions disintegrated. The intrusive images and nightmares were eclipsed by my happiness with Lena and work in *aspirantura*. But in Soviet society, where fear and suffering ruled, the lessening of one person's suffering only meant that someone else's increased.

One afternoon in the spring of 1952 I went to meet Lena in Gorky Park. I'd had a good day in the operating room. I wandered down a distant alley near the bench where we usually met and looked for Lena's silhouette in the distance. Instead I saw Professor Weinstock from the department of internal medicine. He didn't see me and continued walking toward me. I had liked his lectures in cardiology and had spoken with him several times after class. "Good afternoon, Arcady Solomonovich," I said, extending my hand. "It's so good to see you." He didn't shake my hand but instead wiped his face with a handkerchief.

"Please, don't mention to anyone that you met me here," he said, glancing around. "I want to be forgotten, to disappear. I don't know how to tell my wife what happened. I've been coming here every day for the last three weeks. They accused me of being a poor doctor and untrustworthy communist."

"Arcady, let's sit down. What happened? Who accused you?"

"The executive Party committee of the institute. They had a special meeting. I was a member of that committee for two years. The accusations were based on two anonymous letters from a patient and a student. I was expelled from the Party and fired from the institute. I don't know what to do. I have a fourteen-year-old son."

I'd heard many stories like Arcady's from prisoners in Kolyma, stories of people who were denounced by their friends and spouses and fired from their jobs. Their bitterness was unending. But I found it much more disturbing to hear Arcady Solomonovich's innocent, uncomprehending lamentations. He was fifty-eight years old, the author of many publications, an acclaimed expert in cardiology, a full professor, and a member of the Academy of Medical Sciences, and now he'd been ousted. He couldn't understand that he was already nobody.

"I'm afraid of my wife finding out what happened. She's Russian, and she's a devoted Party member. She might divorce me. She's capable of it. So I pretend to go to work every day, but I come here instead. I don't know what to do."

"My best advice is to get out of here. Disappear. Run away as far as you can. Maybe you have family elsewhere—go there today, tomorrow. Don't wait a day longer. Nothing good waits for you here. And remember, keep a low profile wherever you go. Lose your passport. Change your name. Just be an ordinary doctor."

"No, no," he murmured, covering his face. "I can't do it. I can't leave my son. I can't leave my life."

"Arcady, listen to me." I tried to find the words to tell him he no longer had a life, but he walked away. I hoped he would turn to look back so I could tell him again to go away, that it was best for everyone, but he didn't.

More Jewish professors were dismissed from their positions, and one day the anti-Semitic campaign hit closer to home, when Sioma told me about the drive to remove Jews from the chemical industry. He was worried that any day he, too, might lose his job. His specialized knowledge protected him somewhat, but not enough to let him sleep easier. In late August 1952 another event showed me how advanced and deep-seated the drive was to eradicate Jews from leading positions in teaching institutions. Professor Bynin, Viktor's father-in-law, died suddenly of a heart attack. Despite our falling out, I went to Viktor's home to express my sympathy. He invited me in, and with great reluctance he told me how his father-in-law died. On August 30, Professor Bynin met with the Council of Professors, of which he was a prominent member, at the institute. He was also the only person in the institute who'd been awarded Stalin's Prize and who wore Stalin's gold medal on his lapel. During the meeting the director of the institute, Professor Beletzky, told Professor Bynin that the Party committee and institute leadership wanted him to dismiss all the Jewish faculty in his department. If he agreed, he would keep his position. Otherwise, he'd be relieved of his duties in the coming academic year. Professor Bynin went home and told his wife what had happened. He went to bed that night and never woke up.

One night when I was sleeping at Lena's apartment, loud knocks on the door woke everyone up. "Open up! Militia!" It was after 2:00 a.m. I dressed and combed my hair. Lena's mother threw on a robe and went out into the hallway. Lova came out of his and Lidia's room and opened the front door. I pushed the bedding under the sofa and sat at the table. Lena put on a dress and joined me. "Do you have any strangers in your apartment? Anyone who isn't registered here?" one of the militiamen asked.

"No strangers live here," Lena's mother said. "Friends visit my daughter, and sometimes they stay late, like tonight."

"Who's staying here tonight?"

"I told you, we have a late visitor, but no one is staying here."

Briefcase in hand, I went out into the hallway. Lena followed and stood in the doorway.

"Don't lie to us," the militiaman said. "You've got someone living in this apartment. We have information on you." He looked at Lena. "Am I right? He lives here with you. You're both breaking the law."

"No," Lena said. "Search this room. You won't find one piece of his clothing here. How can he live here without any of his things?" Knowing her temper, I feared a sudden explosion on her part.

The militiaman, a sergeant, turned to me and said, "Who are you and what are you doing here?"

I told him my name and that I was a Polish *aspirant* at the institute. "Lena and I are friends. We were talking and didn't realize it was so late."

"Your passport." I gave it to him, and he rifled through the pages and studied my photograph and the entrance and exit visas. "Don't you know that foreigners aren't allowed to be out at night?"

"I've lived in Moscow for over six years, and I've never heard such a thing. The embassy keeps us informed of any changes in Soviet law regarding foreigners."

"You can go back to your dormitory, but I'll keep your passport. You'll get it back at your embassy or at OVIR. Let's go."

"I'm not going anywhere without my passport. Drive me straight to the Polish embassy, if you'd like. You can tell the authorities there that I broke the law by staying outside my dormitory at night. But I refuse to leave this apartment without my passport."

The sergeant turned to his partner as if asking for advice. The younger man shrugged. He looked tired and bored. "Just give him back the passport," he said.

The sergeant gave me the passport. "I'm going to report tonight's event to my superiors and to your embassy. You won't get off that easy. I know what's going on. You're not fooling me." He pointed at Lena and her mother. "I'm going to watch all of you." They left, slamming the door as they walked out of the building.

When I left ten minutes later, they were still standing at the entrance. I passed them and heard their steps fall in behind me on the pavement. They finally split off at the Garden Ring. Walking back to the dormitory, I thought over the night's events. One thing stuck out more than anything else: there was only one person who didn't open her door and show interest in the visit—Alexandra Ivanovna, the older nurse living in the third room. She was the one who had informed on us.

Lena and I had been preparing ourselves for that nighttime visit for a long time, but still, it left us badly shaken. We decided I wouldn't come to her apartment anymore. I felt guilty for pulling Lena into an unpredictable and possibly dangerous future. She sensed my uneasiness and reassured me not only of her love but also of her unshakeable intention for us to be together for as long as possible.

It didn't take long before I faced the consequences of the midnight visit. A week later the Polish embassy called me to report to the executive Party committee of the Association of Polish Students. Inside the small conference room, five students sat behind a table smoking and whispering to each other. I sat in front of them.

As a stipendiary of the Polish government, I was a member of the association. But not being a Party member and not having social connections with other Polish students, I'd never been close to anyone in the clique in charge of the organization. The obligatory monthly meetings were a cross between Abgarian's classes and a court-martial, and I always left them as fast as possible.

Adam Kruchkovsky, son of the most famous Polish writer of the time, presided. He read from an open file: " 'On the night of September 21, 1952, Polish citizen Janusz Bardach was found at 2:00 a.m. in the apartment of Elena Laneyeva. We received information that he visits the apartment frequently and has slept there many times. We suspect that he is breaking Soviet law by establishing a relationship with a Soviet citizen, Elena Laneyeva. We present this information to the Polish embassy so that you may take steps to curb this activity by your citizen. Signed, senior sergeant of precinct 472.' Do you have any comments about these allegations?"

"Lena Laneyeva and I are good friends, but she's no different from other Soviet friends I have in Moscow. I've lived here long enough to know that we aren't allowed to marry Soviet citizens. But we are encouraged to become friends with them and learn the socialist way of life. That's what I'm doing. I'm not breaking Soviet law, which I highly respect. The only true fact in this report is my late-hour visit with Lena. But I also have late-night talks with other friends. All other allegations in the report are false. I feel deeply insulted being called here. I've never had a problem living in Moscow or attending the institute. You can request the opinions of my mentors in the institute."

Adam asked me to leave the room and wait in the hall while they discussed the charge. Half an hour later he called me back.

"We're deeply concerned by the report," Kruchkovsky said. "If the militia caught you at your friend's apartment at 2:00 a.m., and they said you often spend the night there, there must be something more than innocent friendship going on. We've given you a chance to admit to the relationship, but you've refused to do it. We tend to trust the Soviet authorities, but since you've never caused any problems and are in good standing at the institute, we'll give you a warning this time. But another incident and you'll be deported, even if it's the last month of your *aspirantura*."

"I've always respected Soviet law and I've always followed it. Thank you for the warning." I got up and left the room.

My ordeal didn't end at the embassy; at the end of October I was called to appear at OVIR at 11:00 p.m.

A middle-aged man in an elegant civilian suit opened the door of the deserted building. I had expected to meet a typical NKVD bureaucrat and was surprised by this smartly dressed man. He pulled out a chair and offered me a cigarette. "Sorry for the late appointment," he said. The suit, cigarette, and apology put me at ease. "Tell me about your studies and life in Moscow."

I rambled on about *aspirantura* and my work in the hospital. I expressed my admiration for and gratefulness to my teachers. He seemed to listen with interest, but then in the middle of a particularly empty story, he slapped his palm down on the desk and yelled in my face, "Cut the bullshit. Don't lie to me. We know everything about you. We have more than one report. You're breaking our law, you and your lover. Both of you are guilty!" I'd seen faces like his before, and I'd heard yelling like this many, many times, but instead of frightening me, the outburst struck me as a challenge.

"No, sir, I'm not involved with one of your citizens. I've lived in Moscow for six years, and I've always respected Soviet law and highly valued the Soviet-Polish friendship. The words in your report aren't true." I knew he didn't have the facts, and if I calmly denied everything, there was nothing he could do.

He took a puff on the cigarette and held it out in front of himself and examined it. "I've called you here to warn you. We don't want you to be in trouble, but one more report and you and your lover, whatever her name is, won't be spared. We're watching you. Nothing escapes our eye."

It was after midnight when I left OVIR. I vowed to be very careful where I met with Lena but to continue seeing her as much as possible.

19

THE END OF TERROR

In the last months of 1952, I wanted to be blind and deaf so I didn't have to see or hear what was going on around me. I wanted to preserve the tiny island of Lena's and my happiness, but it had already been eroded by the militia's nighttime visit. I wondered if I could withstand another personal disaster—being deported to Poland and separated from Lena forever—and the stress of the threat made me take a hard look at myself to see if I could endure another loss. For the last several years I hadn't attempted to perform a vivisection on myself, knowing I'd changed a great deal but unsure of whether I'd like the changes. I wasn't the same person I was when I arrived in Moscow. Life moved quickly, my thoughts and feelings shuffling around so much that a new me emerged again and again. I wondered if the changes made me a better or worse or just different person. I realized that looking at myself might be painful or just pointless, because it wasn't like watching myself in the mirror. It was like diving into murky water and finding only slight traces of the unknown, only to lose them again. But I wanted to remove the layers of denials and deceits I'd been living with to reach beneath to my true self, whoever it might be.

A long time passed, I can't even say how long, before I felt that my life was normal and not an aberration. I was becoming familiar to myself again. I was still me, but a slightly other me. The memories of my family became more bearable the more I thrived. I took great comfort in knowing that my parents, Taubcia, and Rachel would have been proud to know what I had become. Instead of taking me farther away from my past, which I'd feared, my future became a bridge to my past, a place from which I could look back safely and remember. I was proud to show Julek that I could succeed and that his efforts to help hadn't been in vain. And loving and being loved by Lena inspired me to work hard and achieve more.

Lena and I lived on the edge, in a nervous, frightening atmosphere of whispered news about more arrests in Moscow and Warsaw. I was worried about what would happen to us, and I was very worried about what would happen to Julek. I called him every Sunday to make sure he was okay, but placing a call abroad was a highly complicated procedure. The call could be placed only from the central telegraph building in downtown Moscow, and the waiting time for a connection was usually between two and five hours. The time allowed for a conversation was a maximum of three minutes, with frequent breaks in the connection. However, I was determined to hear his voice, and I continued to call him every week.

I found it almost amusing that in this secretive state, nothing was secret. News leaked constantly from the government and Party committees, even from the Politburo. Rumors flourished. A story I heard in early morning would come back later in the day completely distorted. Even though it was impossible to verify the whispered news, everyone relied on it because it alerted us to possible danger. Increasingly, bad news came in the form of living proof, like my meeting in the park with Dr. Weinstock and shortly afterward an early morning encounter with Dr. Zausayev.

I had arrived at the hospital very early to prepare the first patient for surgery, and when I opened Dr. Zausayev's office door I saw him sleeping at his desk. He started awake and got up to splash water on his face.

"Did you operate at night?" I asked.

"No, no." He dried his hands and looked for his cigarettes.

Not wanting to ask about his personal life, I said, "Go home and get some rest. I'll perform surgery today." I actually wanted him to leave so I could be in charge in the operating room. I'd assisted enough and was always looking for an opportunity to be independent even for a day.

"You can't tell anyone that you found me here, okay, or we might both end up in Lubyanka." I nodded and sat down. "You see, someone else is staying in my apartment." Dr. Zausayev took off his glasses and rubbed his face. "Look, this is more than my secret, but I want you to know about it because one day you might be the only one who knows the truth. You're going back to Poland. You'll be safe." His disheveled appearance and fearful eyes made me very nervous. I didn't want to hear the news.

"Yesterday evening Professor Yevdokimov came to my apartment and asked if he could stay overnight. He was in a panic, out of his mind. He didn't know what to do or where to go. He wanted me to leave him alone for the night. I was afraid he was going to hurt himself and said I'd stay with him while my wife and son stayed with her parents, but he insisted on being left alone. Finally, he told me that several of the most renowned Kremlin doctors have recently been arrested. Professors Vinogradov, Vovsi, Greinstein, Yegorov, Feldman, and others have been accused of heinous crimes."

Dr. Zausayev got up and opened the door to check the corridor. "Professor Vinogradov was Stalin's personal physician. Professor Vovsi was the chief internist of the Soviet army during the war. Everyone else is a leading specialist in his field. They've all been accused of murdering Soviet leaders and plotting to kill Stalin. Yevdokimov is afraid he might be next, so he's hiding out at my apartment. I know I could be arrested for it, but I couldn't refuse him. He's been Stalin's oral surgeon for twenty years." Dr. Zausayev wiped the sweat from his face and looked at me closely to see if I believed him.

I did. I'd heard a variation of this story before, while in the camps. Colonel Vladimir Antoshyn, who had been in charge of daytime food service in the Kremlin for several years, told me how he and his crew had been arrested one night at the end of 1938. All were accused of plotting to kill Stalin and Politburo members. His two superiors were shot. He was sentenced to ten years of hard labor. "For years I had a chance to poison him," he used to lament. "I could've done it. I don't know why I didn't."

A week later, exhausted and resigned to his fate, Professor Yevdokimov returned to sleep at home, and Dr. Zausayev went back to his apartment with his family.

In late November and December of 1952, my life ran in two parallel currents. On the surface I worked in the hospital, went to staff meetings at the institute, and worked on my dissertation. Underneath, I met secretly with Lena and tried to make sense of the increasingly frightening rumors that more doctors and professors were being arrested.

Lena wasn't sure how much longer she'd be able to continue our relationship. Her mother pressured her to break up with me, and her friends wanted her to get back to her normal life. No one wanted trouble from the authorities. Meeting in small cafés, I'd look at Lena's red eyes and feel guilty for getting her into such a hopeless situation. I didn't know how to console her anymore because I myself was losing hope that the law would change. Every time we parted, we weren't sure we'd see each other again. We didn't talk about it, because that led us nowhere except to despair. We just bore the strain, holding on for as long as possible.

Shortly after the new year began, the avalanche that had been hanging over every doctor, hospital, and institute fell. As I was eating breakfast on the morning of January 13, a report titled "Arrest of a Group of Saboteur Doctors" came over the loudspeaker. The announcer said that several Kremlin doctors, most of whom were Jewish, had murdered Politburo members Zhdanov and Shcherbakov and plotted against other Party, state, and military leaders, including Stalin. A headline on the front page of *Pravda* read, "Miserable Spies and Assassins under the Masks of Professors and Physicians." The doctors named in the report were accused of being imperialist spies for the United States, Great Britain, and the Jewish Zionist organization Joint. The arrested were called "murderers in white gowns," "degenerates," and "poisonous reptiles." Although somewhat prepared for the announcement by what I'd heard from Dr. Zausayev, I wasn't prepared for the reaction of my roommate, Fedya, and other medical students. Fedya was a third-year student who was usually quiet and self-absorbed. He'd stopped loading his briefcase to listen to the report, and when it was over he declared, "All of them should be shot immediately. Today. They don't need to be tried. How could they hide their true identities and sneak into the Kremlin. They aren't doctors, they're assassins."

That morning the hospital was in an uproar. The patients tried to figure out which doctors were Jewish and vilified them. The doctors were edgy, especially Dr. Rima Aronovna Turetzkaya, the only Jewish professor in the department. Dr. Zausayev held a meeting and told everyone to stay calm and follow the schedule of surgeries. "And don't discuss any of this with the patients," he said.

For several days I didn't see Dr. Turetzkaya in the hospital. I assumed she was sick, but Dr. Zausayev had advised her to stay home for a few days until things cooled down. A few days later the fallout hit me.

I thought I'd been taking good care of my patients and that they trusted me. But one morning when I was changing a patient's dressing, he said loudly, "I heard from some people that you're Polish, but others tell me you're Jewish. I don't want to have a Jew as a doctor. I don't trust Jews. None of us want Jews to treat us."

It was one thing to read about traitors, assassins, and murderers in white coats, but quite another to have my patient, a person I cared for and had operated on successfully, spit in my face and try to provoke me. I wanted to humiliate him, which would have been easy to do, but stayed calm. "It's up to you what you'd like to do. If you don't want me as your doctor because I'm Jewish, it's perfectly fine with me. As of this moment, I don't consider you my patient. If you wish, you can go to another hospital. I'm staying here and taking care of patients who don't care if I'm Jewish." I walked out the door. Dr. Zausayev took me off the case.

The unfolding of what became known as the Doctors' Plot terrified every doctor in the country, but especially Jewish doctors. At the institute and in the hospital, they slunk through the halls and talked in hushed voices. I felt the same way they did—sneered at, spit on, and dragged through the mud. I wanted to talk to the other Jewish doctors to share my indignation and frustration, but they didn't want to talk to me. Rima Aronovna told me they were afraid to associate with me because I was a foreigner. This added twist terrified me. I no longer felt protected by my Polish citizenship. Now, as a foreigner, Jew, doctor, and ex-convict, I was in more danger of being rearrested than ever before. Day after day the Soviet newspapers, especially *Pravda*, published editorials not only condemning the assassins in white gowns but emphasizing their connections with Zionist spy organizations worldwide. Mark, Lova, and Misha talked about leaving the city, thinking the hysteria was limited to Moscow, but they were wrong. Reports poured in from Minsk, Kiev, Omsk, Tashkent, and Vladivostock denouncing Jewish doctors for poisoning and killing local dignitaries. The media called for the arrests of the "monsters" and "anthropoid beasts," along with Zionist spies and traitors. The news led quickly to a mass psychosis.

The Doctors' Plot arrived on the heels of the escalating campaigns against "rootless cosmopolites," Zionist traitors, and the plotters in the Leningrad case. Not only doctors and Jews were threatened but most Soviet citizens as well. The Great Terror of 1937–1938 was fresh in everyone's memory, and it seemed that a second wave had started and was quickly reaching its apogee.

The beginning of the Doctors' Plot could be traced to one person: Lidia Timoshuk, an X-ray technician in the Kremlin hospital. She'd written a letter to Stalin accusing leading Kremlin physicians of deliberately attempting to kill the leadership of the Party. Because she was a secret police informer, her letter landed on Stalin's desk. She was praised as a Hero of the Soviet Union, awarded the highest honors and decorations, and pronounced the Soviet Joan of Arc. Every institution and Party organization held special meetings and rallies to express unequivocal support for Stalin's policy of eradicating foreign and hostile elements from Soviet society. At the embassy, the staff and Polish students gathered for a special meeting. A Polish Politburo member stood at the podium clenching his fist and urging a cleansing of the Communist Party and Polish society of "poisonous, Zionist snakes." He continued, "Killing under cover of the white gown and professorial title is the most heinous, cowardly crime that can be committed. I call for active vigilance. We all need to keep our eyes and ears open to uncover the enemies in our midst." He praised the Soviets for liberating Poland from Nazi occupation and for their brotherly support and enlightenment after the war. At the mention of Stalin's or Bierut's names, everyone cheered and chanted, "STA-LIN, BIE-RUT. BIE-RUT, STA-LIN."

I have a hard time even now, after so many years, describing the atmosphere in Moscow and in the country in January and February of 1953. In only two months the anti-Semitic hysteria gathered great momentum. The postwar atmosphere of victory and brotherhood dissipated. Jews were harassed and beaten in buses, food stores, and on the streets, while the perpetrators, now called True Soviet Patriots, were cheered on. Everyone was afraid pogroms might start again. The anti-Semitism was more frightening to me than it had been under Hitler in the 1930s. Then, everyone knew about Hitler's plan to exterminate Jews, but the Soviet Union had always proclaimed itself a safe haven for the oppressed, with no distinction as to race or nationality. Now, the anti-Semitism in the Soviet Union began to resemble that in Nazi Germany. Jews were being laid off work. Sioma was transferred from his high-clearance job in the chemical research institute to an ordinary position in the laboratory. He suffered a large salary cut. For over fifteen years he'd been in charge of special projects, and several of his inventions had been adopted by the arms industry. His superior told him that the only reason he wasn't fired was because of his excellent work record. Sioma insisted that I go to Poland and stay with Julek, believing Poland was safer than the Soviet Union, and he urged both of us to look for a chance to escape to the west.

In the middle of February, Sioma told me that mass deportations of Jews were being prepared and that thousands of cattle cars were amassed on the side tracks of the train stations around Moscow. A few days earlier, Mark had told me that all apartment managers and personnel directors in all institutions were preparing lists of Jews and their home addresses. He'd heard it from his apartment manager, an old school friend. Two copies of the lists were requested: one by the local Party committee, another by the local division of the NKVD. The deportations were scheduled for late March or April. Mark and his parents planned to leave Moscow for Uzbekistan. We didn't know to where people would be deported but guessed Kazakhstan or Birobidzhan in the far east. In the late 1920s, Stalin had established Birobidzhan as a Jewish Autonomous Region and encouraged Jews to emigrate there.

I didn't know what to do. On the one hand, I felt protected from deportations because I was a foreigner; on the other, I knew that being blind to such warnings could end in disaster. If I could hold out for another year and a half I could finish *aspirantura* and go back to Poland. But when I finished *aspirantura*, I would never see Lena again. When I wasn't sleeping or working on my dissertation, I alternated between worrying about being deported and despairing over graduating. I turned the problem of how to be with Lena over and over in my mind. I couldn't imagine being away from her. She'd become my anchor in life. I wanted to believe that things would change because Moscow was flooded with students from all over the world. Plenty of foreigners were having relationships with Soviet citizens. Sometimes I felt so desperate that I thought of changing my citizenship back to Soviet; but then I thought of the Doctors' Plot and the cattle cars. Sometimes I felt the pull of my father's fate. Perhaps Lena and I crushing the cyanide capsules together would be the best solution.

It was in this spirit of worry and despair that I heard, on the morning of March 2, 1953, the announcement over the loudspeaker in my dormitory. I was lying in bed waiting for my roommates to leave before getting up when Moscow's most famous radio announcer, Boris Levitan, read from a special bulletin that the Supreme Leader was in failing health. He repeated the communiqué several times, and I lay still, absorbing every word.

It was the most unusual announcement ever heard in the Soviet Union. Prior to this announcement, saying that Stalin was mortal wasn't just inconceivable, it was treason. A person could be arrested for saying the Great Leader had mental or physical problems. I was more than convinced that his condition was extremely serious—or that he was already dead and the leadership was preparing the people for the announcement—because never before had Stalin's health or any of his personal affairs been brought to public attention.

The news affected me in a way I didn't expect; I realized how much I had come to believe in Stalin's immortality. For me Stalin was always alive, omnipresent and omnipotent. In some way he was above mortals. He had murdered millions of his real and imaginary enemies but was never harmed himself. Lenin had been assassinated, but Stalin had made it to the age of seventy-three. However, on that first day, rather than feeling liberated over Stalin's impending death, I felt anxious and alert, cautious not to reveal my true feelings to my colleagues. I wouldn't even talk to my close friend Dr. Zausayev about it. I was afraid that at a moment like this no one could be trusted, because emotions were running high and my words could be misinterpreted. My roommates tried to pull me into their heated discussions, blaming Jewish doctors in the Kremlin for mistreating Stalin, but I didn't say a word to defend the doctors, afraid that any comments I made would draw attention to me.

After the announcement that Stalin was in the hospital in serious condition, something very strange happened in the country: there was no more news about the Doctors' Plot, nor was there another newspaper article advocating the cleansing of Zionist spies from the ranks of devoted Soviet citizens. Radio broadcasts and newspaper articles focused only on the health reports of the Greatest Genius of Mankind, which had been signed by the remaining Kremlin doctors. With all the attention now focused on Stalin's health, I felt safe to go to Lena's apartment for the first time in four months.

We could hardly contain our hope that Stalin would never leave the hospital, believing that with his death, the law prohibiting Soviet citizens from marrying foreigners would change. Although for Lena and me every report about Stalin's worsening health was a cause for celebration, most of the citizens seemed to be waiting for the apocalypse. In two days public expressions of love and devotion to Stalin escalated to mass hysteria. How could the Leader of Mankind be sick? How could Stalin be like an ordinary human being? Men and women cried openly in public, but I couldn't tell how much of the sorrow was genuine. Certainly a great deal of it was raw grief, even terror of being abandoned, but much of it was a mask that had to be put on because the occasion called for it. Although the Great Leader was no longer watching, no one knew what would happen next or how his or her behavior would later be interpreted by the Party and secret police.

For the next three days Stalin didn't regain consciousness, and on March 5, Levitan read from a communiqué that the Greatest Genius of Mankind was dead. A Party- and state-appointed funeral commission chaired by Nikita Khrushchev announced that Stalin's body would be displayed the following day in the Hall of Columns, and the funeral would be held on March 9.

The most secretive of dictators also had a secretive death. Aside from the announcement that he had died, there was no official report on the events preceding the massive stroke he had suffered, but gossip raged about the real cause of death. Mark and Lova heard that he had been dead for quite a while and that all the communiqués were faked. It was rumored that he'd been murdered in his villa by members of the NKVD at the command of Lavrenti Beria, chief of the secret police. Lena's mother brought gossip from the pharmacy that Stalin had been poisoned by his maid, also a member of the secret police. Sioma told me about a rumor that Beria, Wiacheslev Molotov, and Klement Voroshilov had arranged for Stalin to be killed because all three were in danger of being executed, as many of Stalin's other close associates had been. At the last Party Congress and for the first time since the Revolution, Molotov and Voroshilov hadn't been elected to the Politburo. Molotov had been prime minister, and

Voroshilov had been the defense minister and a Politburo member for many years. Excluding them and others from the Politburo was an ominous sign that they might share the same fate as their predecessors. When the Doctors' Plot had begun to unfold, Stalin had publicly denounced Beria for lack of vigilance.

That evening Lena and I invited Mark, Lova, Misha, and their girlfriends to Lena's apartment for a grand celebration. We danced with the drapes closed and made many toasts. Mark said that he and his family were no longer planning to leave Moscow and that he would go back to work. "This one goes to Stalin, who lived long enough and died at the right time!" Mark said. We all laughed and drank the shots. The bottle went around again.

"Here's to Stalin, may he rot in his grave!"

"Here's to our professors, that they may all be released!"

"Here's to our future, that we may live where we want and be with the women we love!"

After a while we couldn't keep up drinking with the number of toasts we made as we peeled off layer after layer of anxiety and fear and expressed our hopes for freer, happier times ahead.

The next day I went to see what was going on around the Hall of Columns. Stalin's body was displayed and guarded around the clock by the members of the Politburo. A mile away from Theatrical Plaza, the crowd thickened and pushed and pulled me forward. Mounted police and army trucks loaded with armed NKVD soldiers furrowed through the mobs of people. Shouting, yelling, crying mourners squeezing me on all sides carried me toward the plaza. When I realized that the force of the crowd would push me all the way to the end of Theatrical Plaza, I panicked, realizing I'd never be able to get back. Tanks and trucks were lined up on the far side of the plaza; there would be no passing them or turning back. The pressure of the forward-moving current squeezed me tighter, and at Bolshoi Theater, out of breath, I clung to one of the columns. Weeping men and women of all ages clad in dark padded jackets or wool overcoats cried out, "How will we live without Our Leader?" "We are orphans!" "Come back! Help us!"

There was no end to the crowds and their hysterical lamentations. Mounted police waded through the crowd and tried to keep order. When one of the mounted policemen turned around and headed away from the plaza, I slipped in behind and followed him out, staying right next to the horse's tail.

I didn't go to the funeral, but millions of people filled the streets to lament and throw flowers. The next day the newspapers were full of reports of people who'd been trampled to death or crushed by tanks and trucks at the Hall of Columns.

In the following days I read every newspaper and listened to the news on the radio. Before Stalin's death it had been obvious that Georgy Malenkov had edged out Molotov as number two in the country and heir apparent. He was considered to be a ruthless Party bureaucrat and devoted Stalinist. From the news now being published on the front page of *Pravda*, it was evident that a power struggle was going on in the Kremlin. The first and most startling information was the return of Molotov and Voroshilov to the ruling Politburo, which had been completely reshuffled. Malenkov was elected first secretary of the Party, assuming Stalin's position but not Stalin's power. He didn't last long, however. In less than a month he was unexpectedly demoted and sent to the deep provinces to be in charge of an electric station.

Khrushchev became the first secretary, accompanied by Bulganin as prime minister and Zukhov, the greatest hero of World War II, as defense minister. The demotion of Malenkov without trial and execution showed that the new rulers had distanced themselves from Stalin's terror tactics. There were no more arrests or expulsions. My friends and I discussed this daily, hopeful that the entire system of cruelty might stop.

More encouraging news was the release and rehabilitation of the surviving former Kremlin doctors, as well as of other doctors who had been arrested before Stalin's death. The leaders of the NKVD who had masterminded and arranged the Doctors' Plot and the anti-Semitic campaign were arrested and tried, and most of them, including the main instigator, vice minister Mikhail Rumin, were sentenced to death. Lidia Timoshuk was publicly deprived of all the honors bestowed on her by Stalin. In December 1953, Beria was executed in the cellars of the NKVD, ending the terror of the secret police.

Although encouraged by the changes and relishing the feeling of personal freedom, I remained skeptical about how far they would go. The Party bureaucracy and the remaining apparatus of the secret police wouldn't easily give up their positions of power. Khrushchev and the new Party leadership impressed me, but on the faces of Khrushchev's supporters I could see the same fervor that was on the faces of those who had supported Stalin. I didn't believe that the political climate would change radically or that a new political and economic system would prevail. I wasn't sure how the informers and millions of Party zealots were reacting to the slight thawing of Soviet society. I wanted to share in the enthusiasm and optimism of my Soviet friends, but I couldn't.

At the beginning of June 1953, I got an unexpected call from Adam Kruchkovsky, the Polish student who had presided at my meeting with the executive Party committee at the embassy. He told me that Stalin's decree banning marriages of Soviet citizens and foreigners was revoked and that my record was wiped clean. In the next breath he invited me to his wedding with his Soviet girlfriend.

That evening I went to see Lena with a bouquet of flowers and bottle of champagne, which surprised both Lena and her mother: vodka was a staple, champagne was only for the New Year. I told them about Adam Kruchkovsky's phone call and asked Lena if she would marry me the next day. We had dreamed of getting married one day and spent hours concocting elaborate schemes that would allow us to leave Moscow and get married in Poland. We called the hospital and told them we were taking the day off, and at ten o'clock the next morning we went to the fourth floor of a crumbling brick building on Sretenka Street. I had passed this building hundreds of times during the three years I dated Lena, but it had never crossed my mind that one day Lena and I would go there to be married.

In the morning I went to the peasants' market to buy fresh flowers and to the jewelry store to buy a pair of gold wedding bands. I dressed in my father's suit, and Lena wore a green calico-print dress, the only good one she had. We invited Lena's mother to come to the ceremony, but she said she couldn't take the day off. I believe she didn't want to go because she didn't feel she could be dressed up enough for the occasion.

Like most occasions in Soviet life, marriage was a purely bureaucratic procedure, annoying to the couple and officials alike. The event was romantic only to the extent that the bride and groom could put up with the rude clerks and ignore the dirty, foul-smelling office. Lena and I waited for nearly an hour in a room with a dusty palm tree dying in the corner before the official in charge came out of his office.

He asked for our passports, looked at them, and pronounced us married. The secretary pounded out a marriage certificate. We exchanged no vows and received no congratulations. The most meaningful thing about getting married wasn't the exchange of rings or dreams we had for the future but the stamped piece of paper, which we both held onto and stared at as we walked out of the building and back to Lena's apartment. We never believed the decree would be lifted, but it happened so quickly that after several months we still had a hard time believing the terror was over.

That night we celebrated our marriage with over thirty friends scattered throughout Lena's and her neighbors' apartments. Sioma and Katia and her sister, Nina, were with us, as well as Professor Yevdokimov and Dr. Zausayev. Lena's and her mother's friends joined us, and we also invited some of the *urki* who guarded the entrance to the building. We celebrated all night, singing, drinking, and even dancing, although we had no space to move. But it didn't matter, because there was such an atmosphere of happiness and joy, something that happens only once in a lifetime.

Soon after Lena and I were married the nurse who Lena and I believed had reported us to the militia moved out, and we were assigned her room. It was a tiny cubicle, with the bed and wardrobe taking up nearly all the space. Chairs on each side of the bed served as nightstands. But compared with the camp barracks, stinky dormitory, and Lena's mother's apartment, the cubicle seemed like a palace. I still remembered the comfort of my rooms in the house on the hill, the apartment on Farna Street, and the embassy, but I was happy for what I had now. For Lena and me, the feeling of privacy and the freedom to come and go as we pleased were all the luxury we needed. We were very poor, but our friends were in similar conditions and we didn't feel deprived. I was sure that I would be able to create better living conditions for us when we moved to Poland, which was less than a year away.

During the next year Khrushchev consolidated his power and became the undisputed leader of the Communist Party and the Soviet Union. The atmosphere in the country was one of optimism, and Lena and I believed that life would get better for the Soviet people under Khrushchev's leadership.

In April 1954, I completed my residency and defended my dissertation, and in May, Lena and I boarded the train for Warsaw.

EPILOGUE

When Lena and I went to Poland in 1954, I was frightened but ready to face the formidable challenges of new colleagues, a new culture, and a new position in life. The Polish Ministry of Health delegated me to work at the Medical Academy in Lodz in the position of assistant professor. Our living conditions were slightly better than those in Moscow—Lena and I were given two rooms in an apartment that also housed three other families. Three years later I became chairman of the Department of Maxillofacial and Reconstructive Surgery. I organized the first Polish Center for the Treatment of Congenital Facial Deformities, and seven years later I created the first academic Department of Plastic and Reconstructive Surgery.

Lena adjusted to life in Poland and worked as a prosthodontist at the Medical Academy but missed the cultural atmosphere in Moscow. I tried to take what I loved about Soviet culture—the people, arts, intellect—and leave behind any bitterness I felt about my experiences in the Soviet Union. I blamed the Stalinist regime more than any individual for my suffering, and Hitler's regime for the murders of my family and friends. Throughout life, whenever good things happened, I attributed them to luck, to the good people who helped me, and to my own hard work. I became aware of my competence and the strength that allowed me to do what I did and to achieve what I wanted. When bad things happened, I refused to let disaster take me down. I learned not to swallow pain, not to let anguish and despair fill me completely, not to let the loss of my family eclipse all hope of a future. My experiences in the labor camps and my years in Moscow taught me what kind of person I really was, and I must admit that I liked myself better the way I was when I left Moscow than the way I was before the war. I learned more about myself and others under the extreme conditions of the labor camps, stripped of the thin cover of civilization, than I ever learned in freedom.

Life in Poland was not easy. The communist regime there established the same authoritarian rule as the one in the Soviet Union. As a newcomer, a professor from Moscow, and a Jew, I provoked strong reactions in people—open hostility in some and blind subservience in others. I lived according to my own ethical code, incorporating some elements of morality from home and elements of camp philosophy: compassion, friendship, justice, and soul-searching, along with resilience and flexibility. Living under communism, I continued to do what was necessary to support people who had no power in a society that had no regard for its citizens.

I was never able to shake off my fear of being rearrested or having my past exposed to the Polish authorities. As time passed I learned to live with these fears. They became integrated into my personality, and I considered them the price I had to pay for my education and professional position. Everyone around me was more or less frightened, and they often didn't even know of what. I became very good at hiding my thoughts and feelings, displaying to the outside world a different persona. If there was any luxury in prison, it was the freedom to be who I was and to know who others were. Honesty and true friendship were extremely difficult to find under communism, and when I found them, I valued them greatly.

The culmination of years of rabid anti-Semitism came in March 1968. It was inspired by a group of Polish nationalists led by General Mieczyslaw Moczar. I was targeted by many of my colleagues. I thought I could weather the tide, but as my Jewish friends and colleagues left Poland, I, too, began to feel the need to seek refuge for my family and myself in another country.

In 1972, the University of Iowa offered me a one-year position as a visiting professor in the Department of Otolaryngology—Head and Neck Surgery. After three months I was offered a permanent position as chairman of the Division of Facial Plastic and Reconstructive Surgery in the department. Under the pretense of their vacationing in the United States, I was able to get exit visas for Lena and our daughter, Ewa, so they could join me—an extremely difficult maneuver, because the Polish government rarely allowed all members of a family to leave Poland at the same time, due to the risk of defection. When

Lena and Ewa arrived from Poland, I accepted the position, and we made our home in Iowa City.

It was fourteen years before I saw Julek again, although I'd continued to call him every week, just as I'd done when I was living in Moscow and he in Warsaw. In 1986 he was allowed to visit me in Iowa, and after the fall of communism in 1991, I made the first of many visits back to Poland. I retired from my position in 1991 but have continued to do research and writing as a professor emeritus.

ACKNOWLEDGMENTS

Several people generously gave their time to read and comment on drafts of this book. Foremost we'd like to thank Adam Hochschild for sharing his editorial knowledge and experience with us. We're also grateful to Mary Gantz, Paul Goldberg, Jim Harris, Bob Kelch, Linda Kerber, Christopher Merrill, and Jan Weissmiller.

Special thanks go to Lynn Franklin, our agent, and Naomi Schneider, executive editor at the University of California Press, for their expertise and friendship. We're also grateful to Sue Heinemann for seeing the book through production, and Jan Spauschus for her critical eye and intelligence in editing the manuscript.

Hyun Joong Kim and Rangaswamy Rajagopal created the maps, and Nathaniel Deutsch kindly shared his photographs of Wlodzimierz-Wolynski, memorializing the city beyond the words in this book. As always, we're thankful to the staff at Prairie Lights Bookstore in Iowa City for their support and friendship.

Our warmest thanks go to the following members of our families for their sustaining love and patience: Phyllis Harper-Bardach, Ewa Bardach, Hani Elkadi, and Suzanne Gleeson.

Mapmaker:	Bill Nelson
Designer:	Victoria Kuskowski
Text:	10/13 Palatino
Display:	Trade Gothic Condensed
Compositor:	Binghamton Valley Composition
Printer and binder:	Edwards Brothers, Inc.